Better Food
for
Public Places

Better Food for Public Places

for

Public Places

A GUIDE FOR IMPROVING INSTITUTIONAL FOOD

by Anne Moyer

 Rodale Press, Emmaus, Pennsylvania

Copyright © 1977 Rodale Press, Inc.

All rights reserved. No part of this publication may be repro-
duced or transmitted in any form or by any means, electronic or
mechanical, including photocopy, recording, or any information
storage and retrieval system without written permission of the
publisher.

Printed in the United States of America

Printed on recycled paper

Book design by T.A. Lepley

Library of Congress Cataloging in Publication Data

Moyer, Anne.
  Better food for public places.

  Includes index.
  1. Food service. 2. Cookery (Natural foods)
I. Title.
TX911.2.M69   642'.5   76-54336
ISBN 0-87857-155-8

            2   4   6   8   10   9   7   5   3   1

Contents

Acknowledgments

My sincere thanks to everyone who supplied information for this book, and especially to Nancy Albright and Anita Hirsch of Fitness House, Genia Lee Roper of Meadowbrook Hospital, Rose McDowell, Elizabeth Benson of Pacific Union College, Jerry Goldstein and Jane Kinderlehrer for so generously contributing their knowledge, experience and enthusiasm to bring it to life.

A.M.

Chapter 1

A Look At
The Institutional
Food Picture

According to the Senate Select Commission on Nutrition, our poor eating habits cost us $30 billion a year in doctor and dentist bills. Living, as we are, in the midst of abundance, Americans should be the healthiest, best fed people on earth. But sadly, such a positive state of affairs does not exist. Some of us are undernourished, not getting enough to eat; some of us are malnourished, from eating the wrong foods; and many of us are actually badly overnourished, taking in far more calories than we need. A growing awareness that chronic and degenerative diseases like diabetes, diverticular disease of the colon and cardiovascular problems are related to our diet is beginning to cause some changes in our eating patterns.

We are experiencing a gradual awakening of food consciousness, of concern for the *quality* of what we put into our stomachs, instead of simply the *quantity*. Once again we are starting to tune into the fact that the reason we eat is not just for enjoyment, but to nourish our bodies and provide them with the fuel they need to function at the highest possible level. Instead of opting for convenience in preparation, we are starting to look for nutritional value in foods.

1

Our new food consciousness is surfacing in many ways. Americans of all ages (and both sexes) are going back into the kitchen, rediscovering the joys of preparing their own delicious meals from fresh, whole foods. Cooking classes are flourishing. Cookbook sales are booming. We've witnessed the birth of various new appliances designed for the person who cooks with whole foods—machines that grind flour, knead dough, chop, shred, grate, beat, puree and whip almost anything. More people are baking their own bread. The family garden has returned, and along with it, home canning and preserving. A growing number of people are eating less meat and getting more of their protein from beans, grains, nuts and dairy products. The term "vegetarian" has become familiar to people in all walks of life; it now encompasses a far broader group of people than just those whose religious convictions have always forbidden the consumption of meat.

In short, the quality of food in American kitchens is on the rise. But what about the food we eat when we're not at home? Our life-style still demands that we spend a good many of our waking hours away from home—at work, at school, in all kinds of occupational and social activities. It is time that we turned our attention toward the kinds of food we eat in our institutions, and who's in charge of feeding us there.

A large percentage of the food we consume is prepared by giant, impersonal food service companies which provide meals by the trillion for nursing homes, hospitals, business dining rooms, schools, colleges, airlines, hotels, motels, restaurants, vending machines and institutions of all kinds. When you stop to think about it, the people who are involved in providing nutriment for so many of us so much of the time are in a way shaping our destiny. Is the food served to your children at school helping them to develop their full mental and physical potential? Are the meals served at the nursing home where your grandad is living designed to make him alert and pleasant? Is the food served at your local hospital really helping patients to build up their strength and recover from disease? How about the company dining room?

Will those lunches help you avoid a heart attack?

The director of one food service told us that he served doughnuts to students at a local college more frequently than apples. Sure, apples may be more nutritious, but they are also more expensive. His board of directors does not ask, "How many cavities are you preventing?" but "How much profit are you showing?"

Our food service system has developed, over the years, into a slick mechanical enterprise where the primary concern is for increased convenience rather than optimum health. As the system grew, corporate brains turned their technological resources toward developing ease of on-site preparation rather than improving nutrient conservation. We were given preportioned frozen dinners instead of new cookware designed to preserve vitamins. We may have grumbled a bit as we loaded a plateful of rubbery, gravy-drenched meat and mushy peas onto a cafeteria tray, but by and large, the American public has meekly accepted the inferior food served in our institutions.

Perhaps we're confused and overwhelmed by developments in technology which have created new foods and new delivery systems. We simply don't know how to cope with them. Because of demands for higher volume, ease of preparation and substantial profit margins, food services depend heavily on preportioned, prepackaged, frozen, canned and instant foods. These foods must be processed into a form suitable for long-term storage and mass transport. As a result, fresh, whole foods are refined, rearranged, repackaged and treated with artificial flavors, colors, preservatives, texturizers and a host of other additives before they are ready for use in the food service kitchen. How can anyone tell what a 30-year accumulation of these substances will do to a once healthy human body?

Dr. Ross Hume Hall, of McMaster University in Ontario, Canada, explains that although the idea of rearranging and repackaging foods to make them easier to transport, store and prepare seems very convenient and sensible, there is a major fallacy to this approach. Convenience foods are being created primarily by people trained in chemistry—the same people who formulate paint, plastic and other synthetic products. To a chemist, food, like any other raw material, is simply the sum of a number of component parts which can be taken apart and rearranged at will to produce new products.[1]

In trying to assess the real value of all of these new products, we must never forget that food is more than just the sum of its parts. When the relationships among nutritional components are severed, part of the value of the food is lost. We cannot reconstitute anything that was originally produced by nature; we can only make clumsy imitations. These manufactured foods do not belong in institutions.

Our children deserve the best food possible to nourish growing bodies and developing minds, to help them mature into healthy, happy adults. Our sick people deserve the best food possible to heal their wounds, restore their bodies' resistance to infection and illness, and return to good health as quickly as possible. Our elderly deserve the best food possible to keep them strong, alert and active in their golden years. In situations where people do not have the option to prepare their own meals, every effort should be made to provide them with the highest quality food.

The time has come to upgrade the food we eat away from home. Consumers must demand higher quality and more nutritional value when eating at work, at school, in the hospital or in a nursing home. And the people who process, prepare and deliver all this food must realize what an awesome responsibility is theirs. It is time they applied more of the discoveries made in nutritional science to the pots and pans that are shaping our destiny.

There is so much information available on good nutritional practice! But so little of this information is actually being applied in institutions which provide nourishment for large numbers of people. How many hospitals or nursing homes in your area serve fresh sprouts on salads or make whole grain breads available? Do you know of any day-care center or school where nutrient-rich brown rice is served instead of

4

its less nutritious counterpart, white rice?

We *know* a great deal.

Now, we must *act* on what we know!

The State of
Institutional Food Today

Recent trends in institutional food service have all been in the direction of the centralized kitchen, where foods are prepared, portioned and frozen to be shipped to satellite kitchens for reheating, holding and serving. Obviously, this kind of a system subjects food to involved handling procedures, whose effects on food are not yet fully understood.

One very definite result of institutional handling techniques is a substantial loss of vitamins from the food. Various studies have found that large amounts of vitamin C, thiamin (vitamin B₁) and riboflavin (vitamin B₂) can be lost from vegetables that are held on a steam table. One research team found that when snap beans and peas were kept hot for three hours, they lost respectively 52 and 94 percent of their vitamin C. This was in addition to the vitamin C that was lost during cooking. The same conditions also resulted in thiamin losses of 30 percent in the beans and 66 percent in the peas.

When cabbage was tested, losses of vitamin C went as high as 80 percent when the cabbage was kept hot for 105 minutes. Substantial amounts of thiamin, riboflavin and carotene (which the body uses to manufacture vitamin A) were also destroyed in the cabbage.

A study of potatoes showed that vitamin C losses were much greater when the potatoes were prepared in a central kitchen and transported to schools than when the potatoes were prepared in on-site kitchens. As much as 60 percent of the vitamin C disappeared from the centrally cooked potatoes, as opposed to losses of 30 percent from potatoes cooked on the premises.[2]

These studies unearthed some valuable evidence of the

nutrient-depleting effects of institutional food handling techniques. The only trouble is that all of them are 20 to 30 years old. Methods of processing, packaging and handling have changed since then, although steam tables are still used. There is every reason to believe that nutrient losses have not been significantly reduced by these changed methods, but we desperately need reliable new information.

In 1974, Dr. Mary K. Head reported some new research findings. The study was conducted in two stages. In Phase 1, samples of hot and cold foods prepared in a central commissary were taken as the food was being loaded into insulated carts for delivery to schools. Similar samples were then collected at the schools shortly after the serving lines opened (an hour to an hour and a half after the original samples were taken), and again shortly before the lines closed (another 30 to 50 minutes later).

In Phase 2 of the study, food samples were collected from school cafeterias which shared a common menu and centralized purchasing procedures, but which prepared the food in on-site kitchens. Phase 2 samples were taken before preparation, immediately after preparation and in the middle of the serving period.

Analysis of the Phase 1 samples indicated significant losses of vitamin C (an average of 19 percent) and iron (an average of 20 percent) from hot foods. Part of the loss was believed to have been incurred even before these foods were prepared at the schools, since many of them were purchased partially prepared. Substantial amounts of thiamin were lost from cold foods prepared in the central kitchen. There was wide variation from school to school.

Phase 2 sample analysis also turned up considerable vitamin C losses, particularly from cooked foods. In fact, the only tested food with any potential as a source of this vitamin was found to be tossed salad, but vitamin C levels varied greatly even here. Also, canned foods were allowed to stand for as long as an hour between opening and cooking. Such practices allow a great deal of unnecessary nutrient loss—depletion of some nutrients begins not when cooking begins, but on exposure to air and light. Average levels of nutrient depletion after preparation were 35 percent for thiamin, 30 to 70 percent for calcium and iron. Holding foods during serving further lowered nutrient levels.

In Phase 2, although nutrient losses were generally less than those incurred in the central kitchen system, there was great variation of nutrient levels among schools using the same brands of food from the same suppliers with the same overall supervision and menus. This variation impressively illustrates the effects of handling techniques on foods. Nutrient content is reduced by any and all of these common practices and probably others: refrigerating foods at temperatures that aren't low enough, allowing too much air circulation during storage, peeling vegetables and opening cans long before you're ready to cook them, cooking foods a few hours before they are needed and then reheating them at serving time, and using equipment made of catalytic materials (materials which react with certain foods).[3] For more information, see chapter 5, "Equipment For The Natural Foods Kitchen."

Some of Dr. Head's figures for nutrient loss may not seem too alarming when compared with the results of the earlier studies.

The most important fact is that a substantial amount of nutrient loss did occur. Since the reason we eat is for nourishment (enjoyment does not make our bodies function better—nutrients do!) every effort should be made to conserve as much of the nutritional value of food as possible. Finally, these studies all prove that the current practice of computing nutrient values of foods in the raw state rather than after cooking is not a valid way to plan a menu. Many meals will be deficient in nutrients if nutrient losses during cooking and handling of foods are not taken into account when the meals are planned.

Working in Food Service

Our convenience-oriented system of food service has undeniably made working in many an institutional kitchen a much easier job than it used to be. In fact, food service is becoming so streamlined that it is losing its resemblance to food preparation as we know it. Consequently, working in a kitchen is becoming as boring and monotonous as working on a factory assembly line.

As we mentioned before, today's trend is toward the central commissary system. But let's take a closer look at that system, and consider the part played by the food service employee.

At the central commissary, food is cleaned and processed in varying degrees. Fresh vegetables, for example, can be prepared for cooking or for use in salads. They are peeled, sliced, chopped, grated or shredded, then they are probably dipped in citric acid and a chemical preservative bath, which might be dubbed a "vegetable freshener" or some similar title. The vegetables may then be packed in plastic bags to be stored in the refrigerator for a week or two. Such methods may save preparation time and labor costs in the on-site kitchen, but someone must pay for the extra processing and also for the chemical preservatives used on the food, not to mention the cost in nutrient value of the extra processing.

The central commissary also prepares meats. Salisbury steaks, for example, are portioned, breaded, packaged and frozen before distribution to on-site kitchens.

In many systems, the central commissary receives foods in these forms from an outside caterer and will actually prepare and then freeze complete individual meals before sending the food out to the on-site kitchens. This procedure is known as "preplating," and it turns the on-site kitchen into no more than a finishing kitchen, where food isn't cooked, only reheated. It doesn't take any culinary skill to slide a bunch of frozen dinners into the oven!

The food service employee's role in convenience-oriented food service is for the most part neither stimulating nor rewarding. The central commissary worker's task is to process raw material into a product, and he or she can hardly relate to that product as food people eat. An extreme statement of the attitude might be, "Who cares if it doesn't look like real food—I don't have to cook it or eat it!" The employee in the on-site kitchen will also have trouble relating to the food as whole food. His job begins with an already-processed "product" instead of fresh, whole foods. He may subscribe to the view that "I don't care what it tastes like—I didn't make it!"

Is it any wonder that food service personnel are not generally a highly motivated lot? It is unreasonable to expect a person to have pride in his work when he can only do half the job.

The Consumer's Experience

Institutional food of all kinds bears little resemblance to food as we have become familiar with it in our homes. For the most part, meals turned out by food service kitchens are uniformly dull and tasteless. Overcooking and steam table holding have destroyed most of the appealing color and texture variations we associate with different foods. Usually most of the flavor is gone too, and the entrée is drowned in a heavy sauce or gravy to compensate.

Food service as we know it has become terribly dehumanized, both in terms of the food itself and the manner in which it is served. To the elementary school child, lunchtime in the cafeteria can be downright intimidating. The child passes mechanically down a line of stainless steel counters holding rows of steam-table pans. Uniform globs of dull-colored food are dished out onto each plate. Probably the child is handed a plate of rather unappealing food by a bored or sullen-looking person in a white uniform.

Hospital patients and bedridden nursing home residents receive the same kind of food when they are handed a covered tray from a stack of identical-looking covered trays. The whole experience is at best dehumanizing and can often be downright cold and impersonal.

Why Natural Foods for Institutions?

The need for better institutional food is obvious. And as we noted before, available research evidence on the relation-

9

ship of processed, additive-laden food products to various allergenic and degenerative disease conditions points to the crucial need for institutional food to be as fresh, pure and unprocessed as possible. Food service must begin to move in a new direction—toward natural foods and away from the impersonal, mechanized world of preportioned, precooked, instant convenience products.

Cooking with natural foods does not mean using expensive specialty or "health" foods. It simply means basing food service on whole, fresh foods prepared and served with nutritional value and optimum flavor and quality in mind rather than convenience, conformity and simplicity of preparation.

Popular foods for the natural kitchen include:
- whole grain breads, cereals and pasta products
- fresh or frozen seafood, poultry and meats, broiled or baked instead of fried or boiled
- brown rice instead of white or instant rice
- honey, molasses and other natural sweeteners instead of white sugar
- complete protein meatless main dishes
- a variety of fresh fruit in season
- real fruit juices instead of fruit drinks with added sugar and water or sodas
- herb teas
- creative salads using an assortment of raw, fresh vegetables
- fresh vegetables steamed, sautéed or baked (not boiled) to preserve flavor and nutrient value
- sprouted beans and seeds, such as alfalfa and mung beans
- vegetable oils (cold-pressed if possible) instead of lard or other solid shortenings
- assorted dried fruits
- unsalted nuts and pumpkin, sunflower and sesame seeds.

Including more natural foods in your menus can upgrade the quality of food service meals in many ways. First of all, the food itself will offer more nutrient value than processed foods. Along with improved nutritional quality will come better taste, texture and appearance—the food will look like real food. Also, natural foods offer new challenges for kitchen personnel. Cooks need to really be cooks, not just "finishers." The kitchen staff will have the opportunity for real involvement in their work, preparing meals from scratch and seeing the end results of their efforts.

Taking on the Opposition

Suggest adding natural foods to institutional menus, and many administrators and food service managers will voice loud and long objections. To a lot of people, the term natural foods is synonymous with health foods, conjuring up visions of unfamiliar, bizarre-tasting and expensive specialty foods popular only among food faddists. In the face of such misconceptions, and in light of the convenience orientation of our entire institutional food service system, the person who wants to integrate natural foods into food service faces a stiff fight.

Several commonly held misconceptions must be confronted, the most basic of which involves simply a definition of what is meant by natural foods. For our purposes here, cooking with natural foods simply means, as we said before, serving high-quality unprocessed foods prepared in the most nutrition-conscious manner possible.

Many food service managers have been taught that preparing food with uniformity in mind yields a better quality product. But the studies on handling techniques and nutrient loss which we discussed earlier seem to indicate the potentially poor quality of the meals turned out in a uniform manner.

A more serious objection to natural foods is that the extra preparation time, increased labor needs and higher cost of whole, fresh foods make this type of food service economically unfeasible. Rising costs are a very real problem. The food service budget does not have to increase by leaps and bounds, but conscientious and skillful management is an absolute necessity. The natural foods kitchen requires some different management techniques from the conventional kitchen. Menus, for example, must be judiciously planned in order to minimize spoilage and waste of fresh foods. Working with production schedules can facilitate wise use of preparation time and insure that all the foods will be ready as they are needed and nothing is forgotten. The production schedule will also reduce waste and help cut costs. Natural foods will require more labor to prepare food for cooking, such as cleaning and chopping raw vegetables, so waste and spoilage must be tightly controlled if the increased labor cost is to be offset.

Another way to cut costs is to serve occasional meatless meals. It isn't hard to put together delicious dishes from combinations of grains, beans, dairy products, nuts and seeds that offer as much protein as sirloin steak. And most people really enjoy these new eating experiences. Of course, purchasing less meat can help to cut costs, as does buying grains, beans, nuts and similar foods in bulk.

Keeping costs down won't be easy—it requires dedicated and efficient management. But the challenge can be met, and it is being met in many institutions right now.

No doubt the old saw that "kids will only eat cheeseburgers and French fries" will also greet the person campaigning for natural food service. But the experiences of the food service directors and cooks whose stories are told in chapter 4 have shown that that statement simply is not true. Kids will eat a variety of foods so long as they are prepared well, so long as they look good, smell good and taste good.

A final misconception about natural foods is that they are too hard to get for institutional use. There are many national and regional distributors, and it should be no problem finding one that will deliver to your area. Also, work as much as possible with local suppliers, especially for meats, produce and dairy products. You need not stick strictly to natural foods distributors either. Any company that sells instant oatmeal, for example, ought to be able to supply rolled oats as well and may be more convenient for your particular needs. If there are no baking facilities on the premises, a local baking firm might be able to supply special products to fill your needs at a reasonable price.

The Problem of Vending

Vending machines are a major source of revenue to many institutions. In fact, most public lunchrooms depend on the sale of snacks and vended products to raise additional funds. In some cases, these items help to allay the cost of the lunch program itself. The very nature of a natural foods program will generate a conflict with vended foods that will in all likelihood become an important area of concern. Since this problem is especially acute in our schools, we'll examine the issue primarily from the public school's perspective, although it applies to hospitals, nursing homes and other institutions as well.

The Child Nutrition Act of 1972 allowed competitive foods to be sold in public school lunchrooms. The term "competitive foods" refers to all foods that are not part of the Type A lunch program, that is, foods sold at snack bars and from vending machines. All of us are familiar with the kinds of food sold in vending machines—sodas, candy, potato chips, corn chips, pretzels, crackers, cookies and so on. These are all high profit items, low in nutritional value and heavily laden with sugar, salt and artificial ingredients. New York Congressman Benjamin Rosenthal, calling for more nutritious vended foods, has stated, "In 1973, 85 percent of the $5 billion spent on vended food was devoted to items low in vitamins, minerals and protein—soda pop, coffee, candy bars and chewing gum."

Children are impressionable and have little experience in what constitutes good nutrition. They can seldom make wise food choices and usually pick foods that taste good to them and that advertising has created a desire for, often sweets. As a result, vending machines do big business in schools, usually to the detriment of the school lunch program itself.

The poor quality of vended foods is the biggest argument against their sale in school lunchrooms. Dentists and nutritionists alike stress the need to reduce our consumption of sugar. Further, the relationship between sugary, high-carbohydrate, high-cholesterol foods and major health problems like diabetes, atherosclerosis, heart trouble and obesity has been clinically demonstrated time and time again. Allowing vending machines in our schools in the face of the medical evidence constitutes gambling with our children's health for the sake of band uniforms or sports equipment. In addition, the school as an educational institution has a responsibility to foster sound nutritional principles, to practice what it preaches.

A spokesman for the American Dental Association, Dr. Louis A. Saporito, has expressed outrage at the way money is placed before children's nutritional needs in school:

"Every parent or parent-teacher group wants its school to have the finest equipment, resource materials, and so forth," contends Dr. Saporito. "Schools are often hard pressed to find the funds to purchase what they should have. All of us, as citizens, need to be sympathetically alert to that need and be responsive in meeting it.

"When all is said and done, however, it is hardly defensible educational policy to tempt a child to rot his teeth in order for his school to have more athletic equipment or better band uniforms."[4]

When confronted with arguments like these, the food industry loudly proclaims that there is no such thing as a junk food. In the eyes of the industry, the only danger in any food is overconsumption. This may be true in the sense that an occasional soda or candy bar won't do any damage. But our kids are being encouraged to overconsume the wrong foods. Consider the commercials presented on Saturday morning television. How many ads for milk or other healthy foods spring to mind? One, perhaps. But how many jingles for soda, candy bars and cereals can your kids recite?

Although most children are exposed to a few hours of nutrition education in school, they are bombarded by hundreds of ads pushing soda pop, candy bars, candy-flavored cereals and all manner of sugar-laden foods. Coca-Cola spends in the neighborhood of $50 million in one year on advertising. All those commercials link the consumption of these foods to fun and peer acceptance. But they make no mention of the link between candy and tooth decay, or that a 12-ounce can of Coke contains nine teaspoons of sugar.

Because the income generated by vending machines is so valuable, the best solution to the problem would be to stock the machines with wholesome snack foods that can make a positive contribution to health. This is not an impossible dream—vending alternatives *do* exist and are being successfully marketed in schools today.

Schools in Indiana, New York, Texas, Washington, D.C., West Virginia and California have replaced junk food with nutritious snacks. Students at seven North Vancouver schools in British Columbia are now being given a choice of vending machine fare. Instead of only the usual items, students can now pick from a selection of nuts, raisins, dates, figs and dried bananas. Beverages include cherry and apple cider, grape drink and fruit punch—all made from natural fruit. Although standard junk foods are still available, school officials reported that the natural products are selling well.

Probably the first widely publicized and successful campaign against junk foods in school took place in Bloomington, Indiana, initiated by the efforts of one concerned mother, Jean Farmer. As of August 1974, the Monroe County school board voted to regulate all food sold on school premises, including vending machines. The ruling permitted only foods that "make a significant contribution to the students' nutritional needs." This meant that all the junk was removed from the vending machines and replaced by nutritious items. The regulations apply throughout the school day, but not during extracurricular activities.

As one school board member explained it, the school is responsible for the welfare of its students and must set an example. The school's duty extends into the area of health as well as classroom instruction. Besides, if kids really want to have sweets, they still have the rest of the day to do it.

In the Greenburgh Central School District No. 7, in Hartsdale, New York, a committee of parents was formed to monitor and improve the quality of the lunches served in cafeterias in the district's schools. One of the first problems the committee decided to tackle was the sale of snacks during lunchtime. They faced a major problem because sales of snacks and a la carte items were the only way the regular lunch program could break even. The caterer could not continue to run the program without that extra revenue.

The parents' committee solved the problem by substituting wholesome snacks that the caterer could also sell at a profit. Instead of sweets, the students are now munching on raisins, fruit, hard-cooked eggs, bread and butter and sunflower seeds. Potato chips, pretzels and cookies are still in evidence, but the brands sold contain no preservatives or artificial additives. How does the committee determine which snack foods are acceptable and which are not? They explained it to local parents in this way:

"All snack items must be approved by the committee whose standards on questionable food additives must be met. There may be times when a product is removed from sale. The committee wishes to make parents aware that the school board has given them the authority to do so, and that the vendor assists willingly in such decisions. A snack is never removed unless a reasonable substitute is offered."[5]

Wholesome vending is a sound, practical idea whose time has surely come. A whole host of nutritious vending machine products is available right now. The list includes nuts, sunflower and pumpkin seeds, granola, yogurt, fruit, fruit juices, and milk. The Planters company markets several different nut packages. Although they come salted, they are a step in the right direction. The Flavor Tree company puts out a whole line of nutritious, additive-free snack foods made from honest ingredients like bulgur, sesame seeds, sunflower seeds, unbleached flour, toasted soybeans, raisins, peanuts and carob (see the Appendix section for their address). Small packages of cheese and crackers are also available. The cheese contains additives to keep it from spoiling, but still offers more nutrient value than a candy bar.

It might even be worthwhile to consider purchasing a commercial heat sealer to package your own vending products.

You may think that wholesome vending requires all new machines and increased expense. But such is not always the case—many nutritious products can be sold in the usual vending machines. Candy machines can dispense packets of nuts, seeds, granola and whole grain cookies. Fruit juice is available in bottles that will fit in soda machines. If we, the consumers, demand new products, industry will sooner or later have to respond. Milk machines could vend yogurt as well, frozen orange juice bars could be sold in an ice cream machine. Many cafeterias have stainless steel milk dispensers which use milk packaged in large plastic bags. Why couldn't cider and juices be supplied the same way? The point is, we *can* improve the quality of vending machine products, and we owe it to our children to do so.

How to Work for Better Vending

Here's a blueprint for action suggested by the Center for Science in the Public Interest, a nonprofit organization dedicated to improving the lot of today's consumer (for more information, write to them at the address supplied in the Appendix):

1. Choose a specific target. Work towards getting soda pop and candy bars banned from school vending machines, or getting at least half of the slots of every vending machine in the community stocked with nutritious products.

2. Solicit the support of health professionals *before* you announce the campaign. Doctors, nutritionists and particularly dentists should be willing to publicly support the project. Also, contact such organizations as the PTA and consumer groups.

3. If your project concerns schools, the school board will

have to vote on the proposal. Lobby individual board members prior to the meeting at which the issue will be raised. Stress the harmful effects of consuming too much sugar. (The average American consumes more than 100 pounds of sugar every year. Degenerative diseases such as heart disease, some intestinal diseases, and obesity are caused, in part, by diets high in sugar, fat and calories. Sugar is also the leading cause of tooth decay. Fluoridated water supplies do *not* totally prevent cavity formation.)

4. If you are working on a community-wide "good vend" program, inform the local vendors that you definitely want to have better foods. Point out that good foods are available in vendable forms. Unsalted nuts, whole grain snacks such as granola, fruit, hard-boiled eggs, yogurt, milk and fruit juices can be easily purchased by the local vending company. These wholesome products cost about the same as products currently vended. Suggest that nutrition information be posted on vending machines to help promote sales of the new offerings. Remind the vendor that favorable publicity will probably accompany the stocking of good foods. If you are turned down flat, proceed to #5.

5. When your plans are well formulated, contact local newspapers and radio stations. The press has shown a great deal of interest in the "good vend" campaigns that have been launched in the past. Encourage the public, through the press, to support your project. Circulate a petition and/or urge everyone to boycott vending machines. Your chances of success are high. And in the process, you'll help make your whole community more sensitive to the importance of good nutrition—at home as well as in school.

Generally speaking, the most effective way to improve the quality of food service meals is to institute changes gradually. We noted before that fresh-baked bread goes a long way toward better meals, and it is universally popular. Perhaps, then, baking your own whole wheat bread is a good place to start your improvement program. Homemade soups might be the next step. Concentrate on serving dishes that taste good, are simple to prepare and use familiar foods, and you can minimize the cooks' resistance. To please the people who eat the food, don't neglect the all-important principle of choice. People must not be forced to accept new foods or they will rebel. Introduce new foods as alternatives—serve your own fresh, fragrant bread next to store-bought white bread and chances are that most people will go for the whole wheat. If the food looks good enough, they'll try it eventually. If it tastes good enough, they'll be back for more. So remember, when bringing natural foods into institutional food service, the keys to success are gradual change and freedom of choice.

Chapter 2

Feeding Our Children

The eating habits of Americans, especially young Americans, are strongly influenced by media advertising and by the constant changes in our life-style. Over the past couple of decades, this combination of influences has pushed us in the direction of convenience foods designed to get the cook out of the kitchen, starchy carbohydrates that appeal to and strengthen our collective sweet tooth, and fast-food establishments that both reflect and cater to the frantic pace of our lives.

Our food choices are further complicated by the multitude of new developments in food technology which inundate us with an endless flood of processed food products which we are told are not only substitutes for foods like hamburger, bacon and eggs, but are for one reason or another better than the real foods. Our children, as new consumers, need to be taught how to deal with the increasingly complex problem of what to eat. If we as adults are often puzzled by the claims of new food products, imagine the effect on children inexperienced in making food choices. How can our children be expected to differentiate between what's good for them and what isn't?

Whether despite or because of the problems created by the complexity of food choices available to so many of us, we cannot escape the fact that child malnutrition is still a serious health problem in this country. Apparently, we have not yet learned to choose our foods wisely. More startling is the realization that undernourished children who just don't have enough to eat are not confined to the underdeveloped parts of the world—there are many hungry children right here within our own borders. The Ten-State Nutrition Survey, conducted from 1968 to 1970 by the Department of Health, Education and Welfare (and monitored by the Center for Disease Control in Atlanta), found that incidence of malnutrition in some regions of the United States is as high as that of much poorer countries. Fifteen percent of the children surveyed suffered retarded growth due to a simple lack of food. Between one-third and one-half of all persons surveyed, adults as well as children, had vitamin deficiencies. A substantial number were deficient in protein.

But the group with the highest incidence of overall poor nutritional status was made up of children between the ages of 10 and 16—school-age children. This group was also found to have a lot of dental problems, associated with between-meals consumption of high-carbohydrate snack foods such as candy, sodas and pastries. And many of the children were found to be either underweight or overweight, another indication of improper eating habits.

There is no excuse for the existence of such nutritional deficiencies in a country as affluent as the United States. As a nation, we have access to more food than anyone else in the world. Why, then, are so many of our children malnourished? One reason is the absence of adequate nutrition education, which Senator George McGovern, Chairman of the Senate Select Commission on Nutrition, calls "nutritional illiteracy." The ignorance of what kind of food is good for us leads to poor food choices, which lead in turn to improper or inadequate nourishment. Other factors responsible for our nutritional problems include poverty and just plain lack of interest in food.

When good nutrition is not practiced at home, it becomes vital in school. Many children get their major meal of the day in school. Thus, the school lunch and breakfast programs are the most effective weapons we have to fight child malnutrition. At the same time, the school should act as a positive influence on shaping children's food habits. The school program should always provide nutritionally sound meals that offer variety, are attractively presented and are planned with young tastes and appetites in mind. Hand in hand with the food itself should go the teaching of good nutritional principles and an awareness of good food habits.

But, as we'll see, the feeding programs set up for American children are largely ineffective in their attempts to provide meals of high nutritional quality, and nutrition education programs are sorely lacking. Inadequacies are present from preschool levels all the way through the secondary and collegiate levels. Our children deserve better from us.

Day Care and Head Start

On October 7, 1975, Congress passed legislation extending government support of child feeding programs. The new law, P.L. 94-105, not only extended the scope of the National School Lunch Program, but provided increased subsidies for summer food programs and day-care programs as well. Under the Child Care Food Program, all nonprofit public or private day-care centers are eligible for government money and food for breakfasts, lunches, snacks and dinners. The program now provides assistance to all types of licensed day-care facilities, including family day-care homes, Head Start centers, settlement houses and recreation centers. In previous years the program was only available to day-care centers located in poverty areas or in neighborhoods with a high proportion of working mothers.

The Child Care Feeding Program is set up along the same general lines as the school lunch program, with the amount of money a day-care center receives being determined by the number of needy children it serves.

With more and more mothers working at full-time jobs, a substantial part of the responsibility for feeding young children has passed from the home to outside agencies. What the extended program amounts to is Congress's recognition of the importance of day-care feeding programs to childhood nutrition. This is an important advance; the next step must be to insure that children are provided with the *best nutrition possible* within the boundaries of the established system.

Of course, a sophisticated network of government regulations and subsidies is not the only way to provide good food for children in day care. The independent route, whereby an enlightened day-care cook prepares food purchased for an individual center, can be just as successful.

To illustrate the point, we'll look at two examples of day-care feeding (a third appears in chapter 4). Both provide highly nourishing meals, but the approaches are vastly different. One is the Lehigh Valley, Pennsylvania, Head Start organization, which took advantage of government commodities to feed the children under its care. The other is the Atlantis Individual Development Center, a Volunteers of America day-care center in Virginia Beach. The cook for the Atlantis Center did all her own shopping and worked in her own way to provide nutritious food for the center children.

As many mothers could attest, it is often easier to get very young children to try a variety of nutritious foods than to convince older children who have more definite food likes and dislikes. The official guidelines for the Head Start program state the following objectives in the area of nutrition:

1. Provide food which will help meet the child's daily nutritional needs in the child's home or in a clean and pleasant environment, recognizing individual differences and cultural patterns, and thereby promote sound physical, social and emotional growth and development.

2. Provide an environment for nutritional services which will support and promote the use of the feeding situation as an opportunity for learning.

3. Help staff, child and family to understand the relationship of nutrition to health, factors which influence food practices, variety of ways to provide for nutritional needs and to apply this knowledge in the development of sound food habits even after leaving the Head Start program.

4. Demonstrate the interrelationships of nutrition to other activities of the Head Start program and its contribution to the overall child development goals.

5. Involve all staff, parents and other community agencies as appropriate in meeting the child's nutritional needs, so that nutritional care provided by Head Start complements and supplements that of the home and community. [1]

Each Head Start center serves one meal, either breakfast or lunch, and a snack. Any child who hasn't had breakfast before arriving at the center is served a nourishing breakfast. In a part-day program, the food served each child must fill at least one-third of his daily nutritional needs (based on the Recommended Daily Allowances, or RDAs). In the full-day program, the food must fill one-half to two-thirds of the child's RDA.

A hot meal is served each day, and menus are planned to include a variety of foods to broaden children's food experiences. An assortment of regional, ethnic and cultural dishes gives children the chance to taste foods they wouldn't get a chance to try at home.

Each day there is served a good to excellent source of vitamin C; a dark green leafy or yellow vegetable every other day; desserts are an integral part of the meal and supply nutrients other than just calories.

In 1975, Head Start of the Lehigh Valley sought a new six-week menu plan that could be used in rotation throughout the year. Such a plan would make it easier to order food. Anita Hirsch, home economist in charge of the Fitness House kitchen here at Rodale Press, was asked to draw up a menu plan that would utilize available government commodities while providing children with good, nutritious meals.

In planning the menus, Anita first looked over a list of available commodities and found out what food was left over from the previous year (powdered milk was one item available in abundance). The next step was to find recipes using those foods. In order to take advantage of the low-cost government foods, some compromises in quality had to be made. For this reason some canned foods and some sugar were used in the Head Start menus.

However, only whole grain breads and cereals were used, and full-strength fruit juices were served with snacks instead of fruit drinks. Not only are fruit juices nutritionally better than fruit drinks, they're also a better economic value. Examining the labels of many fruit drinks shows that the first ingredient listed is water, meaning that the product contains more water than anything else. The second ingredient is usually sugar, and fruit juice ends up in third place. What this means is that when you buy fruit drinks, you're really paying for sugar and water.

Along with the fruit juice, children received a graham cracker, fresh or dried fruit, a cookie or peanut butter. Cookies were limited to three kinds which contained oatmeal, raisins or peanut butter, to provide some food value other than the carbohydrates supplied by sugar and flour. The Head Start guidelines stress the importance of snacks, and specify a number of wholesome snack foods to be served instead of pretzels and sweets.

Anita prepared the following list of suggested snack foods for use in all the Head Start centers:

Fresh Fruits

Apples	Grapefruit	Peaches
Oranges	Grapes	Pineapple
Tangerines	Pears	Cantaloupe
Tangelos	Plums	Berries

Canned fruits packed in water or own juices

Fresh Vegetables

Asparagus	Cucumbers	Peas
Broccoli	Green beans	Radishes
Carrots	Green peppers	Tomatoes
Cauliflower	Mushrooms	Turnips
Celery		

Protein Foods

Cheese, cottage cheese, yogurt (plain)
Eggs
Fish
Meats
Nuts and seeds
Popcorn
Poultry (chicken, turkey)
Soups and dips made from dried beans or peas
Soy nuts

Thirst Quenchers

Buttermilk and plain milk (low fat or skimmed)*
Fruit juices, canned, fresh, frozen, but no sugar added
    (Look for word "juice" when purchasing; the label indicat-
    ing "fruit drink" usually says "sugar added.")
Vegetable juices, without sugar
Water
*Milk can also be considered a protein food.

Along with the breakfast foods kept on hand for children who needed them, bread, cereal, milk, fresh fruit, dried fruit and nuts were always available.

The lunches followed this pattern: vegetable and/or fruit; main dish (protein); bread and butter; milk. Each meal contained at least one hot food. Portions were small so children had enough but those with small appetites weren't forced to eat, and seconds were always available. Anita recommended substitute foods for children with various food allergies.

In line with the Head Start regulations, menus were planned to broaden children's food experiences, as well as to offer ethnic and cultural favorites with which children were familiar. (The menus for Head Start of the Lehigh Valley appear in the menus section, chapter 8.) Hamburgers and grilled cheese sandwiches were served, but so were spaghetti, chow mein and liver. Instead of sticking with vegetables like peas, carrots and corn which most children know and like, menus also included broccoli, Brussels sprouts and other more unusual vegetables which children might not get the chance to try at home. Everyone was encouraged to try a little of everything, but no one was forced to eat foods he or she didn't like. Having the teachers eat at the tables with the children set a good example for reluctant appetites. Also, serving vegetables in different ways was often successful; many children didn't like cabbage but enjoyed cole slaw. To their surprise, the cooks and teachers found that children ate liver, Brussels sprouts, spinach, squash, lentil soup, meatballs and beans, broccoli, and spinach and rice casserole.

A very commendable feature of the Head Start program is the system of meal evaluation. Meals are monitored periodically to see that certain standards are met in terms of nutritional quality, to see that children are eating the food and cooks are preparing it properly. The program as it has been set up is a generally good one and offers a real opportunity to provide children with high quality meals in an atmosphere of learning.

To encourage the close connection between eating and learning, Anita suggested growing sprouts in the classroom, where children can watch them grow, then using them in salads and other dishes where children will taste the end result of the growth process.

Quite a different approach to meal planning was taken at the Atlantis Individual Development Center in Virginia Beach. During the 1974–1975 term, Ms. Page Cullen was responsible for feeding 60 three- to five-year-olds lunch and a snack each day. She did it for a remarkable $60 a week, without any government commodities. The center received some government funds, but no food.

Page explains that her biggest secret was cooking from scratch, using foods as free of additives as possible. Every other meal was vegetarian, with complete-protein combinations of beans, grains, nuts and dairy products based on the information in *Diet for a Small Planet* and *Recipes for a Small Planet* (see the Appendix). Ms. Cullen used organic beans, whole grain noodles, eggs and cheese, nitrate- and nitrite-free bacon and hot dogs, and fresh produce.

Much of the food was purchased at supermarkets and a local farmers' market. Ms. Cullen did all the shopping herself and found that most supermarkets carry items like honey and commercial brands of whole wheat and rye flours. For the special items, such as nitrate- and nitrite-free meats, she joined a co-op where foods were sold at wholesale price plus a 10 percent markup. Yearly co-op membership for the day-care center cost $15.

Although there was ample storage space (one refrigerator full of milk and another for flours, raisins, eggs, butter, vegetables and fruits; freezer space for the meats), Page went shopping nearly every day to have a continuous supply of the freshest possible foods. It sounds like a lot of time for the cook to put in, but she prepared all the food in just three and a half hours a day, and this time included the shopping.

In addition to frequent vegetarian meals, cost-cutting practices included using meat scraps to make soup stock and doing all the baking from scratch. Ms. Cullen found that mentioning to the fish market man, the grocer or the farmer that she was cooking for a government-subsidized group resulted in discounts she didn't even ask for. On a nice day, the children had fun picking vegetables in a "pick-your-own" field, while they learned how vegetables grow and also supplied the cook with some fine, fresh, inexpensive produce for their lunches.

Another very important way to save money is to reduce food waste by tailoring portions to small appetites. At the Atlantis Center, apples were served in quarters and grapes a few at a time. It's always better to give some children second and third helpings than to throw out a lot of partially eaten apples.

Ms. Cullen also found that in the long run, whole grain products cost less than white-flour products because they are more filling. The children could easily consume two pieces of white bread, but usually only half a piece of homemade whole wheat.

Page used many standard recipes in her kitchen, substituting whole wheat flour for white, honey for sugar and tahini (sesame seed paste) for butter. She used no luncheon meats, no chocolate and no MSG. Snack foods included raw vegetables, fresh fruit, crackers, cookies, milk and unsweetened diluted fruit juices.

Some foods the children especially liked were cheese rarebit, miso soup, chick-peas, corn on the cob, salads with cheese cubes and Italian dressing, stuffed eggs, baked beans, poached fish, nitrate- and nitrite-free hot dogs, zucchini bread and whole wheat doughnuts. Raw cucumbers, carrots, string beans, turnips, rutabagas, black olives and sugar peas were also well accepted.

To be sure, there were some things that just didn't go over, such as cream soups, any thin soups, hollandaise sauce and cheesecake. Noses were turned up at vegetables that weren't attractively chopped. Oddly enough, that all-American favorite, steak, was also unpopular.

Each day, six children were sent to help in the kitchen, and menus were planned so that each meal contained a food that three- to five-year-olds could help to prepare. This kind of experience can help to lay the foundation for future nutrition education activities by introducing children to various foods and how they are prepared.

Several rewarding experiences came out of the natural foods meals at the Atlantis Center. One hyperactive little girl took her first nap—an event credited to the additive-free foods. The teachers stopped bringing their lunches and started having lunch at the center. To her great delight, one of the teachers lost 15 pounds because the filling lunches enabled her to cut down on the food she ate for dinner. Another teacher who suffered from arthritis and whose doctor had forbidden her to eat meat and eggs was overjoyed by the profusion of vegetarian meals. Most gratifying of all were the showers of compliments that rained down on the cook from her young charges.

You can't start too early to steer children away from foods that are filled with additives and sugar and toward foods that build strong muscles, good teeth and happy smiles. Day care offers the perfect opportunity for children to experience new foods in the company of their peers. We've seen two approaches, one working a government program and one working independently, both of which supplied varied, nourishing meals for preschoolers.

Elementary and Secondary Schools
—The National School Lunch Program

The magnitude of the problems involved with feeding children on a large scale, as well as the potential for improvement, can perhaps best be seen in the National School Lunch Program. Our schools constitute a major food market, exceeded only by separate eating places (restaurants, public cafeterias, etc.) and the military services.[2] *Food and Nutrition* magazine stated that during the 1974–1975 school year, more than 43 million children attended schools participating in the National School Lunch Program—the largest number in the program's history.[3] Further evidence of the increasing numbers of children relying on the school for their lunch was collected in October of 1975 by state and regional USDA offices. Data showed that although the number of kids enrolled in school dropped by 370,000 from the 1973–1974 school year to 1974–1975, enrollment in the school lunch program rose by 415,000 during the same time. Also, the USDA reported that fewer children attended schools without food service in 1975–1976 than in previous years.

What all this means in day-to-day terms is that the school bears an enormous responsibility for the feeding of

American children, and thus should provide the most nutritious food possible. Every day, millions of children eat a lunch that must comply with government regulations. Many eat breakfast in school as well. The guidelines presently allow for such products as "Breakfast Squares" and "Super Doughnuts" to be served for breakfast, and highly refined carbohydrate foods and sugar-laden desserts appear in many of the lunches.

In 1972, Congress changed the lunch program to allow vending machines to compete with the hot lunches served in school cafeterias. In July 1975, an attempt to restore the former ban on the vending of junk foods during the lunch period was passed by the Senate, but killed in conference with the House. What this means in many schools is that a hot meal is being served in the cafeteria while vending machines dispense soda and candy in the halls, surely a situation which discourages many students from eating a good lunch. This issue is discussed more fully in "The Problem of Vending" in chapter 1.

In a USDA bulletin, the following goals are outlined for the National School Lunch Program by Dr. Ruth M. Leverton of the Agricultural Research Service:

> Close the nutrition gap between food available at home and total food needs, thus meeting current nutritional needs for the child's growth and development;
> Shore up some nutritive reserves for the child's future growth, development and well-being;
> Establish good eating habits through repeated experience with desirable practice;
> Reach parents with aids for maintaining nutritional health of their children; and
> Acquaint teaching staff with the value of encouraging children to eat and enjoy a variety of good foods.[4]

These are very admirable goals and define for the school an important role in the health of all children. Unfortunately, these goals are seldom, if ever, attained in actual practice,

31

and school lunches are still generally of relatively poor quality.

For one thing, the meals served have been found to be often low in nutritional value, due for the most part to poor planning and handling techniques. The Type A lunch requirements specify that each lunch must contain the following rather modest components (minimum amounts):

- ½ pint whole or skim milk
- 2 ounces lean meat, poultry or fish; or 2 ounces cheese; or 1 egg; or 4 tablespoons peanut butter; or a quantitatively equivalent combination of the above
- ¾ cup serving of two or more vegetables or fruit, or both
- 1 slice whole grain or enriched bread
- 1 teaspoon butter or margarine.

The Type A lunch is supposed to provide at least one-third of the nutrients and food energy a child needs in a day, based on the RDA (recommended daily allowance). (The Type B lunch, a sandwich and milk, and Type C pattern, only milk, are not currently in use.) But a USDA study conducted in 1967 found that two-thirds of the school lunches surveyed did not meet even the modest Type A requirements.[5] Some of the lunches were simply too small, and many were lacking in iron.

About a third of the lunches did not provide enough vitamin A. It wasn't that the deficient lunches didn't include vitamin A-containing foods, the problem was that they contained only fair sources of vitamin A, such as tomatoes, instead of good sources like dark green and yellow vegetables.

Many of the lunches had too much fat (over one-third of the lunches derived more than 40 percent of their calories from fat!), but surprisingly, many of the lunches didn't provide enough calories.

As we discussed in an earlier chapter, many common handling techniques, such as distributing prepared foods from a central kitchen, holding food in steam tables for extended periods during serving, and preparing vegetables by boiling them in large amounts of water substantially deplete nutrient values. Thus, the chance that an already poorly planned meal will fulfill the nutritional requirements of the Type A lunch is even slimmer. The problem is further compounded when a sizable part of the lunch regularly ends up in the garbage can instead of in the student's stomach.

Thus, even when the lunches do meet the Type A requirements, kids don't get the nutrients if they don't eat the food. The USDA regulations stipulate what must be served in the Type A lunch, but they don't say students have to eat it or like it. And many kids *don't* eat the school lunch. The amounts of food thrown away in many of our schools is something to behold.

A couple of years ago, a team of researchers conducted a study on plate waste in which they analyzed what nutrients were actually consumed from the lunches in a group of schools.[6]

Three groups of students were studied—fifth, seventh and tenth graders. The researchers found that none of the groups consumed the required one-third of their minimum daily allowance of calories, vitamin C or thiamin (vitamin B_1). Only the fifth graders consumed enough iron and calcium. However, all the groups did get enough protein, vitamin A and riboflavin (vitamin B_2).

It is interesting to note that in the case of vitamin A, students consumed on the average of only 64 percent of the vitamin A served in the lunches, but that amount was more than enough to fill one-third of their daily requirement. This finding illustrates the importance of serving the best possible food sources of all nutrients. On the other hand, the researchers found that no really good sources of iron were included in any of the lunches. And vitamin C was not even served in adequate amounts, so students could not possibly fill their vitamin C requirements even if they ate the whole meal. When you stop to consider that the government's recommended daily allowances (RDAs) for vitamins and minerals are under fire by many nutrition advocates for being too low, serving less than a third of the RDA in school lunch might be encouraging marginal or subclinical deficiencies in our children. The child who gets a good breakfast and a good nutritious dinner at home probably makes up for any nutritional inadequacies in the school lunch. But what about the kids for whom school lunch is the main meal of the day? How will they get all the nutrients they need to develop to their full physical and mental potential? It should be the school's responsibility to provide the most nourishing and appealing lunch possible to the students under its care, a lunch that students will want to eat.

Why don't students eat their school lunches? The USDA study cited above included a survey of high school students to find out what made them decide to buy the school lunch.[7] The most common answers were:

- how the food is prepared,
- the quality of the food,
- the appearance of the lunchroom,
- time spent waiting in line, and
- length of the lunch period.

While the latter three points may be primarily administrative matters, the first two are certainly problems with which the food service director must be concerned. Quite simply, kids just won't eat a lunch that is unappealing. Consider the following examples of lunches served in one Pennsylvania school district:

- tomato soup with saltines
- fish sticks on bun
- buttered peas
- buttered potatoes
- chocolate pudding
- ½ pint milk

- chicken pot pie (a dish made from chicken, noodles, potatoes and carrots)
- buttered corn
- bread and butter
- shoo-fly pie (a type of pie with a cakelike filling and a gooey, sweet bottom layer)
- ½ pint milk

Both these meals are full of heavy, starchy, high-carbohydrate foods and sweets. Noticeably lacking are good sources of vitamin C and crisp, fresh foods such as salads and raw vegetables and fruits. There is also little dietary fiber. Such an assortment of foods doesn't offer much contrast in texture or color, nothing to break up the heaviness. In short, the meals are unimaginative and unappealing.

Meals like these lead to the large amounts of plate waste uncovered by studies such as the one conducted by the USDA.

Part of the problem is that the school food service is limited in the foods it can serve because it must take advantage of the foods donated under the government commodities program in order to keep costs down. The school food service is both helped and hampered by the commodities program because the foods made available to schools at no cost are not based on the needs of children, but on the need of farmers and industry to dispose of excess foodstuffs. As Margaret Mead, the noted anthropologist, described the situation in the *Journal of Nutrition Education* (Summer 1970), "We are separating food that nourishes people from food out of which some people derive their incomes."

The USDA has listed among its available commodities canned and frozen beef, canned and frozen chicken, frozen turkeys, canned pork, canned applesauce, grapefruit, peaches, pineapple and plums, canned string beans, peas, sweet potatoes and tomatoes, dried peas and beans, dehydrated sweet potatoes, dried eggs, canned chopped meat, lard, margarine, peanut butter, grape juice, orange juice, cornmeal, rice, bulgur, rolled oats, rolled wheat, flour, white potatoes and honey.*

This may sound like a pretty good selection of basic foods, but on closer examination it becomes evident that in many cases the same foods in less processed form, although more difficult to ship and store, would be markedly better in terms of nutritional value. Consider these points:

The canned fruit is packed in sugar syrup which adds many useless calories.

The cornmeal is degermed, meaning that the heart of the corn kernel, its most nutritious part, has been removed.

The rice is white—the brown outer layer, where the vitamins and minerals are concentrated, has been polished off.

The flour is ground from only the middle portion of the wheat kernel. The fiber-rich bran and nutritious germ have been removed. Also, the flour has been bleached and treated with chemical preservatives.

Lard and margarine are not very desirable shortenings. Lard is highly saturated fat, the type of substance doctors now believe helps to cause heart and circulatory ailments. Margarine, while not as bad as lard, is still saturated to a degree and contains various artificial ingredients as well. Some margarines are made from vegetable oils, which are often high in polyunsaturates. But the oils must be hydrogenated (saturated) to harden them. If margarine was truly polyunsaturated it would be a liquid. Further, the manufacturing process turns the oils into a dark, greasy mass. It has to be bleached and deodorized, then treated with dyes and flavorings to produce the sunny yellow spread we know as margarine.

But there are ways in which a clever, resourceful food service director can use government commodities and still serve meals that are tasty as well as wonderfully nutritious. The Milwaukee School District has won many awards for its

*Current copies of the USDA's quarterly report on donated foods are available from them on request.

lunch program. Food Service Director Tom Farley never refuses government commodities, and his department turns out lunches of such high quality that they won an award for the best food service operation in the United States. The Milwaukee story is told in "A School Lunch Program To Be Proud Of," in chapter 4.

One of the pioneers in the field was Gena Larson, who set about to improve the lunch program at Helix High School in La Mesa, California. The remarkable thing about Ms. Larson's successful campaign was that it began back in the 1950s when the climate of public opinion was still a tremendous hurdle. At that time, before the advent of the natural foods movement, people weren't as food conscious as they are becoming today, and there was little concern over the effects of processing on the nutrient value of food.

Ms. Larson's approach was to institute her changes gradually. "The first day as director I asked permission to remove the candy," she told newspaper editor Don C. Matchan. "And that year we were content to have made that stride. The next year we introduced the low-calorie but high-protein diet, with the salad line divided into three sections: protein foods, vegetable section and fruit tray.

"The next year we introduced box lunches. These varied in foods, but they were always high in essential nutrients. Sometimes the box lunch consisted of a peanut butter cupcake, slaw or salad in a carton, choice of seven kinds of sandwiches on whole grain bread, a hot dish, milk, and dessert which was fruit." The box lunch was usually eaten outdoors, picnic style, which added to the fun.

Another innovation introduced by Ms. Larson was the extra-high-protein line for athletes and students carrying heavy scholastic loads. Anyone could choose this food but the portions were heavier, and if a youngster repeatedly did not eat all of it, he was gently but firmly directed to another line.

Ms. Larson naturally had to watch every penny since, like all school cafeteria directors, she worked on a tight budget. The only year the cafeteria operated at a slight deficit, three assistants were out for illness, resulting in extra payroll. But after her assistants had been with her a while, they too learned how to eat, and sick leaves were rarely necessary.

Ms. Larson's success was due largely to the fact that she cleverly adapted her resources and facilities within the framework of the federal-state program. She used all the most nutritious foods provided under the government commodities program. The foods that were processed she reinforced and supplemented with highly nutritious substances—wheat germ, brewer's yeast, brown rice flour, soy flour. Whenever possible, she removed unnecessary sugar from a commodity food. For instance, instead of feeding youngsters the sugar syrup with canned fruit, she drained it off and served the fruit plain. When there was a choice she bought water-packed fruit in No. 10 cans. Then she would pour off the juice, sweeten it with one-quarter to one-half cup of honey and return the syrup to the fruit. This method proved most popular with the students.

Many schools use instant mashed potatoes that have had practically all the nutrients processed out of them and various chemical substances added to them. Ms. Larson used the whole potato, skin and all. She found that potatoes scrubbed in their jackets can be diced, creamed, hash-browned, prepared with cheese sauce or even used in salads. This practice preserves valuable nutrients and fiber and saves peeling time as well.

Ms. Larson used various techniques to stretch foods and not only added nutrients but saved money as well. Ground beef was extended with cheese, cottage cheese, powdered milk or soy meal. She asked her meat supplier to make hamburger of one part ground heart to three parts ground beef. This mixture is more nutritious and less expensive than ground beef alone, and the Helix High students enjoyed the difference without knowing what made the difference. Whenever Ms. Larson used white flour, she added wheat germ. She made her own mayonnaise and catsup using honey, her own cake frosting with carob and honey.

Other schools have found wide acceptance of special "diet

lunches." Teenage obesity is often reported in nutrition surveys, and even teenagers who aren't overweight are notorious calorie counters. To deal with this problem in Tuscon, Arizona, Canyon del Oro High School offers a diet plate which meets Type A requirements. It was reported that 50 to 90 students a day ate the diet lunch, and not all of them had weight problems. It was also popular among athletes, especially wrestlers who had to maintain a certain weight.

A sample menu included tuna salad, green beans, a tomato slice, bread and butter, fruit and milk. Other entrées were cottage cheese, beef patties, surf patties (made from tuna) and a taco salad.

In conjunction with the diet lunches, the principal organized a class in "weight awareness" to discuss nutritional needs and maintaining a proper weight.[8]

From her successful experience at Helix High, Ms. Larson compiled a list of nutrition tips for school food service directors.

Nutrition Tips for Your School's Food Manager

In baking, replace some of the commodity flour with whole grain flour, plus wheat germ, soy flour and rice polish. No need to change the other ingredients. Use your favorite recipe, she advises. Use arrowroot flour with its high mineral content as a replacement for cornstarch in all recipes. In sauces and gravies, use ⅓ cup arrowroot for each one cup of cornstarch called for. In puddings sweetened with honey or molasses, you will need ¾ cup arrowroot for each one cup of cornstarch called for. The lesser quantity needed makes the cost comparable to that of cornstarch.

In order to bring the commodity white rice nutrients up, sprinkle it with raw rice polish just as it goes on the food line. It is convenient to use a large shaker-top jar for this.

To sweeten cakes and cookies, use honey—⅓ to ½ cup for each one cup of sugar called for in the recipe. Simply blend with shortening as in standard recipes.

For a brown sugar flavor, use part molasses.

Date sugar or date butter can also replace white sugar about cup for cup.

In order to substitute carob for cocoa or chocolate, use one teaspoon of cocoa in each cup of carob for the aroma of chocolate, as carob does not otherwise have it. When the students learn to like the carob taste, discontinue the cocoa.

Multiply food values, avoid toxic sprays, and help balance the food budget by using sprouts. (See "Grow Your Own Sprouts" in chapter 8 for directions on sprouting.)

Sunflower or pumpkin seeds are delicious snacks. Serve them in a one-ounce souffle cup as an "extra" once in a while. Suggest that students add sunflower seeds to salads, applesauce or other fruits. Mix seeds with raisins and nuts in a three-ounce cup for a fine winter dessert.

For a new taste experience, try a mock lobster salad made with grated raw parsnips. Dress with lemon, seasoned salt, black olives and mayonnaise.

Here's a great dessert: Roll one-half banana in yogurt or lemon, then in chopped nuts. Decorate with whipped dried milk topping.

Here are some additional ideas for better quality school food:

Try making your own applesauce instead of always relying on canned. At a local vo-tech school, leftover apples that begin to go soft before they are used are cooked and made into applesauce.

Assorted fresh vegetables and cheese sticks served with a tangy dip make a nutritious and tasty accompaniment for soup or a sandwich, and can be especially welcome in hot weather. In addition to carrot and celery sticks and radishes, try green pepper slices, whole cherry tomatoes, raw broccoli and cauliflower florets.

Fill sandwiches with natural cheese, meats, eggs, peanut butter and various spreads, instead of luncheon meats or processed cheeses.

Don't overlook cottage cheese when planning menus. It's

high in protein and less expensive than similar cheeses, such as ricotta.

Dried fruits can be used as snack or dessert items. In addition to raisins, try apples, apricots, dates, figs, peaches and pears.

For a new kind of dessert, try a yogurt fruit cup, made from plain yogurt, fresh berries or other fruit, diced dried fruit, nuts and honey.

Pudding topped with granola makes a nice crunchy dessert.

For high-protein beverage to serve athletes or use in a snack bar, make milk shakes with whole milk, non instant powdered milk, fresh or frozen berries, bananas, honey and eggs.

The single most important factor in successfully introducing new foods into the school lunch program appears to be to make the change gradual. On this point food service people in schools where the lunch program was overhauled largely agree. Students of all ages will rebel at the idea of being forced to accept new foods, whether the food is better for them or not. The element of choice is an absolute necessity if the transition is to occur smoothly. This may mean concessions and compromises such as offering a choice of sandwiches made with whole grain or white bread at first or perhaps, for younger children, making sandwiches with one slice of whole grain bread and one slice of white bread.

Providing some sort of orientation to the student body to explain the reasons for the change in lunchroom fare is also helpful and may become necessary. One food service director reported that when natural foods were introduced in her school, many students were dismayed at the disappearance of their favorite junk foods. However, a humorous assembly hall presentation explaining the change in food proved highly successful, and after a few weeks, the backers of the natural foods line just about equalled the hard-line traditionalists who refused to switch. Consequently, the idea of offering both natural and conventional foods stuck, and satisfied both factions.

Parents Can Help, Too

Parents can play an important role in upgrading the lunch program in local schools. If you are among the increasing number of parents who have been working with dedication to establish good nutrition habits in your children, you probably look with dismay at the kind of food your children are eating at school, for two important reasons. These foods can undermine their health, as you know. They can also undo much of the good work you have been doing. Children, especially young children, tend to accept the authority of the school as gospel. If white bread, white rice and doughnuts can be served under the aegis of such a powerful authority, then how can you hope to compete?

You must, of course, insist on better nutrition at home to compensate for its lack at school. But you must do more than that. With tact, diplomacy and gentle persuasion, you should bring your knowledge of the importance of good nutrition to the school.

You might understandably have qualms about such an undertaking. Can you, a mere parent, educate the food service manager at your school in the importance of high-nutrition snacks, whole foods and a cut-back in sweets and refined starches? Can you, a mere parent, show the cafeteria manager how he can improve his nutritional index?

After you have learned the modus operandi of one eminently successful nutritional adventure in a public school, you'll feel confident that you can and you most definitely should.

You must bear in mind that the director of the food service is usually schooled in nutrition and may be just as dismayed as you are because of the empty calories on the menu. He may be eager for some show of concern on the part of parents. As one food service director remarked, "Parents are more concerned about getting new uniforms for the band than they are about getting decent food for their children to eat at school." We'd all like to tell ourselves this isn't so, but if the PTA continually goes gung ho over new uniforms or new playground equipment and never spends an evening discussing nutrition and whether the food service is meeting the requirements of their growing children, you can't blame a food director if he feels there is little parental interest in this most important subject.

In the Greenburgh Central School District No. 7 in Hartsdale, New York, a committee of parents was given authority by the school board to decide what kinds of food should be served in district schools. The parents got rid of all foods containing artificial flavors, colors and preservatives. They replaced white bread with whole wheat and got rid of the sodas—only milk and fruit juice are now available. In general, the amount of sugar in the food served was reduced. Canned fruit, for example, is served with only a teaspoon of syrup instead of the usual dishful.

Why did the parents decide to make all these changes? For one thing, they just don't believe processed foods have been proven safe and don't want to expose their kids to possible harm from the additives and artificial ingredients present in such foods. The parents are also aware of the harm that sugar can do to young teeth and its potential to encourage obesity, coronary and circulatory problems later in life. The actions of the Greenburgh parents' committee are further discussed in "The Problem of Vending" in chapter 1.

Increasing Participation in the School Lunch Program

Of course, spending so much time and effort to make school lunch better is a lost investment if students don't buy their lunch in school. After years of unappealing food have brought participation in the local school lunch program to an all-time low, it may be necessary to look for ways of getting the students back in the cafeteria, and for ways of expanding the program to allow as many children as possible to take advantage of the nutritious lunches.

Officials from the Cheltenham, Pennsylvania, School District increased participation in the elementary school lunch program by allowing fifth and sixth graders to eat anytime between 11:30 A.M. and 12:15 P.M. A red flag, visible from the playground, is raised when 15 minutes remain in the lunch period. Besides increasing participation, the system has reduced long cafeteria lines.

A few years ago, the Maryland Food Committee increased participation in the lunch program in Maryland schools by more than 600 percent. First, the committee was aware that the state and federal governments had allotted money to feed needy children but weren't in much of a hurry to spend it. The committee brought public pressure to bear on the government agencies to get the money released.

Since all religious groups are concerned with feeding hungry people, committee members went to the churches for help. The first fund drive back in 1969 brought in almost $70,000, and more in following years. This money was used to buy equipment and hire workers for school cafeterias. In return, the schools that got help were expected to explore every available means to feed more children, from applying for more government aid to simply letting parents know when their children were eligible for free or reduced-price lunches.

The Maryland Food Committee isn't composed of paid professionals. It is a volunteer organization of over 100 private citizens. And it works. By 1974, over 130,000 children in Maryland were getting free or reduced price school lunches.[9]

A Plan for Improving Your School Lunch Program

The following plan for taking positive action to get better food in your school's cafeteria was developed by Mary T. Goodwin, public health nutritionist with the Montgomery County, Maryland Health Department. It is part of an excellent paper entitled "How To Improve Your School Lunch Program," which is available from the county health department (see the Appendix).

1. Do the administrators and teachers feel that the school food service program is important to the growth, develop-

ment, learning and behavior of children? If so, are they committed to making the program succeed? Do parents feel the program is important, and are they willing to support it? In a recent study, the USDA found positive attitudes in administrators, teachers and school food service workers in schools with high cafeteria participation (high school level—average of 80 percent daily). Concerned groups could survey administrators, teachers, food service workers, parents and students, regarding their perceptions of the purpose and state of the program.

2. Are the school food service personnel adequately trained? Many programs fail because personnel are poorly trained. Comprehensive courses should be required in food purchasing, preparation, servicing, storage, management, nutrition, human relations and sanitation for all school food service personnel.

3. Is the nutrition education classroom instruction coordinated with the food service program? The school food service program provides an ideal laboratory for nutrition education and vocational training. Promotion of energy-intensive convenience foods, such as preplated lunches through classroom instruction, is hardly in the best interests of our children. Be sure the nutrition education is responsible and is not a time to promote highly processed foods. Remember children are establishing lifelong eating patterns.

4. Is the school lunch a model for teaching good nutrition? School lunches should be a model of good nutrition, an example of a well-balanced meal. With mothers working and the popularity of snack foods, the teaching role of the school feeding program is more important than ever. In addition, the school lunch is with students from kindergarten through high school graduation. Consider the Chinese proverb, "I hear and I forget, I see and I remember, I do and I understand."

5. Do students creatively participate in planning, preparing and serving the school lunch? Student committees on school food service can be valuable if students are given realistic guidelines and reasonable suggestions are imple-

mented. Students could learn food service skills useful for summer jobs and part-time employment.

6. Is a variety of nutritious foods, seasonal foods and regional foods frequently served? A wide variety of nutritious food is more likely to provide the essential nutrients; various fruits and vegetables contain different kinds and amounts of nutrients. Use of regional foods may give students a sense of belonging and helps support small local farmers who would supply fresh foods and more variety than the international corporate conglomerates. Natural foods are best.

7. Do at least 60 percent of the students participate in the Type A lunch? Ideally, the lunches should be so appealing and low cost that every student would want to eat the lunch.

8. Do the students have a choice in the Type A lunch; a salad bar or low calorie lunch; a hot lunch; a bag lunch; a natural foods lunch; a soup and sandwich bar? Today's children have to take more responsibility for their own health than in the past. They need to be given the opportunity to make decisions which will benefit their health. Availability is one of the most important factors in food selection.

9. Is the food in the Type A lunch carefully selected to provide a wide variety of wholesome foods? At least 50 known nutrients are important for human nutrition. A diet containing a wide variety of natural foods is best. Raw fruit and vegetables and whole grain bread and cereal contain fiber. Foods high in fiber promote healthy teeth and gums, as well as a healthy colon.

10. Is the Type A lunch carefully prepared? The foods selected and prepared should provide a variety of nutrients and a variety of colors, textures, flavors and forms. Hot foods should be served hot and cold foods served cold. If food is overcooked and mushy, not only does loss of taste and appeal result, but nutrient loss occurs also.

11. Is the Type A lunch attractively merchandised? The eye eats first. If the food looks good, the chances are the students will taste it.

12. Do the students have more junk food to select from

than wholesome foods? Are a la carte items competing with the Type A lunch? Bombarding children with a variety of junk foods may undermine their health. Educational institutions should be setting an example and not encouraging children to eat foods that are debased by excessive amounts of sugar, saturated fat and potentially harmful food additives. Fabricated, formulated, fake foods are making huge inroads into institutional feeding.

13. Does the food service staff spend more than 10 percent of their time ordering, preparing, merchandising and selling junk foods? The school food service program is subsidized by your tax dollars. Using time and energy for pushing junk food may not be the best use of tax dollars, or more importantly, not in the best interests of your children.

14. Was the school kitchen closed and preplated lunches substituted for lunches prepared on site? Closing school kitchens is closing alternatives. Preplated lunches are inferior in nutrition, taste, texture and color to lunches prepared on-site. In addition, some foods used are diluted with extenders, and others are laced with food additives. Little is known about the additive, accumulative and synergistic effects of many food additives. Why test them out on children?

15. Are throwaway plastics, paper and aluminum containers used in serving the lunch? Our resources are not unlimited. The ecological ramification of throwaways is far reaching. Consider the value system that is being encouraged in children.

16. Is more than 10 percent of the food served wasted? Try an archaeology study and measure the waste. What is the cost of the food wasted? How many people could be fed with this food? What is the educational message? Why is the food being wasted? Consider the high cost of food, the world food shortages and world famine.

17. Do the students have adequate time to eat and savor their food (20 to 30 minutes)? When students are rushed and hurried, there is a tendency to waste food, and a negative attitude toward eating may result.

18. Is the environment in the cafeteria pleasant, relaxing

and conducive to enjoyment? The environment in which students eat may be as important as the food. A noisy or regimented atmosphere may result in rejection of food. A pleasant atmosphere is far more conducive to development of good eating habits.

19. Is the food offered under psychologically acceptable conditions with proper regard to the students' self-respect? If positive emotions are aroused, the program is contributing to the emotional well-being of children. If negative emotions are aroused and the meal is unenjoyable, the lunch program may be detrimental to the child's self-respect. Eating and being fed are intimately connected with one's deepest feelings. Food offered without due regard for childrens' self-respect may result in their disliking school, thereby poisoning their relationship to school and learning.

20. Do the teachers eat the same food as the students? If the teachers have different food from the students, one may suspect that it is not good enough for them, perhaps a suggestion of classism.

21. Does your school protect the rights of students on a free or reduced-price lunch? Students receiving free or reduced-price lunches have the right to remain anonymous, and they should not be treated differently from those who pay. This means no separate lines, they should *not* work for their meals, and they should not eat in a separate room or have a special kind of identification. If the rights of one are violated, the rights of all are in jeopardy.

22. If your school serves breakfast, is it adequate? Breakfast is a very important meal. In areas where there is a high percentage of low income families, serious consideration should be given to providing an adequate breakfast program.

23. Does your school have a vegetable garden? Vegetable gardens could provide food for its cafeteria and for classroom demonstration, as well as an opportunity for students to learn gardening skills and provide worthwhile contact with nature.

24. Does your school have celebrations, ethnic happen-

ings or festivals with food as an important part? Celebrations around favorite people, past and present, in the community give children a sense of community, of belonging. Collect recipes from local heroes and heroines, leaders and favorite people to use in menu planning, then invite the local celebrities to come and celebrate.

The School Breakfast Program

The School Breakfast Program can fill a real need among many school-age children today. Too many Americans of all ages skip breakfast. Adults should know better—everyone knows you can't do your best work on an empty stomach. But what lots of people don't know is that a doughnut or pastry or slice of toast in the morning is little better than skipping breakfast altogether. All those carbohydrates rush pell-mell through your bloodstream, and by 10:00 you're hungry again and haven't got the energy to concentrate on your work.

Skipping breakfast has just as strong an effect on a child's ability to concentrate in school, perhaps an even greater effect. It's a well-documented fact that missing breakfast seriously hinders academic performance. A good breakfast is especially vital for children who don't get an adequate meal in the evening. If a child doesn't have enough good, nourishing food to eat at dinnertime, his blood sugar level drops to fasting level by the next morning. Fasting level is the point at which there isn't enough sugar in your blood to give you energy, and you feel hungry and weakened. If the child doesn't eat breakfast, he has no energy left to begin a new day. He is listless, unable to concentrate, and can't pay attention to class work. In short, it would seem that a hungry child just can't learn easily, no matter how intelligent he is.

And research conducted by the Food Research and Action Center (published in their book *If We Had Ham, We Could Have Ham and Eggs...If We Had Eggs*) has shown just that— hungry children can't work up to their full ability in school,

49

no matter how skillful the teacher or how eager the child is to learn.

Lest we are tempted to assign the breakfast skippers to lower income families who may not be able to afford enough food, it is a known fact that lots of kids from all social and economic backgrounds either have an inadequate breakfast or skip the meal entirely. The number of children who are not getting a proper breakfast is known to increase with age, and girls are worse culprits than boys. Also, children who don't eat properly in the morning generally have poor food habits during the rest of the day, too.[10]

A Massachusetts survey of 80,000 school children turned up the amazing statistic that only 5 percent of the elementary students and 4 percent of secondary students ate a proper breakfast in the morning! And middle and upper class kids ate only slightly better than lower class kids.[11]

The reasons why so many children skip breakfast are varied. The excuse may be not having enough time, lack of appetite and so on. Many mothers are simply not aware of the need for a good breakfast.

Teachers and school administrators generally recognize that children must be fed if they are to learn. When legislators recognized that need, the School Breakfast Program was established.

The idea behind the breakfast program is a worthy one, and indeed, a study conducted in Atlanta showed that the program had a positive effect. In this study, one class of fourth graders was given milk in the morning when they got to school, while another fourth-grade class was given milk and breakfast. The report on the study said:

"Almost immediately following the introduction of the supplementation program, the teacher reported marked changes in the classroom. Not one child fell asleep during the school day....The apathy all but disappeared and the hyperirritability was greatly reduced. Furthermore, the teacher reported subjectively that she felt that the children were better able to master and retain conceptual lessons."[12]

At the end of the year, the two classes showed a 21 percent

difference on reading test scores as compared to their scores at the beginning of the year.

Unfortunately, the value inherent in the School Breakfast Program is negated, at least to an extent, by the many drawbacks also involved in the program. For one thing, insufficient funding and reels of administrative red tape are keeping many schools from serving breakfast, even where the need is recognized. Further, the program is based on a meal pattern of one-half cup of juice, one-half pint of milk and one slice of bread or cold cereal—a woefully inadequate breakfast in terms of students' nutritional needs. Many school administrators feel that instituting the breakfast program is just not worth the trouble; it is financially impossible and nutritionally inadequate.

Program regulations don't provide any funds to cover the labor costs required to serve a decent hot breakfast. Nor is money provided for purchasing the necessary food for such a meal. The funds allow for only the three-part meal described above, which nutritionally cognizant administrators would not in good conscience pass off to their students as a sound breakfast.

As a final blow, government commodities cannot be used in the program because they require labor to prepare. Using free commodities for school breakfast would actually *raise* the cost of the program to the school. Here's an example of how it works: A school principal decides it would be a good idea to take advantage of the frozen orange juice concentrate available under the commodities program and use it for breakfast. Now, someone must mix the juice with water and pour it into cups. The principal finds that it takes a cafeteria worker half an hour to prepare the juice for 100 breakfasts (assuming that number is needed). At a salary of $2.50 an hour, the labor cost of using the frozen juice concentrate is $1.25—a modest sum, but under the School Breakfast Program, the government will not reimburse that expenditure.

As the yearly budget won't cover the extra labor cost (it would add up over the course of an entire school year), the principal decides instead to serve orange juice that is pre-packaged in individual containers. He finds the juice in this form can be purchased commercially for eight cents a piece, making the total cost $8.00. Since the cost now represents only the juice purchased and not the labor required to prepare it, the government would reimburse the school. In this way, the USDA has to pay $8.00 when only $1.25 was required.

The failure of the program to reimburse labor costs usually forces up the cost of the whole operation, because disposable dishes and utensils and preportioned products (like the orange juice in cartons) must be used. The government's practice of paying for excess waste instead of a little extra employment amounts to subsidizing inefficiency, not to mention creating an ecological nightmare. And of course, the quality and variety of breakfasts that schools can serve is sharply limited, which in turn can deny many students the chance to learn up to their full scholastic capacity.

Many valuable foods could be made available for school breakfast under the government commodities program, if labor costs would be reimbursed. Then, instead of just a slice of bread or a doughnut, kids could have freshly prepared frozen orange juice, some fruit (fresh or canned), peanut butter, grains, cheese and butter.

If a school could afford the labor costs involved with the commodities, there would still be other hindrances to the use of these foods for breakfast. For one thing, some of the foods are made available at irregular intervals and only on short notice, so it would be difficult to plan for them in a large-volume program which has to be figured out well in advance. Also, schools must pay shipping and storage costs for the government foods, which adds another expense to the food service budget.

School Breakfast Should Be a Good Breakfast

So OK, you say, maybe the government isn't helping schools to give kids a great breakfast, but it's at least adequate, right? After all, Type A lunch is based on a sound standard, even if it isn't always met, and since there's no preparation involved in the breakfast program, it probably meets those standards. Not necessarily so. In order to understand the problem, let's first define what is meant by a "good breakfast."

In order to be of any real value, breakfast should fill one-fourth to one-third of your nutrient needs for the day. But some nutrients are more important than others. The typical American breakfast of a pastry or bowl of sweetened cereal and coffee is high in carbohydrates, but it is protein that we need at breakfast, not carbohydrates. A high-protein breakfast keeps your blood sugar level steadier, allowing it to drop slowly through the morning hours. This means you have a more or less constant supply of energy until lunchtime. A higher blood sugar level means more attentiveness, better ability to concentrate and less apathy and restlessness.

On the other hand, a high-carbohydrate breakfast causes your blood sugar level to shoot up for a burst of "quick energy," then plummet downward just as quickly, and you've got that familiar midmorning slump. This means in effect that the large proportion of carbohydrates served in school breakfast programs could be contributing to the very learning problems the breakfast programs was designed to overcome!

Taking a closer look at the actual foods involved leads to the classical pattern for a good breakfast universally endorsed by nutritionists:

- a serving of fresh fruit, fruit juice or vegetable juice
- a good protein source
- cereal or bread (with butter) and milk.

The necessary amounts of each vary with age and sex. The school breakfast program is based on the daily requirements for boys aged 10 to 12 (for the elementary school breakfast) and boys aged 14 to 18 (for the secondary school breakfast).

The USDA requires the school breakfast to include:

- one-half pint of milk either as a beverage or on cereal,
- one-half cup of fruit or full-strength fruit or vegetable juice,
- one slice of whole grain or enriched bread or its equivalent (rolls, corn bread, etc.); or three-fourths cup of whole grain, enriched or fortified cereal; or an equivalent combination of these foods.[13]

Note that the pattern includes no protein (milk does contain protein, but in too small an amount to rely on it as a primary protein source). The program regulations state that protein foods should be included in school breakfasts "whenever practicable," but it is not required. Since availability of protein foods is so erratic under the commodities program, and these foods are among the more expensive items to purchase commercially, it's a good bet that school breakfasts will seldom, if ever, contain foods like meat and cheese.

In terms of overall nutrient value, the USDA breakfast is nutritionally inadequate. At the elementary school level, the meal fails to provide even one-quarter of the RDA of calories, iron, vitamin A and the B vitamins thiamin and niacin. One-third of the RDA is supplied only for vitamin C and riboflavin. High school students fare even worse. They don't get a third of their RDA for *any* nutrient, and the one-fourth level is reached only for vitamin C and riboflavin. The breakfast supplies only 5 percent of the needed iron, and 9 percent of niacin and calories. The meal doesn't contain enough protein to maintain an acceptable blood sugar level.

Such an inadequate meal is of negligible value to kids who get insufficient meals at home. Under the federal food stamp program, the Economy Diet Plan, the diet recommended for the lowest level of purchasing power, which is known to be nutritionally inadequate and is regarded as suitable for emergency sustenance only, provides BETTER breakfasts than the school program! Of what help can the school breakfast program be to children who can't learn because they're undernourished?

And Yet More Problems...

Although the USDA guidelines specify *minimum* requirements, it is easy to lose sight of that, and to interpret the requirements as *maximum*, especially in light of the low rate of reimbursement provided by the government. Also, a catering service which administers a school's lunch and breakfast programs could interpret the requirements as maximum for economic reasons. Further, sticking right to the letter of the scanty regulations will make for boring, repetitive breakfasts that are bound to decrease participation in the program.

Let Them Eat Cake

In 1974, the USDA approved cupcakes and milk as an acceptable breakfast under the Federal School Breakfast Program. The cakes are "fortified" with such nutrients as B vitamins and iron, and may therefore replace the required juice and bread or cereal. Among the various brands of breakfast cakes and doughnuts approved for use in the program are Astrofood, manufactured by ITT, Supercake, made by Tasty Bakery, and Krispee Creme from the company of the same name.[14] Other breakfast cakes are Morning Break made by Keebler, and Prestige Donuts' Superdonut.

The reasoning behind permitting such foods in the school breakfast program was that these cakes would be so formulated as to supply the same nutrients as the foods they were replacing, with the bonuses that the cakes would need no refrigeration or preparation, would cost relatively little and would appeal to the innate desire of children for sweets.

The proposal to allow the cupcakes for school breakfast provoked widespread opposition from many quarters, from members of Congress to the New York City Health Department to the Society for Nutrition Education, not to mention parents and nutritionists. But, as usual, industry got its way and the government neatly circumvented the opposition. The USDA decided to permit the cupcakes, then accepted public comments as a simple formality, because the law requires that such a proposal must be submitted for public approval. The USDA's mind was made up before the proposal ever hit the Federal Register; public opposition had no effect.

The USDA's action amounts to telling kids that sweets for breakfast are good. A child isn't going to recognize the difference between a "fortified" cake and any other kind of cake. To him or to her, a cupcake is a cupcake, because after all, one tastes pretty much the same as another.

Encouraging such poor eating habits in school contradicts the purpose of the school feeding program (to promote good food habits) and effectively negates any genuine attempts at nutrition education in the classroom. If a balanced breakfast is so important, the student will reason, why does the school give us cupcakes and doughnuts? The school says cakes are OK, so they must be OK. Mom is wrong.

Psychological factors aside, from a strictly nutritional point of view, these "fortified" breakfast cakes are a disaster. They are loaded with sugar (in the neighborhood of 30 percent), which we all know is bad for teeth, especially children's developing teeth. Dietary fiber is missing, and a few currently popular vitamins have been added to an essentially nonnutritious (except for abundant carbohydrates from sugar) product, without regard for the essential relationships existing between the nutritional components in whole foods such as whole wheat kernels and pure, fresh orange juice.

But now that the USDA has sanctioned one artificial food for use in school feeding, the practice will undoubtedly spread. The supercake is precisely the kind of product the food industry likes best, and various companies will be sure to capitalize on it. That the USDA has not officially "endorsed" the cake but merely "approved" it will not matter. The terms are synonymous to many.

What Can Be Done?

The problem of serving better food under the Federal School Breakfast Program is complex, and for the present all but defies solution in schools where no additional funding beyond that provided by the government is available. But in schools that can muster some additional means of financing, the breakfast program has great potential. In a report on the National School Breakfast Program, the Food Research and Action Center (funded by the United States Office of Economic Opportunity) presented two sample breakfast menus drawn from successful programs in various schools that illustrate the possibilities of school breakfast. [15]

The first menu offered high school students a cup of juice, an egg, one ounce of ham, two slices of whole wheat bread with peanut butter and one-half pint of milk. Younger students get one-half cup of juice, an egg, one-half ounce of ham, one slice of whole wheat bread with a tablespoon of peanut butter and one-half pint of milk.

Both meals stack up well against the standards that determine a good breakfast. The high school meal supplies over one-fourth of the RDA of every nutrient except calories, which can usually be made up during the course of the day. Over a third of the RDA is supplied for protein, thiamin, riboflavin, niacin and vitamin C. The smaller breakfast provides a similar proportion of nutrients.

The second sample menu, which is low in fat in addition to being quite nourishing, is based on a hot cereal such as oatmeal. High school students receive one cup of tomato juice (which contains more iron, vitamin A and niacin than orange juice, but fewer calories), one cup of hot cereal with a pat of butter and one-half cup of fruit, one slice of whole wheat bread with peanut butter and a cup of milk. Again, nutrient values are high, with calories being the only low value.

There are several very desirable features to this meal. First, it uses an alternative source of protein (peanut butter) which is cheaper than meat. Serving fruit (such as raisins) with the cereal helps to boost nutrient values. Also, the meal uses government commodities—flour, butter, peanut butter, oats and raisins. When the commodities are available and the labor can be budgeted, schools can serve this breakfast at very low cost.

Getting Better Breakfasts in Your School

The biggest hindrance to serving a good hot breakfast in school instead of cupcakes and milk is, of course, limited funds. In many schools, there are no extra funds to buy food and pay labor costs beyond the amounts provided by the government. About the only way to get around the problem, other than increasing the school's own budget, is to take advantage of money available under other related federal training programs.

For example, in one high school in California, home economics students were enrolled in a work-study program funded by the Federal Vocation Education Act. As part of their work project, four students helped plan menus and prepare meals for the school's food service department, thus providing additional labor without the need for additional lunch or breakfast program funds.[16]

Increasing Participation in the Breakfast Program

The school with a good breakfast program will naturally want as many of its students as possible to take advantage of the program. Washington, D.C., elementary schools held a "Stick Up for Breakfast Week" to teach all their students the importance of a good breakfast. Schools were visited by their very own caped crusader, Mr. Super Breakfast, who came bounding into classrooms to tell the kids about nutritious breakfasts. They learned that cake, candy or pudding does not make a good breakfast.

The campaign was funded by a grant from the Kellogg cereal company and included nutrition education teaching materials, media messages, a free breakfast at the end of the week and a trip to Disney World for the two classes who wrote the best song about nutrition.[17]

The school district decided to sponsor the Stick Up for Breakfast Week because only 20,000 of the 54,000 children eligible for free school breakfasts were taking advantage of the meals.

Unfortunately, the Kellogg-sponsored campaign encouraged children to eat various cold cereals which are not whole grain and contain as much as 50 percent sugar. But the basic idea behind the Stick Up for Breakfast Week is a good one. This kind of a campaign could be conducted (preferably without industry support) in any school, even on a smaller scale, to get more children involved in the breakfast program.

School Food and Hyperactivity

Another factor that may further complicate school feeding programs is the possibility that food may be related to some kinds of childhood ailments or learning disabilities. Hyperkinesis, one of the most difficult to treat learning disabilities to afflict our children, has reached epidemic proportions in recent years. No one really knows what causes hyperactivity, but one current theory links it to synthetic food additives. Although the connection has not been indisputably proven, it is another aspect of child feeding that should be looked into more closely.

Pioneering research into the relationship between food additives and hyperactivity was conducted by Dr. Ben Feingold, a San Francisco allergist. Dr. Feingold believes that the molecular structure of the substances used as synthetic colors and flavors causes them to behave in the body much like drugs, causing allergic reactions in sensitive people. Hyperactivity, he feels, is the reaction that can occur in people with a susceptible genetic structure.

The usual treatment for hyperactivity involves strong stimulant drugs, but Dr. Feingold's discoveries about the relationship between food additives and hyperactivity led him to devise a dietary treatment for hyperkinesis. The program eliminates all foods and all drugs containing artificial flavors or artificial colors, and all foods containing salicylate (a naturally occurring compound known to cause allergic reactions). So far, the elimination diet has proven highly successful—about 50 percent of the children Dr. Feingold treated found full relief of their symptoms, and 75 percent could at least go off their drug regimens.

The elimination diet offers new hope for sufferers of hyperkinesis. But it isn't always easy to avoid artificial colors and flavors. Virtually all children's medicines contain them, and children are exposed to offending foods everywhere, especially in school. Dry cereals, hot dogs, cakes, cookies, ice cream Popsicles, fruit punches, soft drinks, quick-mix drink powders, luncheon meats, processed cheese food and cheese spreads, salad dressings, jams and jellies, soup mixes—all contain the forbidden additives that mean suffering for the hyperkinetic.[18]

The failure of government agencies to require adequate labeling of artificial ingredients in processed foods is unforgivable. Federal law does not require many of these additives to be listed on product labels, which makes it a real problem to avoid them. "U.S. Certified Color" is no help to the person whose health depends on avoiding specific chemicals.

Equally dangerous is the fact that the government has little control over the composition of the flavors and colors themselves. For example, three different brands of flavoring may be mixed in a single product, with the end result that the total content of a specific chemical used in one or all three brands can't be determined in the final product. The formulas for many artificial flavors are jealously guarded secrets among the manufacturers. Raspberry flavor from Company X probably has a different composition from Company Y's raspberry flavor, and nobody outside the company knows what's in either of them. Government monitoring of these additives is largely ineffective because the responsibility is split up among a whole group of agencies.

The first scientific study of the effectiveness of the elimination diet was completed in 1975 by Dr. C. Keith Connors of the University of Pittsburgh. Results indicated that the elimination diet did bring improvement, although Dr. Connors stressed the need for more extensive and closely controlled research.

If diet is the all-important factor for hyperactive children, the food they get in school should be as natural, as unprocessed as possible. Every effort should be made to provide wholesome food without unnecessary flavors and colors whose chief value is cosmetic. Such food would not only benefit children already suffering from hyperkinesis, but might also help protect those with the genetic susceptibility from developing the syndrome.

It is up to us to demand purer foods from industry. In fact, the movement has already begun. The parents' lunch committee in the Greenburgh Central School District No. 7 in Hartsdale, New York (who we mentioned earlier), confronted the issue of synthetic food additives in cafeteria food. One of the first things the committee did was get rid of all the snack foods that contained artificial flavors and colors and inform the manufacturers of those products why they had been removed from sale. And they got response from industry. Here is their story:

In September of 1974, the Drake's Baking Company asked to meet with us because we had removed Yodels and Ring Dings from our snack shelves. They came to convince us that artificial additives were necessary to their products. We, in turn, pointed out to them that our growing concern regarding artificial flavors and colors was a trend they should not ignore. Since they were unable to provide a reason for the use of artificial coloring other than cosmetic, we asked them if they could use their vast research resources to come up with a natural product which, combined with an educational advertising campaign, would sell as well as their current product.

In May, 1975, the Drake's Manager of Research and Development called to inform us that they had been experimenting with the use of a natural coloring agent made from turmeric instead of artificial yellow in their yellow cakes. Again, last month [December, 1975], Drake's called to say that the turmeric yellow is being sold in all their yellow cakes and they are proceeding with experiments to find an alternate natural red.[19]

The fight for better food can be won, but it will not be an easy victory or a quick one. For each manufacturer closely attuned to public wishes and the importance of good nutrition, there are many more that remain coldly unresponsive. Here is another example of the kind of corporate attitude encountered by the Greenburgh Central 7 Lunch Committee:

"Another incidence of the Committee's research into the use of food additives was our experience in trying to track down the chemical composition of the artificial flavoring in an ice cream product our District was selling. We were referred by the ice cream manufacturer to American Food Labs, a company that makes flavorings and colorings. We were told that their company was not required by law to divulge the ingredients that they are putting in their products. This truly frightened us, and we decided to remove some questionable...products from sale.[20]

The College Scene

Probably the greatest potential for change in institutional food service exists in the college cafeteria. College students have a reputation for the kind of progressive thought and conscious awareness of the needs of the individual, both biological and psychological, that typifies no other group in society. The desire for unprocessed, natural foods was primarily expressed by isolated individuals until it hit the college campus. This age group was responsible more than any other for the start of the natural foods boom. As a result, natural and vegetarian foods are finding their way into more and more colleges and universities.

Of course, traditional cafeteria fare still outnumbers by far the innovative menus on the college food scene. Mushy vegetables, processed and canned foods, thick fatty gravies, heavy, starchy dishes and lots of nonnutritional junk still remains the only meal choice at most schools. Results of a study done at 50 colleges in 31 states to analyze the fat and fatty acid content of typical college meals attest to the generally poor quality of most of the meals. Researchers analyzed breakfasts, lunches and dinners at the sample schools.

Although there is no recommended daily allowance (RDA) for fat or fatty acids, the Food and Nutrition Board of the National Research Council has recommended as a moderate amount that no more than 35 percent of the total calories found in a meal come from fat. The fat content of the meals studied averaged between 36 and 47 percent of total caloric value. None of the colleges served meals with only 35 percent of the calories from fat; in fact, most of the meals were well above the 40 percent level.

Fatty acids are components of fat and come in three varieties, saturated, mono-unsaturated and polyunsaturated. The need for two polyunsaturated fatty acids, linoleic and arachidonic acids, has been established in human nutrition, but saturated fatty acids are considered undesirable in large amounts. The Inter-Society Commission for Heart Disease Resources has recommended that less than 10 percent of a meal's total calories should come from saturated fatty acids and that polyunsaturated fatty acids should supply up to 10 percent. In the colleges surveyed, none of the meals contained less than 13 percent of the calories from saturated fatty acids, and the average was 15.63 percent. Most of the meals fell well below the 10 percent mark for polyunsaturated fatty acids, with the mean level at 6.4 percent.[21]

In general, four problems characteristic of the American diet are reflected in college fare: too much sugar, too much fat, too little fiber and too many chemical additives. Fortunately, however, many colleges are adopting alternative meal plans, often under pressure from students. And these programs are proving successful.

An outstanding example of an alternative meal plan is discussed in the success story on Lewis and Clark College. Their new approach to food concentrated on those four problem areas, and menus were planned around simple dishes prepared with optimum nutritional value in mind. Over 76 percent of the students participating in a survey said they liked the new meal program.

One school that has been serving alternative meals for

many years is Pacific Union College in Angwin, California. Because it is associated with the Seventh-Day Adventist church, the college has served vegetarian meals since its establishment in the nineteenth century, long before vegetarian meals were popular. Today Pacific Union College owns a bakery, where most of the school's baked goods are made, all without artificial preservatives. All the herbs used in the kitchen are grown on campus; vegetables were too, before the school got too large. Fresh and dried fruits, nuts and fruit juices are always available in the dining hall. Some sweets are still in evidence, to cater to that ever-present demand, but they are kept to a minimum.

At the State University of New York campus at Purchase, New York, Peter Donovan, who directed the food service, and his staff, employees of one of the nation's giant-volume feeding companies, had the job of providing meals for 750 students. In just a few months, they did what most food service entrepreneurs maintain is impossible. They improved the nutrient value of the food offered, cut down on processed and empty calorie foods, devised recipes to make the food more acceptable than it had been previously, and miracle of miracles, they did it on a lower budget—spending approximately 10 percent less. Since total food costs ran around $7,000 per week, 10 percent meant a substantial saving of $700 per week.

How did they do it? Here is part of the blueprint.

1. They used sprouts, bushels of them, as one of their fresh raw vegetables. Some vegetables are costly, especially in winter. But one pound of mung beans at about 40 cents a pound (wholesale price) provides three gallons of fresh, delicious sprouts bursting with vitamins, minerals and enzymes. The staff grew the sprouts in steam table pans, rotating them so that a fresh crop was always ready for use. Sprouts enhanced the taste, texture and nutrient value of many dishes at the college. Sprout and spinach salad was a favorite item on the menu.

2. By offering delicious vegetarian dishes that combined

beans, grains, fresh vegetables and dairy products, Donovan was able to meet protein requirements while cutting down on meat, the most expensive item in any food operation. The usual food budget called for a 13 percent allocation for meat. Offering a vegetarian alternative cut down on the quantity of meat that had to be purchased for a given meal, with the result that meat purchases were cut down to 10 percent of the total food budget.

3. Brown rice, millet, buckwheat, wheat germ, soybeans and seeds were introduced in combinations with other foods that made complete protein patterns. Whenever a new dish was presented, the staff let students know everything in it and explained the relationship of the new dish to other foods on the menu. In this way, they encouraged a better selection of foods and were able to serve new, nutrition-rich dishes without much hassle from the students.

At Northland College, a small liberal arts school in Ashland, Wisconsin, a total food awareness program which included natural foods in the cafeteria was introduced on an experimental basis and proved quite successful. The underlying philosophy of the experiment, as described by Kenneth R. Nielsen, Vice President for Student Affairs, concerns the perception of the role of the college that

> It is our responsibility to introduce students to different concepts of lifelong learning. We deal essentially with the life experience aspect of the educational process here at Northland College....It was our intention, and I believe we reached much of the goal, to develop an interest and sensitivity to what we eat, and how we eat. Very often individuals are not really conscious of the effect of the food which they take into their bodies. By the consciousness raising methods which we have developed, we found that students became more aware of what they ate, how they ate, as well as the effect of those foods on their bodies.[22]

A four-part program was presented on campus to stimulate in the students an awareness of needs to remain in a state of optimum health. Phase I consisted of a lecture/discussion of various methods of meditation, exercise and diet that can help to develop one's human potential. Phase II was a six-session workshop on meditation and mantram (chanting). Phase III was a ten-session workshop entitled "Psycho Calisthenics." Phase IV was the special diet program implemented by the college food service.

To introduce the experimental diet, an information campaign was conducted to ensure that everyone understood the reason for it. A questionnaire was passed out to students to assess their basic knowledge of nutritional principles and their eating habits, and to determine how they made food choices in the cafeteria. Then the following letter explaining the experimental diet program was given out to students in the cafeteria:

Dear Student,

For the next two weeks the Food Service will present a food alternative, a test run offering you new tastes of natural beverages, whole grain breads, raw and not the usual overcooked vegetables, creative salads, and fish and poultry prepared with a new awareness.

Yes, we are discarding the canned fruits, vegetables, soup and dessert mixes with additives and preservatives, the bleach and processed grains and flours. The meals will not taste as though they are from the same pot. Besides being fresh, the meals will be nutritious as well; we are offering a high protein-low carbohydrate diet.

You might ask why the program? The answer is simply we want to present a healthy balanced diet that gets us out of our unconscious attitudes. You might be familiar with some of them described below:

1. Consuming the same amount of food while studying as we did in the summer and finding out weeks later after the semester has begun that we have gained considerable weight.
2. Starving ourselves for a few days and gorging ourselves with any food that is in sight. Counting calories and eating only carbohydrates and fats, forgetting about nutrients.

3. Believing that as long as we have lean meat, potatoes, and a salad on a regular basis, we can eat packaged meals, soups, and processed cheese and breads. It is now common fact in the medical profession that we need to consume raw fruits, vegetables, nuts and whole grains to create bulk without which the digestive system will not effectively operate. Refined foods slow down the digestive process causing a residue to be left in the gut; studies show that these conditions are found in cases of intestinal, colon cancer.

4. We are all concerned with health and consider ourselves to be healthy as long as we have no major disease. The fact is that many conditions which lead in later years to serious illness can be *prevented* by conscious food selection and eating habits.

We want you to participate, experiment, and give your mind and body a new feeling towards dining hall food. At the end of the program we will be handing you a questionnaire for your feedback and we hope your support of this new program.

To orientate yourself, we suggest you read the attached sheets.

Bon Appetit!
The Food Service

Descriptions of the kinds of meals to be served accompanied the letter:

BREAKFASTS
To accompany breakfasts we will serve fresh fruit, homemade granola, and eggs with herbs, cheeses or sprouts.

LUNCHES
With crisp salads offering color, seasonings, and textures we will be serving one of a variety of hot soups each day: hearty vegetable, miso, lentil, split pea, Greek egg-lemon soup, chicken, and chili. Sandwiches will be self-service; fillings will include vegetarian spreads, cheese, sprouts, vegetables, peanut and sesame butter with honey and seeds, besides egg and tuna salad.

DINNERS
Poultry, fish, and vegetable entrées will be prepared according to international recipes: chicken cacciatore, shrimp-fried rice, baked chicken with herbs, trout almondine, and ratatouille.

DESSERTS

Desserts will be served at lunch and dinner. Ingredients are all natural fruits and unprocessed flours. Sweets will range from traditional brownies, cakes, cookies to yummy seed, nut, coconut, and honey combinations. Fruit and yogurt will be served as well.

BEVERAGES

Hot and iced herbal teas will be served along with fruit juices and coffee. Natural herbal teas contain no dyes or chemical treatments. According to Chinese thought they provide a way to soothing harmony in the body and help to maintain the yin-yang balance. Oriental healers prescribed herbal teas: peppermint for headaches, indigestion; camomile flowers for the stomach and digestive system and rose hips for aiding blood circulation and providing vitamin C.

Finally, a list of new ingredients, their nutritional value and why they were being used was presented so students would gain a better understanding of what they were eating and why. The list included sea salt, tamari soy sauce, miso, seaweed, garlic, kelp powder, honey, sprouts, grains, beans, tahini, peanut butter and sesame butter.

Northland's meal plan is built on a 19-meal per week system which costs the students $2.48 a day (1975–1976 price), for a weekly total of about $20. Students are allowed as many additional helpings as they wish. Students choosing the natural foods were found to eat less than those on the regular meal plan.

Some schools have found that alternative menus are necessary to keep vegetarian and other diet-conscious students involved in the meal plan. In October of 1971, Yale University began a natural foods line in its Commons Dining Hall, primarily to keep vegetarians from drifting away from the dining halls.

Natural foods were served each day at dinner. Menus emphasized fresh vegetables cooked for as short a time as possible, to preserve their flavor, appearance and nutrient value. Safflower and peanut oils were used in salad dressings, and a variety of natural foods was presented with each meal.

A typical dinner menu would include a vegetable dish such as lentil casserole; a side dish of fish or poultry or a vegetable omelet; assorted salads and the standard selection of natural foods. At each dinner, granola and familia, yogurt, fresh fruits, organic peanut butter, raw honey, wheat germ, brewer's yeast, assorted teas, breads made from unbleached flour and without any artificial chemical additives, fresh vegetable salads and raw sugar.

The new foods were a big hit with the students. So big, in fact, that for the first few months students were helping themselves to one of every main course, and taking main dish salads as side dishes. But in time, consumption leveled off, the budget which began exceedingly high came down to a reasonable level, and the program really began to work.

At the Massachusetts Institute of Technology, where the meal program wasn't mandatory, attendance was dropping off. A natural foods line was begun in an attempt to lure disenchanted students back into the dining hall.

Natural foods were an entirely new experience for the dietitian and the food service staff, but after a little practice they became quite competent with preparation of foods like brown rice. Students reacted favorably to the new menus, and a lively interaction between students and food service staff resulted in even better meals.

In order to make students aware of what they were eating, the food service issued a detailed listing of the ingredients in each new dish served. In addition to letting everyone know what they were getting in their meals, the ingredient lists made it easier for vegetarian students to pick out things they didn't wish to eat.

There were some surprises along the way, too. For example, when the food service decided to serve unsulfured dried fruits, they felt that the fruits would have to be stewed or served in some other type of dish because they looked so unappealing that students wouldn't eat them plain. But when they served the disguised fruits, students asked to have them raw instead.

Cornell University took a slightly different approach to

natural foods. Many students there formed purchasing co-ops and prepared their own meals. The dining room began to bake bread, pancakes and doughnuts from whole wheat flour. Campus vending machines were stocked with apples and sandwiches made with whole grain bread—and they sold well.

On the West Coast, the food revolution was headed by the University of California at Santa Cruz, where the four-acre Student Garden Project led to insistence that the organic produce they were growing be made available in an alternative choice line. By 1971, when the project was in its third year, more than 40 percent of the campus diners steadily chose the organic food line—with many others crossing over to get the better whole grain or sprouted grain bread.

The college food service field is an area of many options. Natural foods are being successfully served in many universities across the country, and indications are that the trend is still growing. Various alternative menu plans have been proven to be not only acceptable to students, but financially feasible as well. The college food service director can choose from among alternative ideas such as serving regular or occasional meatless meals; baking whole grain breads, cereals and desserts; a salad bar with sprouts, assorted raw vegetables cooked for as short a time as possible; homemade soups and whole grain sandwiches made with natural cheeses, various vegetables and spreads instead of processed cheese products and luncheon meats; ethnic, regional and international dishes; always available granola, yogurt, wheat germ, fresh fruit, peanut butter and honey; fruit juices, low-fat milk and herbal teas. The natural foods meal plan should be tailored to the needs and desires of the students, and the limitations of budget and facilities.

The Role of Nutrition Education

The single most important factor responsible for the admittedly poor quality of today's American diet, both at home and in institutional or commercial settings, is the simple lack of awareness of food and proper food habits that pervades every segment of our society. From Mom in the family kitchen to the child going through the cafeteria serving line to the cook in the hospital kitchen—we just don't understand what's good for us and even lose sight of why we eat in the first place.

Senator George McGovern, introducing the bill which became the Nutrition Education Act of 1975, stated the problems:

> Today nearly the entire nation is misnourished because of the misuse of abundance. Tens of millions have the resources to buy sufficient food, but lack the knowledge to choose correctly. Too often we eat enough, but we are not well fed.
>
> Many who are not hungry are the new misnourished.
>
> The new misnourished consume too many processed foods and an unbalanced diet.
>
> The new misnourished are most of us, most of our children, and too many of those who seem most healthy.
>
> This new misnourishment requires a new program of nutrition education.[23]

McGovern further declares that we have ignored the opportunity the School Lunch Act provides to teach children about good food habits and the nutrient content of food. Such opportunities we cannot afford to miss, because our need for nutrition education is vital.

Optimum nutrition is the best preventive medicine available. Even the best medicine isn't as effective as preventing illness in the first place, especially in regard to the degenerative diseases, such as diabetes, obesity, tooth decay and heart disease. Preventing illness means there is less need for crisis health care (our method of treating symptoms instead of causes) and, therefore, fewer expensive medical bills.

The costly industry advertising, which for many exerts a major influence on food choices, often dwells on half-truths and does not present a clear picture of the product. Media ads push glamorous junk foods to the masses at inflated prices, urging people to choose exotic, high-priced food products instead of basic wholesome foods. The consumer with no background in nutrition and no knowledge of processing techniques can't possibly judge the value of these products and thus is easily manipulated by advertisements.

If people are to gain the nutritional knowledge they need to provide themselves with the best possible nutrition, educational programs must be expanded and improved. The expense of such programs would be well justified, for in McGovern's words, "A tax dollar spent to give consumers a sensible scientific guide to spending their food dollars is an investment...in our schools and our children."

Learning what food does in our bodies and which foods are good for us can and should begin at an early age, even before a child starts school. Day-care and Head Start programs offer a unique opportunity for the teaching of nutrition to children who often need such instruction most—children whose mothers work. The child whose parents both work will probably be making more of his or her own food choices sooner than many other children. His mother might not have the time to cook good meals very often and might not be home to oversee which foods her children choose for snacks. Children who don't get nutrition instruction at home really need exposure to good eating habits in their Head Start or day-care centers to prepare them to make good food choices in the future. When they get to school there's a good chance they'll be confronted with vending machine goodies, and who's to keep them from eating potato chips and candy for lunch if they don't know any better?

Nutrition education is an integral part of the Head Start program. The Head Start guidelines state that "There must be an organized program of nutrition education integrated into the educational aspects of all components of the Head Start program for staff, parents, and children."

This program is to include meal time and the foods served as an important part of the total education program. Special activities are planned to teach children to select and enjoy foods that are suited to their individual needs. Nutrition education and counseling are extended to the rest of the family as well, in order that good food habits can be maintained in the home.

All staff members, including administrative personnel, are prepared for the active role they will take in building better nutrition in the youngsters and families by a special course in nutrition. The course includes instruction in principles of nutrition and their applications to child development and family health, ways to create tne kind of physical, social and emotional environment which fosters the growth of good food habits.

Care is taken to involve parents in Head Start's nutrition education program, from planning the program to evaluating its success.

The food service staff also receives instruction in nutritional principles. Cooks take a special course which explores the areas of menu planning, food purchasing, preparation and storage, sanitation and personal hygiene.

This sort of basic program of nutrition education provides children with a sound base on which to build a lifetime of healthy eating habits. The educational program should be continued throughout the school years, each level of instruction building on those which preceded it.

There is no better place to teach nutrition than in the schools, and no time like the present to begin. The Nutrition Education bill states that "nutrition education in the schools has the potential for improving substantially the health and well-being of students and of significantly reducing many health problems which adversely affect the learning processes of students."

Throughout their school careers, kids are generally exposed to a few hours' worth of instruction about the four food groups and the necessity of eating a balanced diet. But nobody learns about the differences between canned and fresh vegetables or how margarine is made or even why our bodies need vitamin A or protein. It is far more likely that a

73

child will be told that everybody needs sugar for quick energy than that he'll learn how to pick out the kind of foods he needs from supermarket shelves.

Besides being generally irrelevant, most of what passes for nutrition education in our schools is abysmally boring. Nutrition class is not an activity one expects to find exciting or even remotely enjoyable. Mostly it consists of the dull old grind about food groups, instead of a genuinely creative effort to get students interested in food. A drudge for the teacher, nutrition education becomes a drag for the students.

Every educator knows (and most of the rest of us do, too) that any concept becomes much more meaningful when it is taught through actual experience. The school cafeteria is a ready-made laboratory for kids to observe the principles of good nutrition in practice. The school lunch and breakfast should always be nutritionally sound and illustrative of the nutrition principles taught in the classroom. This means that the school lunch should consist of a nutritionally balanced, attractive assortment of high-quality foods, all prepared to conserve optimum nutrient values.

The school acts as a symbol of authority and "rightness" to elementary-age children especially, who are still easily and profoundly impressed by what they see there. Throughout the duration of the school career, peer pressure exerts perhaps an equally strong influence on behavior, and kids are naturally more willing to try new and different foods when they see their friends doing it.

The food service director can play a most important role in the teaching of nutrition in school. As head of the kitchen, the director forms the connecting link between the kitchen and the classroom. He or she can help teachers plan nutrition studies—in fact, as long as no nutrition courses are required for a teaching certificate, the food service director may need to teach the teachers first. When students visit the kitchen, the director can explain why the foods on the menu for lunch that day are being served. Meals can also be planned to coincide with classroom lessons. On a day when the lesson is about leafy green vegetables there should certainly be some in the lunch menu.

Under the Five State Nutrition Education Project (a two-year program funded by the Food and Nutrition Service in Tennessee, Alabama, Georgia, Florida and Mississippi), the collaboration of teacher and food service director formed an essential part of the teaching of nutrition. The team idea combines the teacher's experience with teaching techniques with the director's skills in food preparation and nutrition. Teamwork resulted in an approach to nutrition education in which students actually practiced what they were being taught. In the J. B. Young Elementary School in Jackson, Tennessee, for example, a first grade class made a big pot of Irish stew right in their classroom for St. Patrick's Day. Children were given the titles of "scrapers" and "choppers" to prepare the vegetables for the pot, and took turns stirring the stew as it cooked. In another lesson on bread and cereal, children went into the school and learned how to make biscuits.

The goal of the program was to make the kids aware of the food they eat both in and out of school. They were taught that the school lunch gives them one-third of the nutrients they need each day, and that they must also eat a good breakfast and a good dinner to get all they need.

Teachers and food service directors who participated in the project did indeed note results. As the children learned about nutrition, more of them bought school lunches and were willing to try foods, like broccoli, they wouldn't touch before. Skinny kids who began to regularly eat breakfast and school lunch put on weight.

The Five State Nutrition Education Project drew an enthusiastic response from students and school staff alike, and the key to success was the cooperation between teacher and director.[24]

Similar things have been done at various schools across the country, but as yet no unified pattern has developed. In recent years, Food Day programs have been held at many schools to set aside that one day for nutrition studies. At least it's a step in the right direction. At Chicago's School for

Exceptional and Retarded Children, the kitchen was used for preparing lunch and for learning. Students had an opportunity to help make whole grain bread with one of the teachers interested in natural foods. They also made orange juice and sometimes carrot juice.

At the Albanesi Education Center, a Montessori method elementary school in Dallas, Texas, children learn and practice good nutrition habits and even bake whole wheat bread.

Mr. and Mrs. Albanesi said that baking whole wheat bread has proven to be a meaningful class experience in nutrition. Children who ordinarily would not even taste dark bread were shown by their peers that tasting new foods can lead to acquiring and enjoying new diet habits.

"Each child is given alone (not as a class project) the responsibility of baking under the direction of the teacher," they explained. "Such an individualized experience ensures success without risking failure and provides a sense of pride and self-fulfillment when the product of his work is shared with the entire class. To enable the child to put his newly acquired knowledge to practical use, he is then asked to be a teacher-assistant when the next turn to bake comes for another child."

For older students, a more sophisticated approach is generally the most successful in teaching nutrition. Getting students involved in the lunch program, by having them plan their own luncheon menus and forming student advisory panels to judge the quality of various food products, can result in changed eating habits and increased participation in the lunch program.

At the high school age, it is most important that students' opinions be solicited and listened to. Teenagers need to feel they are being listened to, and in most cases, their ideas can really contribute to the school's lunch program. In Milwaukee, a student testing panel decides which new foods can be included in the lunch program, and helps plan menus. As a result of having student input in the planning stages, the food service is able to serve the same meal in all district schools with a minimum of student complaints at the remarkable price of 30 cents elementary and 35 cents secondary (see chapter 4 for the Milwaukee story). The motivation to change eating habits just isn't there with the traditional classroom course in food groups. A feeling of involvement is necessary to generate change.

Nutrition Education and Job Training Programs at the College Level

Except for assorted cooking classes, some of which emphasize natural foods, colleges and universities generally neglect to offer courses in basic nutrition for those who don't want to go into the food service field.

Most of the professional people in a position to strongly influence our dietary habits are given no nutrition education when they prepare for their chosen careers. Teachers, for example, are given no nutrition training. Neither are most doctors—about 72 percent of the medical schools in this country have no required nutrition courses. Nutrition education is offered only as a part of the various training programs for food service work, and these programs are geared to the current convenience-oriented food delivery systems. A one-year program can qualify one to work as a cook, baker or food service worker. A two-year associate degree program may train the student to become a head cook, run his or her own restaurant, or supervise a food service (such as in a nursing home) under the direction of a registered dietitian. Graduates of this kind of program receive the title of dietetic assistant, and in situations where there is only a consulting dietitian (as exists in many nursing homes), the dietetic assistant not only runs the food service but is responsible for patient diets as well.

Some colleges offer a four-year program which yields a B.S. degree in foods and nutrition and qualifies the graduate to go on and become a registered dietitian.

The most practical, valuable program in nutrition and management to come to our attention is the dietetic internship program conducted for college graduates by the

Milwaukee School District. This 10-month program provides on-the-job instruction on a one-to-one basis with professionals who specialize in the areas of food specifications and quality control, menu planning and recipe testing, equipment specifications and kitchen planning, central purchasing and data processing, annual budgeting and cost accounting, supervision of personnel, employee training programs and union negotiations, child nutrition and elderly feeding programs, public relations and community projects. The internship program prepares graduates to fill management positions in all kinds of food service and to take the examination for Registered Dietitian. In addition, graduates are eligible for membership in the American Dietetic Association.

During various phases of their training, interns learn all areas of food service work. First they are given three weeks of kitchen experience, working with food service managers and assistants in school kitchens to learn every aspect of kitchen operation. The next two weeks are spent in the company of the school district's supervising dietitians, where interns receive individual training in all management areas and gain experience in on-site supervision of school food service. Eight weeks of clinical experience follow, as the interns go out into two private hospitals for therapeutic and teaching experience. Work with community agencies is scheduled throughout the internship, according to the interests of each intern.

During the second half of the program, interns assume the responsibilities of a supervising dietitian (under the dietitian's guidance) both in an area of management and in the on-site supervision of a school food service. Interns rotate to spend two weeks with each of the school district's six supervising dietitians.

As we have seen, steps can be taken, even within the bounds of government lunch programs and the present cafeteria system, to serve better food to students. But we must go even further, and work toward the goal of insuring a satisfying, nutritious lunch for all of the students in all of our schools.

Chapter 3

Feeding The Sick And Elderly

Our contemporary system of hospitalization has developed into an awe-inspiring institution. New miracle drugs and surgical techniques have made curable many illnesses that were once fatal. This is the age of heart transplants and computerized body scanners. Our crisis-oriented health care system with its drugs, its machines and its emphasis on treating disease rather than promoting health has spawned a hospital food service system based on mass production, convenience and profit.

Many hospital kitchens are run by outside catering companies and are operated on a profit basis. Centralized or off-premise food preparation, computer-assisted management procedures, and pre-prepared and portion-controlled foods are part and parcel of today's health care system. This intensive concentration on machinery and manufactured foods has led to some rather remarkable systems.

Here's an example. According to a story in the *Cedar Rapids Gazette*, St. Luke's Hospital in Cedar Rapids, Iowa, installed 14,000 feet of tubing to facilitate the distribution of soft drinks to patients. Prior to installing the system, an executive of the hospital explained, some 24,000 cans of soda pop

79

had to be served every month. Under the new system, a battery of 30 five-gallon containers provides each dispenser with five different syrups which are mixed with carbonated water at the point of serving.

St. Luke's of Cedar Rapids was by no means the first hospital to install the automated soft drink system. Hospitals in Boston and Indianapolis already had similar systems. But in the true spirit of today's health care establishment, a St. Luke's spokesman proudly pointed out that the Boston hospital's system only delivered one flavor, ginger ale, and St. Luke's offered a choice of root beer, orange, Teem, Diet 7-Up and Pepsi-Cola.

These sophisticated food-delivery systems certainly do fulfill the objectives of feeding great numbers of people and making sizable profits for the catering companies. But the important question, which the food service industry and hospital administrators don't seem to be asking, is whether this food service system is providing patients with appetizing and optimally nutritious meals that facilitate the return to health. It seems that this question is left to the consumer, in whose lap the responsibility for changing our health care system must ultimately fall.

How many patients would honestly say that the food they were served in the hospital was appealing and genuinely tasty? Hospital food has a universally notorious reputation, and it seems to be well deserved in too many cases. One British doctor offers the following description of a meal he was served while awaiting minor surgery in a large hospital.

> One morning my breakfast choice was scrambled egg. Now I make a good scrambled egg myself: it sits perched on its bit of toast golden, glowing, appetizing, tempting. On this morning mine arrived solitary, positively lonely, in the middle of a plate, a clean cut brick of pale yellow 'substance' and lukewarm at that. This jaundiced briquette was one of the most unappetizing objects I ever set eyes on, and I in good health and appetite. It tasted as it looked. All the food

had this same anonymity, mass-produced, machine divided, impersonal, wholly unappetizing.

Recently a friend of mine endured two months in another of our great hospitals. He lost over a stone [14 pounds], not due to his illness, which was not debilitating but from simple lack of food, which he could not face.[1]

It seems reasonable to assume that hospital patients should be served the most appealing and palatable food possible. Unappetizing food isn't going to stimulate a sick person's flagging appetite, and not eating surely will not hasten the patient's recovery.

But even more serious than the lack of appeal of the usual hospital meal is the fairly recent discovery that many of the meals are not providing proper nutrition even when they are eaten. It's not just a matter of the food not providing *optimal* nutrition, much of it isn't even *adequate*.

The startling charge that malnutrition is widespread in American hospitals was leveled by Dr. Charles E. Butterworth, Chairman of the Council on Foods and Nutrition of the AMA in 1974. He stated that "I suspect...that one of the largest pockets of unrecognized malnutrition in America, and Canada, too, exists, not in rural slums or urban ghettos, but in the private rooms and wards of big city hospitals."[2] Dr. Butterworth supported his claims with several case histories, and in-depth clinical research conducted by other physicians confirmed that the evidence of malnutrition among hospital patients is indeed widespread.[3]

In fact, at least five percent of the patients in our major hospitals suffer from severe malnutrition *as a result of their hospital stays,* according to clinical evidence uncovered in a study by Dr. George L. Blackburn of Harvard Medical School. Dr. Blackburn reported the incredible finding that the rate of malnutrition in American hospitals is higher than that in Biafra, the poverty-stricken section of Nigeria that was so much in the news a few years ago.[4]

Of course, all these cases of malnutrition aren't caused intentionally, they simply go unrecognized because so little attention is given to the overall nutritional status of hospital patients. Dr. Butterworth and Dr. Elizabeth A. Prevost surveyed the nutritional status of 100 medical and surgical patients who were hospitalized for at least two weeks, and uncovered the following examples of neglect:

- Almost a third of the patients were never weighed during their hospital stays.
- Two-thirds of those who were weighed lost weight.
- Almost a third had symptoms that indicated possible nutritional problems which weren't investigated.
- About one-fourth of the patients were suspected to have vitamin depletion, but no vitamins were prescribed.
- Almost a third were anemic when admitted, and one-fifth became anemic during their hospitalization. [5]

Dr. Butterworth believes this sort of inattention results from the lack of nutrition education in our medical schools. Doctors are simply not made aware of the importance of good nutritional status in maintaining or restoring health. It is a well-known fact that malnutrition slows the healing of wounds and makes patients more susceptible to infections, but this fact is not impressed upon medical students. Consequently, a few enlightened doctors keep careful tabs on their patients' nutritional status, but most don't bother because it just doesn't occur to them.

Most medical personnel only recognize nutritional deficiency when the classical deficiency diseases appear. Scurvy, pellagra, beri-beri, kwashiorkor and the like almost never occur in our hospitals these days, but a more subtle form of malnutrition does. Known as protein-calorie malnutrition, or PCM, this kind of deficiency has been found to afflict from one-fourth to one-half of all medical and surgical patients hospitalized for two weeks or longer. [6]

Patients suffering from PCM are more susceptible to infection and other complications than are well-nourished patients. Their wounds and incisions heal more slowly, and they have less resistance to concurrent illness. The patient whose PCM goes unrecognized can become caught in a vicious cycle: malnutrition allows complications to develop, the complications prolong the patient's hospital stay, which worsens the nutritional status, which causes more complications, and so on. The end result is a lot more suffering for the patient, in addition to a longer and more costly hospital stay.

Dr. Butterworth cites a number of common hospital practices which adversely affect the nutritional status of patients:

- Failure to record height and weight
- Frequent rotation of attending physicians and other staff, which hinders continuity of patient care
- Diffusion of responsibility for patient care among many staff members
- Prolonged use of glucose and saline intravenous feedings
- Failure to observe patients' food intake
- Withholding meals in order to perform diagnostic tests
- Using tube feedings of uncertain composition, in inadequate amounts, and under unsanitary conditions
- Ignorance of the composition of vitamin mixtures and other nutritional products
- Failing to recognize when injury or illness increases patients' nutritional needs
- Performing surgery without first making sure that patients are optimally nourished, and failing to provide nutritional support after surgery
- Failure to appreciate the role of nutrition in preventing and recovering from infection, and relying too heavily on antibiotics to prevent and cure infection
- Lack of communication and interaction between physicians and dietitians
- Delay of nutrition support until the patient is in an advanced state of depletion, which is sometimes irreversible
- Limited availability of laboratory tests to assess nutritional status, and failure to use those that are available.[7]

Certainly there are various additional factors which contribute indirectly to patient malnutrition. For example, high food prices are undoubtedly causing more of the poor and elderly to be malnourished when they enter the hospital. But the real cause, at the bottom of everything else, is the hospital system itself. It is our system of crisis health care that has caused the poor practices set forth by Dr. Butterworth, and it is this system that has created the unwieldy bureaucracy which Dr. Richard L. Meiling describes as an "army of people who influence the food that goes on the patient's tray and when and how it's served."[8]

This army includes dietitians, food service managers, nurses, ward secretaries, aides, pharmacy technicians, housekeepers, kitchen help, cooks, storage managers and purchasing agents. All these people come between the doctor's orders and the patient, with the result that the doctor usually doesn't know if his orders are being followed. This, says Dr. Meiling, is the first potential strike against patient nutritional status: Even if a doctor *is* concerned about his or her patients' nutrition, it's practically impossible for the doctor to keep track of all the people between the diet order and the patient to see that the patient is getting the right food.

The second strike is the food's frequent unpalatability. Nobody asks patients how they like to have their food seasoned, whether they like their hamburgers rare or well done. There's usually not even much of a choice of condiments. Most hospitals use preportioned condiment packets based on the patient's diet. For example, the regular diet packet would include salt, pepper and sugar, and maybe ketchup. Bland diet packets would contain only salt and sugar, low-carbohydrate diet packs would eliminate the sugar, and so forth. All these little color-coded packages are handy for the tray line, but less than inspiring to the patient.

Strike three occurs when the food is served. Patients don't get to eat when they're hungry; they eat when the army has the food ready. If it means being awakened at the crack of dawn for breakfast or feeling starved halfway through the night, little can be done about it. After all this mass-produced food is handed out, does anyone check to see if it's being eaten? Chances are a patient could slip into malnutrition without anyone realizing he just wasn't eating.

So far, most of the blame for neglecting patients' nutritional well-being has been placed on the shoulders of personnel coming between doctors' prescriptions and patients' meal trays. But the medical staff must also be held accountable. New instructional methods being applied in a lot of teaching hospitals allow attending physicians to rotate every week, or sometimes every day. The rotation schedule also includes residents and interns, all of whom are permitted to prescribe for the patient and to change existing prescriptions. Such frequent rotation destroys continuity of patient care. Malnutrition is a gradual process and needs continuing observation to be detected. In Dr. Meiling's words, "Rejection of food that goes unobserved; steady weight loss because no one bothers to weigh the patient; the emergence of signs and symptoms of nutritional deficiencies few physicians and virtually none of the house staff, including most dietitians, recognize—these are the major causes of malnutrition."[9]

Why Hospital Malnutrition Must Be Eliminated

If the shameful problem of hospital malnutrition is to be overcome, doctors, nurses, dietitians and administrators must all become concerned with the nutritional states of the patients under their care. Malnutrition in most hospital patients *is preventable* and inexcusable. The high costs of hospital care and overcrowded conditions make the quickest possible recovery a necessity for most patients today. Now that health care people are finally becoming aware that good nutrition can hasten recovery time and poor nutrition can lead to complications which delay recovery and wound healing, a serious effort must be made to insure that patients are kept in a state of optimal nutrition.

Doctors Blackburn and Butterworth proposed, as a solution to the problem of how to maintain patient nutritional status at a high level, the establishment in every hospital of a Nutrition Support Service.[10] Under such a program, patients with a high risk of malnutrition (such as the elderly, members of low-income families, obese patients, etc.) would be identified within 24 hours of their entry into the hospital by a notation on their hospital records. This information would then be passed to the Nutrition Support Service, whose duty it would be to assemble a file of nutritional information on each patient and dispense this information to the people directly involved with the patients' care—the attending physician, the nurse and the dietitian.

It should be the attending physician's duty to determine the patient's nutritional needs and to involve nurses, dietitians, pharmacists and other staff members as necessary to fill the patient's dietary requirements. The doctor's involvement with patient nutrition should go far beyond the diet prescription. The physician should always be aware of the patient's nutritional status and any problems that develop. To do this he or she uses the medical history, physical examination, laboratory results and personal observation of the patient's condition.

The dietitian also plays a key role in the patient's nutritional progress. Many times, the right questions asked by the dietitian can turn up surprising information about the patient's eating habits, both at home and in the hospital. It is the dietitian's job to find out if the patient really understands why he is on a particular diet, and how to stick to that diet.

Nurses can be on the lookout for which foods the patient eats and which get thrown away. The nurse is also in a position to determine if the patient is losing or gaining weight. One reliable nurse's manual urges nurses to observe the nutritional status of their patients.[11] The manual suggests that although the dietitian is in charge of planning a patient's diet, it is the nurse's job to:

- Know what foods are included in the diet prescribed for the patient and learn how the foods should be served (hot, cold, etc.)

- Be aware of what the diet is supposed to do for the patient
- Be familiar with the special nutritional needs created by the patient's ailment
- Keep checking the patient's reactions to the diet to help him stay on it
- Be aware of the patient's home environment to help plan for his care to be continued by his family.

A Look at the System As It Operates

In a system where so little regard is given to keeping patients well nourished in order to promote healing and recovery, it is not surprising that equally little regard is given to preserving the nutritive content of foods by employing conservative processing and preparation techniques. The hospital food service system has been geared entirely toward saving labor and increasing profit, which has resulted in dependence on automated meal delivery equipment like the soda dispensing tubes described at the beginning of this chapter. Models of engineering efficiency one and all, but what does all this machinery really contribute to health and well-being? Getting a cup of soda from a machine is a quick and simple way to gratify a momentary desire, but it can't encourage recovery like the feeling that someone actively cares if you feel thirsty, cares whether you get well. You can't get a feeling of personal concern from all the impersonal mass production apparent in today's hospital system.

The kitchen area of even a moderate-sized hospital today is something to behold. In a typical setup, there is a room where all hot foods are prepared and another room for cold foods such as salads and desserts. Cooks must work at least a meal ahead of the one being served; that is, at lunchtime they're cooking dinner. The food must then be reheated at serving time. If the cooks are rushed or less than conscientious, already cooked foods may be left standing uncovered on the counter while other foods are being cooked.

87

A visit to one hospital kitchen revealed huge open bowls of oven-fried chicken pieces standing neglected on a counter, while the cooks were busy cooking vegetables and slicing sandwich meats. Such practices not only increase the chance of contamination, they also increase nutrient depletion through prolonged exposure of food to air and light. Imagine the effect of cooking-standing-reheating on the easily destroyed vitamin content of most vegetables.

Cooking methods in most cases are also less than desirable. Vegetables are routinely boiled in enormous pots of water at high heat. Not only is boiling the most nutrient-wasteful method of cooking, boiling also encourages over-cooking, which results in minimum palatability and eye appeal, and maximum loss of vitamins and minerals. Most of the vitamins are tossed out with the cooking water.

The practice of steaming vegetables in smaller batches is catching on in some institutional kitchens, due to the marketing of new pieces of steaming equipment. Steaming vegetables just until they're done conserves most of their nutrient value, color, texture and flavor. But even if the vegetables come out of the steamer cooked to perfection, an hour or two of holding in the steam table while patient trays are assembled pretty effectively negates the benefits obtained by steam cooking.

An essential feature of any hospital food service, whether antiquated or ultramodern, is the tray line, where workers place the various food items and utensils on trays for individual patients. The tray line in action resembles not so much an activity connected with the serving of food to sick people as it does the assembly-line manufacture of some sort of product at a large industrial plant. Anyone who has ever worked on a factory assembly line knows the tedium of such a job, and the haphazard attitude which develops after a couple of hours of standing in the same spot. So it is with the hospital tray line. Workers must stand in one place in extreme heat for hours, each performing the same, single motion over and over again. Every chicken leg placed on a tray looks like every other chicken leg on every other tray.

Under these conditions, who could take much of an honest interest in their job, and more importantly, who could feel they were helping to make sick people well? Even watching a tray line operation, you lose the sense of food being served. It seems like just another factory.

The completed trays are covered, stacked up and loaded into the elevator to be delivered to the patients. Special insulated plates, trays and carts designed to keep "hot foods hot and cold foods cold" are used, but don't always perform their intended function too well.

The food service which is truly "advanced" by today's standards operates along the same lines, except that it has completely transcended the lowly art of cooking and deals in precooked frozen meals. The up-to-date hospital food service is exemplified in this description of a Brooklyn hospital:

> On the day of service, foods are removed from the freezer and thawed at room temperature. Since bacteria can build up at temperatures between 40 and 160 degrees, food is taken from the freezer only shortly before serving. Still in their storage containers, the foods are placed on either side of a 30-foot conveyor belt at which seven diet attendants have taken up their assembly-line stations. The patient's menu, which he has selected from three alternatives of his prescribed diet, is placed on the tray. Then, the tray is moved down the line by each aide after the various menu items have been placed on it: utensils, juice, soup, bread and crackers, butter, condiments, main course, vegetables, dessert, beverage. All utensils and dishes are plastic and disposable.[12]

The meals are removed from their containers and heated in microwave ovens located on each floor of the hospital, then delivered to the patients.

The backbone of the individual frozen entrée system is the portion-controlled food. For the uninitiated, a portion-controlled food is a product which is always a standard weight and a uniform size. One portion-controlled fish fillet is the same size and shape as every other portion-controlled fish fillet, no matter what size fish it came from.

It is hard to relate most of these products to the whole foods they once were. For example, if you were to slice up a whole potato into French fries, all the slices would not be the same size. Since potatoes aren't square, the slices taken from the ends would naturally be smaller than those from the middle. But portion-controlled French fries are all the same size, so that a given number of slices will always have the same weight. If the brand of French fries used comes six to an ounce, the server knows to dish out exactly 12 French fries for a two-ounce serving. Everybody's serving looks exactly alike. No fuss, no confusion...and no variety.

Portion-controlled, frozen, canned, powdered, instant and all the other kinds of convenience products are obviously different from fresh, whole natural foods. They look different, smell different, taste different, are handled differently. These are only the apparent physical differences between whole and processed foods. We must also take into account that some processing techniques so alter the internal composition of foods that the relationships among nutrients in the original foods are altered, as in the manufacture of textured vegetable protein, described in chapter 1. As sophisticated delivery systems evolved to accommodate the increasing dependence on these foods, we might expect that the standards on which therapeutic diets are based would be overhauled to allow for the differences between the new food products and the original unprocessed foods. But the nutrient values assigned to foods when diets are formulated are based on the nutrient content of raw foods.

Let's take the potato as our example. Food technologists base the nutritive value of the potato on its raw, untouched state. When mixed with other foods, whether stewed, mashed, fried, baked, boiled or otherwise cooked—regardless of the cooking process—it is still considered to possess its original raw food value.

No allowances are made for the nutrient losses known to

occur during cooking, storing (freezing or canning) and handling of foods both before preparation and during serving. The nutrient losses these techniques created in school lunches (see page 6) apply to hospital foods as well, at least insofar as the same handling and preparation techniques are used. No matter how it is treated, that potato is expected to retain its full nutritional value.

Equal nutritional credit is given to various forms of foods too. When diets are planned, a whole baked potato is assigned the same nutrient value as an equal weight of French fries, which contain oil, and mashed potatoes, which contain milk and probably butter as well. All forms of milk are given equal status—whole, evaporated, skim, buttermilk, dried whole and dried skim alike. Yet an analysis of these different milks will not support the assumption that they are all the same.

Ice cream is a classic illustration of the misguided reasoning employed in formulating too many diets. One pint of ice cream is considered to contain the equivalent of eight ounces of milk. But all pints of ice cream do not equal eight ounces of milk. In fact, it's hard to imagine that any pint of ice cream does. In addition to the large amounts of sugar and flavorings used in most ice creams, some brands use so many artificial ingredients that they contain practically no milk at all. Yet no allowance is made for the variation in ingredients among brands, or for the fact that ice cream and milk are simply two different foods.

Planning diets on raw food values when the foods served no longer have the same nutrient values can only mean that we cannot be sure the meals actually supply all the nutrients they are supposed to supply. Small wonder that so many hospital patients become malnourished!

Another undesirable practice must be noted here. When special diets must be followed and certain foods are to be avoided, artificial substitutes are recommended. Diets to control cholesterol, for example, generally forbid or severely limit consumption of eggs and butter while allowing the patient to have refined starches and sugars. Instead of re-planning the diet to obtain necessary nutrients from other foods which have no cholesterol, the patient is simply instructed to use egg substitutes and margarine.

The fallacy of this approach is that it does nothing to educate the patient or retrain his unsound dietary habits. To be effective, a therapeutic diet must get at the cause of the problem, not just the symptoms. In the case of the patient with a high cholesterol count, his or her eating patterns are at fault. Substituting artificial foods may lower the cholesterol level, but will not change the patient's eating patterns. What will this person do when the substitutes aren't available, for instance in a restaurant? Will this person be able to choose acceptable foods instead of his or her favorite dishes?

The Problem of Therapeutic Diets

Introducing substantial changes in hospital food service operations would create more problems than in any other institutional setting, because of the battery of special diets that must be handled. The usual array of diets includes the general or house diet, light, high protein, low protein, high carbohydrate, low carbohydrate, high iron, high fiber, low fiber, bland, low calorie, liquid and diabetic.

Briefly, the general hospital diet supplies about 2,000 to 2,500 calories a day and permits most foods, except those which often upset the stomach (like hot peppers, for example). A light diet omits fatty, coarse and spicy foods. Meats generally preferred are lamb, chicken and fish.

A high-protein diet is basically a general diet with extra portions of lean meat, eggs, cheese and other protein foods. Fatty foods are not allowed. The high-carbohydrate diet stresses additional portions of fruits, vegetables, sugars and starches. Fatty and spicy foods are avoided. The high-iron diet emphasizes good sources of iron and vitamin B_{12}, such as organ meats, leafy green vegetables, dried beans and peas, egg yolks and whole grain cereals.

A high-fiber diet is simply a general-type diet with special attention paid to fibrous (roughage-containing) foods. It includes lots of raw fruits and vegetables (served with their skins whenever possible), whole grain cereal products and leafy green vegetables. In a progressive-minded hospital, this diet might also include wheat bran, but the prevailing attitude is one of reluctance toward its use. Not permitted in a high-fiber diet are refined cereals, concentrated foods and heavy seasonings.

The low-fiber, or soft, diet, which should not be confused with the bland diet, is intended to give the gastrointestinal tract a rest. Foods are meant to be completely absorbed. This is only a temporary diet; it is noticeably lacking in vitamins and minerals. The soft diet is built around clear (fat-free) soups, tender lean meats, eggs, refined cereals, fruit juices and gelatin. Forbidden foods include milk, whole grain cereals, fruits, vegetables, cheese and heavy seasonings.

The low-protein diet is designed to keep protein intake at a low but still adequate level. It allows for limited amounts of milk, cheese, eggs and meat, and also permits bland, easy-to-digest fruits and vegetables. The diet eliminates incomplete proteins and heavy seasonings.

In the low-fat diet, all but the most easily digested of fats are forbidden. This means no egg yolks, fatty meats, sauces or gravies. Foods permitted are lean meats, egg whites, cottage cheese, skim milk, and fruits and vegetables low in fat. This diet does not supply enough vitamin A, and patients on it must take supplements.

The bland diet is intended to prevent peristalsis (the muscular contractions which move food through the intestines to be eliminated), and to slow the flow of gastric juices in the stomach. Soft, smooth foods are emphasized, in frequent small feedings to keep food in the stomach without overloading it. The patient eats primarily refined cereals and pasta products, white rice, potatoes, milk, eggs, tender meats, pureed fruits and vegetables, custards and gelatin. Strictly taboo are strongly flavored and highly seasoned foods, fibrous foods, and raw fruits and vegetables.

A low-calorie diet is a normal diet with a reduced number of calories for the purpose of weight loss. Calorie intake is reduced by eliminating some fats and carbohydrates; protein intake remains the same. The emphasis is placed on bulky, low-calorie fruits and vegetables, lean meats, eggs, skim milk and plenty of fluids. Fatty foods, pastries, creams, sauces and gravies are not allowed.

Liquid diets are used for short-term maintenance. A clear liquid diet is mostly water and carbohydrates, and is used only to prevent dehydration and to start peristalsis in post-operative patients. It consists mainly of frequent feedings of clear broth, coffee, tea and other clear beverages, often including certain soft drinks. In most cases, the patient progresses from the clear liquid diet to a full liquid diet before returning to solid foods. The full liquid diet, while providing more calories, should also be used strictly on a temporary basis. This diet includes milk beverages, strained soups, tea, coffee, fruit juices, ice cream, gelatin and carbonated drinks.

Diabetic diet programs allow a lot more flexibility than they used to. This is made possible because of a system known as "food exchange lists," in which foods are grouped according to the amounts of protein, fat and carbohydrate they contain. This system eliminates the need for diabetics to weigh food portions. The patient simply selects the number and category of food exchanges (fruit, meat, fat, etc.) that his or her diet calls for.

Admittedly, working with natural foods presents some new problems for the dietitian planning many special diets. Dietitians are trained and required by law to work with a group of standards established by the American Dietetic Association. These standards, as we noted before, are based on raw food values and fail to take into account the changes caused in foods by processing and handling techniques. They also permit the use of highly processed convenience products and nonnutritious foods such as white sugar.

The answer is not to throw out the standard diets and start over, but to use the standard diets as a starting point and substitute whole foods for their processed counterparts wherever possible. This method proved the best at

Meadowbrook Hospital (discussed later in this chapter and in chapter 4), satisfying the desire for natural foods as well as the demands of the ADA, Medicare and various insurance companies that all diets be computed according to the ADA standards.

To show you how the system can work, here is a sample of a low cholesterol diet using natural foods in the ADA standard diet.

Low Cholesterol Diet

	Foods Included	**Foods Excluded**
Beverages	buttermilk, cereal beverages such as Postum, Sano-caf	milk, chocolate products, "soft" drinks, alcohol
Breads	whole grain: wheat, rye, soya, mixed grains; crackers such as Rye Krisp, Ak mak, flat breads; home baked with natural ingredients	products made with bleached flours, hydrogenated oils, preservatives and additives
Cereals	all whole grain and unrefined	refined and those with sugars, preservatives and additives
Desserts	fresh fruits, fruit whips, simple custards and puddings (honey or maple syrup in small amount)	rich desserts, meaning those high in sugar and fats
Fats	liquid vegetable oils, limited amounts of butter, cream, half-and-half, cream cheese, salad dressings (best if homemade)	margarine, "hardened" (hydrogenated) shortenings (those solid at room temperature)
Fruits Juices	all fresh fruits; frozen or canned (no sugar); juices with no added sugar or additives	none with sugar and additives; best to eat whole fruits and drink juices in moderation
Protein Foods	one to two eggs daily, if desired; cottage cheese, natural cheeses; tofu (bean curd); lean beef, lamb, poultry, fish (fresh when possible); tuna (water packed); raw or lightly toasted seeds and nuts	egg substitutes, processed cheeses and substitutes, regular ground meat, bacon, ham, or any smoked or cured meats, fatty cuts or cooked in fat—no fried foods; "roasted" nuts with oil, seafoods such as oysters, shrimp, lobster and crabs

Low Cholesterol Diet (Cont.)

	Foods Included	Foods Excluded
Soups	homemade using acceptable foods	commercially prepared made with starches, sugars and fats
Sweets	honey, natural maple syrup, natural molasses; fruit butter with no sugar	refined sugars, jams, jellies, marmalades, syrups, candies
Vegetables	all vegetables, brown rice, pastas made with unrefined products	fried potatoes, potato chips, any fried foods, white rice, pastas made with refined products

Can the System Be Changed?

If any significant improvements are ever to be made in the quality of hospital food, the change will have to come from two avenues—the food service system itself and the area of diet planning. The task would be gargantuan and would require a complete change of attitude in almost everyone connected with hospital care.

Revising the system is a lot more complicated than telling the caterer to throw out the convenience foods. Cooking from scratch for the numbers of patients in today's huge hospitals would mean more storage and preparation space, more cooking equipment and more labor. New pieces of equipment designed to conserve nutrients instead of to save time and labor would be needed. Delivery systems would have to be changed. Food products themselves would be different—no more preportioned convenience foods. The food service would no longer be run for profit and would have to be developed internally.

Staffing the food service would also present a major stumbling block. Strong, efficient management would be an absolute necessity. Food storage would have to be tightly controlled and menus carefully planned to prevent waste.

Under the present externally operated system, the outside caterer supplies all food, personnel and even some of the equipment used in a particular food service, amounting to a monopoly over all aspects of the operation. This domination creates inflated prices and guaranteed profit for the catering firm. It also means employee loyalty goes to the caterer rather than to the welfare of the patients.

This is the major difficulty encountered by those institutions where a natural food service is desired. Produce and other food is supplied by the caterer and is accepted for the hospital by their own employees. Poor quality (and high profit) food is much more likely to be accepted, and is then disguised under gravies, sauces and dressings, or in casseroles and similar dishes.

Cooks generally present another problem in developing natural food service. They are employed by the caterer, and are therefore accustomed to the company's procedures, recipes and convenience foods. Foods such as whole grains are probably unfamiliar to them. In addition, cooking from scratch requires a lot more work, and cooks' salaries are notoriously low.

Change Must Start Somewhere

Although the immensity of the existing hospital food service system makes drastic changes extremely complicated and difficult for the large metropolitan hospital, less dramatic reforms are possible. Many of the improvements suggested for the school lunch program (see "Nutrition Tips for Your School's Food Manager" in chapter 2) should be possible in hospitals as well.

Such simple procedures as covering pots during cooking and not allowing foods to stand uncovered at room temperature could help to save nutrients. Cans should be opened when they are needed, not hours before. Fresh vegetables should be rinsed thoroughly, and when necessary, scrubbed as well (as for root vegetables), but there's no need to soak them. Soaking serves no real purpose and depletes nutrients. Cooks and assistants should be aware that some vitamins are water soluble.

More whole grain baked goods should be made available. At the very least, patients should be given a choice of having

100 percent whole wheat bread with meals unless their diet restrictions forbid it.

• More fresh fruit could be served as desserts, or as part of breakfast. Canned fruits could be served without the syrup. It also seems that the use of fatty gravies could be cut down, and occasional meatless meals could be served. The present system allows pitifully few alternatives for vegetarian patients. In fact, the usual approach is to treat the vegetarian as a troublemaker whose food preferences disrupt the smooth functioning of the food service operation. The possibility of making allowances for vegetarians needs to be explored. There are no good reasons why concerned management personnel cannot upgrade the quality of hospital food service at least a few notches. Could it be that these people don't have enough concern for the patients under their care to make the extra effort?

Private Hospitals and Nursing Homes

The situation in smaller, private facilities is far brighter. Although similar problems in regard to special diets and food service employees must be faced, the smaller scale of the food service operation allows more opportunity for change than the large hospital system. "A Natural Food Service for Meadowbrook Hospital" (see chapter 4) attests to the kind of wholesome, delicious food that *can* be served in the private hospital or nursing home.

Because of limited budget and lack of space, most small institutions don't have the latest in kitchen equipment and food-delivery systems. But this is a blessing in disguise, for it means that these institutions still have the equipment needed to prepare meals without a lot of convenience products. The nursing home cook might not have microwave ovens to heat up frozen portions of roast beef, but she does have an old-fashioned gas or convection oven to roast a real piece of beef and slice it herself.

To attest to the kind of food service that is possible in the smaller hospital or nursing home with a concerned, enlightened staff, here is a description of how the various food service operations are conducted at Meadowbrook Hospital, from the dietitian there, Genia Lee Roper:

Fresh and frozen foods are served, when possible, instead of canned. Vegetables are steamed instead of boiled to death, and the patient receives the most food value that can be received from the vegetables. To enhance the flavor of the vegetables sea salt and different herbs are used.

Fresh fruits are before the patients at all times. A fresh fruit basket is placed in each patient's room at the beginning of his or her stay and is replenished daily. Because of the continuous availability of the fruit baskets, sweet desserts are seldom prepared. When foods do require sweetening, honey is used instead of white sugar.

Meadowbrook uses the freshest dairy products obtainable. The law states that it is illegal to sell raw milk in Louisiana, so only pasteurized milk is used. Most of the milk is nonfat skim milk; buttermilk and additive-free yogurt from the local dairy are also served frequently. Butter is bought from the local dairy and is individually wrapped for patients' protection. All cheeses used in the department are natural cheeses; processed cheeses like American cheese and cheese spreads are not used. Patients are served fertile eggs purchased from a local farm where the chickens are allowed to run on the grass instead of being kept in cages. All patients receive three-minute eggs for breakfast unless diet does not permit.

Meats of the best available grade are bought from a local source. Whenever possible, only homegrown beef that was raised without the use of hormones is used at Meadowbrook: they serve no commercially processed meats like hot dogs and luncheon meats. The prepared meats that are used are purchased from Shiloh Farms (a national distributor) and contain no artificial preservatives and no nitrates or nitrites. Poultry products and fish also come from Shiloh Farms and have no artificial preservatives.

Breads are baked at the hospital with all natural ingredients. Whole wheat pasta products are bought from local health food stores. Brown rice is the only kind of rice normally used in the food service. Special dishes are sometimes prepared with wild rice. Natural cereals are served both hot and cold. Hot cereals such as cracked wheat, rolled oats, millet, seven grain, barley grits and soy grits are served. Pancakes are a specialty at Meadowbrook. Most of the time, the dietary department makes up their own pancake mixes. When prepared mixes are used, they are all natural products purchased from Shiloh Farms Baking House.

Beverages are served to patients three times daily or at the patient's request. The beverage selection includes natural fruit juices, fresh lemonade, fresh carrot and celery juices made with the dietary department's juice extractor. These freshly extracted juices are available whenever patients request them.

All patients receive midmorning, afternoon and nighttime snacks of assorted nuts, seeds and unsulfured dried fruits. At 10 A.M. and 2 P.M. the food service prepares a high-protein drink for all patients. The high-protein beverage has been found to be especially beneficial to hypoglycemic and diabetic patients.

Another unique feature of Meadowbrook's food service is that great effort is put forth to try to accommodate patients' special dietary requests. Vegetarians can receive good, balanced meals without causing trauma to the kitchen staff.

Now that natural foods have been served at Meadowbrook for a few years, the program seems to be running smoothly, and the staff has adjusted to the new approach to food. "In fact," says Ms. Roper, "there is not one cook in the kitchen who could not explain to you the reason we cook and prepare foods the way we do. Their reward not only comes in salary, but in seeing patients change, become well and able to eat good, wholesome food. I have seen the dietary personnel work after hours in order to please patients; not patients alone, but also to help out a very fair and generous employer, Dr. Evers. He too gives us encouragement to prepare the right and wholesome diets, because of his sincere desire to help supervise the good health of his patients and encourage them in a better way of life."

Imagine how wonderful it would be if all hospital patients got this kind of dedicated care!

Feeding the Elderly

In the case of older people, the difference between an appetizing and attractive meal, and one that is tasteless, colorless and uniform can be the difference between people eating and refusing to eat. Pleasant meals are important to psychological as well as physical health.

In a nursing home environment, mealtime is an important social occasion, and every effort ought to be made to provide the most nutritious, tastiest food possible. But we must not forget that many elderly people not in nursing homes live alone and have neither the economic means nor the motivation to prepare wholesome meals for themselves.

We have a vast obligation to our elderly. They are our parents and grandparents, and we need to show more concern for their well-being. Rampant inflation has wiped out the savings of many of our Seniors, and they've been reduced to the poverty level through no fault of their own. A few years ago, Congress took the first step toward genuine recognition of the plight of elderly Americans.

In 1972, the federal government established the Title VII Nutrition Program for the Elderly, to provide a hot meal five days a week for Americans over 60 with low income levels. Over 30 million Americans are now 60 years of age or older, and almost seven million of them exist below or on the borderline of the poverty level. All these people are eligible for Title VII meals, yet in 1976, only 200,000 were actually receiving the meals to which they are entitled.

The Title VII program allots funds for the preparation and serving of meals to elderly persons at strategically located community sites. Schools, churches and any similarly available facilities may all be used to serve Title VII meals. All local projects under the Title VII program are eligible for government commodities, but many are run by outside caterers who refuse the donated foods. The cost of producing the meals averages $1.96 per meal. Reimbursements are made on the basis of total project cost (including administrative expenses) instead of by means of a set fee for each meal served.

The Senate Select Commission on Nutrition and Human Needs conducted a nationwide survey of Title VII projects early in 1976, to assess the successes and shortcomings of the program. The biggest problem uncovered was the sheer inadequacy of the program. It cannot reach many of the people who need the free meals. Most of the local projects participating in the survey had long waiting lists. And Seniors who are housebound and unable to get to the places where the Title VII meals are served usually miss out entirely. Less than 30,000 of them receive meals delivered to their homes.

Introducing a tabulation of survey results, Senator George McGovern, chairman of the Commission, cited the critical need for more elderly feeding programs. "Tragically," he writes, "we spend billions of dollars on hospitalization and nursing homes for these persons, and relatively nothing to provide them with meals in their own homes which might make such institutionalization unnecessary. I think that this shameful fact, as well as the results of this survey, should again remind us that, despite our best efforts, much remains to be done."

Despite the difficulties involved in finding funds to create feeding programs for our senior citizens, some very good programs have been set up.

The state of Massachusetts has pioneered in providing meals and related services for its Seniors. In 1975, the state had funded 18 projects which served approximately 6,200 meals a day at 125 locations throughout the state. The projects were set up with 2.835 million dollars in federal funds that were matched on a local basis.

Seniors eligible to receive meals through the projects are those who:

- cannot afford to eat adequately,
- lack the skill and/or knowledge to select and prepare nourishing meals,
- have limited mobility which may impair their capacity to shop and cook for themselves, or
- have feelings of rejection and loneliness which obliterate the incentive to prepare and eat a meal alone.[13]

Those who are able, pay for their meals. But for most, the meals are free.

Each local project serves at least 150 meals a day five or more days each week. A project council is set up along with each project to serve as an advisory and governing body to help the project run smoothly. Half the members of the council are project participants, and the other half are professionals, local government officials and other interested citizens.

Places where meals are served have to meet the following requirements:

- They must be as close as possible, preferably within walking distance, to the target group of eligible people.
- Each site must have a volunteer or paid manager who is in charge of all activities conducted there.
- All sites must meet several standards in regard to cleanliness, safety, equipment and furniture, space and layout, and so forth.

Schools, churches, community centers, apartment complexes and senior citizen centers are all being successfully used as project sites.

The Massachusetts nutrition projects provide more than just meals for their clients. Transportation is provided for anyone who has trouble getting to and from the meal sites. Information and referral services are available for people with special dietary needs and for those who just want to learn more about the food they eat. Health and welfare counseling are provided. Nutrition education is provided so that Seniors can learn how to prepare the most nutritious, satisfying meals possible. Participants can get help with their shopping to enable them to spend their food dollars wisely and to learn to cope with the increasing complexity and diversity of new products lining supermarket shelves. Finally, recreational activities are conducted at the centers to provide the warmth and social contact so many of our elderly need. The centers are not just places where Seniors can go to eat, but friendly places where they can feel they belong.

School Lunch for the Elderly

Milwaukee is offering a hot, nourishing noon meal to Seniors of 60 years and over in 150 public schools, in conjunction with school lunches. This program differs from Massachusetts' in that it is purely a local effort, conducted without any state or federal subsidies whatsoever. Tom Farley, Director of Food Services for the Milwaukee School District (whom we met in chapter 2) explains the program this way: "We're not offering charity. Our new lunch customers have paid for these facilities with their hard work and taxes. The modest charge of 50 cents a meal plus an optional beverage at a dime, pays for all direct costs. There is no means test." Farley's enthusiasm is matched by the response of his new customers.

Many people were afraid that elderly people would not enjoy a children's Type A lunch, but the program has worked splendidly.

In the Milwaukee School System, there is only one basic hot meal for all 170 schools. Only the portions vary in size. The first major American city to offer Type A hot lunches to all its students, Milwaukee offers other pluses to its lunch customers. The schools bake their own bread and rolls without preservatives. Nothing is fried, so the foods are lower in calories and easier to digest. There are no heavy flavorings to disguise the good flavors of the high-quality foods. Nearly everything is prepared from scratch. Texture, color and taste harmony are important to Farley's family of dietitians.

As a public service, newspapers and local radio stations announce each day's menu. Since there is no a la carte, Seniors are not tempted to buy a cheap dessert and coffee.

Another advantage is the flexibility of the lunch program. Some principals, like Ms. Jennie Brodi of 35th Street School, have the Seniors eat in the privacy of the library. The children act as hosts and hostesses, delivering utensils, napkins and milk, then carrying the empty trays back to the cafeteria. In other schools, Seniors thoroughly enjoy eating with the children.

The value of this kind of program shows up in other ways beyond the day-to-day satisfaction of putting good food in empty stomachs and happy smiles on lonely faces. Remarks Mr. Farley, "Everybody seems to forget that Seniors are taxpayers. You show them the good things our schools are doing, and the Seniors are going to support us. I call it voting with a fork."

Asked to compare Milwaukee's feeding program for the elderly with the usual government program, Farley said, "Let's look at it from the standpoint of cost. I feed school children a deluxe, well-balanced meal for 30 cents for grammar school, 35 for high school. I can give Seniors that same fine meal for 50 cents, 60 if they choose beverage. That's the same price the teachers pay."

By contrast, many government meals for the elderly run from $1.25 to $1.50. Transportation costs and small production runs escalate meal cost.

Since he uses existing facilities that are geared to mass production—his operation serves an average of 75,000 lunches daily—Farley can afford to charge so little. Quantity purchasing and careful planning make the difference.

Which do Seniors really prefer—a meal for nothing or a "donation" of a quarter, or a meal at school for sixty cents full cost? Farley has strong feelings on the subject, and recognizes the need of many of our elderly. "There's no denying there is terrible suffering among the aged poor. The government estimates that from December 1970 to March 1974, low-priced food jumped 41.7 percent. When you're already eating beans, and beans double in price, what do you do?" he asks.

Senior citizens, by and large, are a proud and sensitive group of people. In a society such as ours, which worships the young and rejects the old, it is to be expected that the elderly are wary of making their needs and problems known. Their self-respect is the most important sense of worth they have—society no longer respects them.

Tom Farley feels that a person's self-image is the most important thing he possesses and must never be destroyed. If the aged poor need money, they should have it, in the form of programs like the SSI (Supplementary Security Income). It is the elderly's rightful share in the riches of this country. But the danger in the government's food programs is that they are like handouts. Accepting charity is painful and demeaning to an elderly person desperately clinging to the image of a self-sufficient person. Free food programs can work, like the Massachusetts program, but they must be handled tactfully and make every effort to maintain Seniors' self-respect.

It is tremendously difficult to plan diets for the elderly. There is wide variation in the kinds and amounts of food that older people can consume and absorb. Perhaps the most sensible approach is the one taken by the Milwaukee feeding program. It is based on generally sound nutritional principles; the goal is to teach children and adults alike the simple, direct tastes of wholesome, made-from-scratch foods.

The lunches approved by the student testing panel appeal to the Seniors as well as the students. An encouraging 64 percent of the Senior guests reported that they could eat everything the schools served, and 34 percent indicated that they only avoided things to a slight degree.

No one knows how much illness and unhappiness proper nutrition can forestall in the elderly. But we do know that one of every four suicides and one of every four admissions to mental hospitals is a person over 65. The Milwaukee program has made all the difference to many of its participants. One housebound Senior suddenly discovered that he could walk after all. All the doctors in the world probably couldn't have gotten that man out of bed, but the chance to have lunch at school gave him something to walk for, a sense of belonging.

Programs like those in Massachusetts and Milwaukee are still all too rare. But there's every reason to believe that regular good meals, plus companionship, could keep thousands of our elderly out of nursing homes, and serving better food in the homes could make them much pleasanter places for those who do need care.

Chapter 4

Success Stories—
Four Pioneers
In Better
Institutional Feeding

This chapter is devoted to four of the best examples of quantity cookery we've seen. Each serves a different clientele, but all share the same dedication and concern for providing the best food possible to the people they serve.

A Day-Care Center
with a Natural Difference

In Allentown, Pennsylvania, some children are being introduced to natural foods before they ever have their first encounter with a school cafeteria. The 40 or more moppets who attend the Volunteers of America (VOA) day-care center are lunching on such unusual fare as cashew-millet casserole, brown rice and spinach casserole, broiled liver and soybean surprise—and they love it.

Sara Bell, official cook for the day-care center and the genie behind a new food program designed to build better eating habits, has brought a new look to the dining room and kindled a keen appetite for lunchtime in the three-, four-, and five-year-olds attending the center.

For some of these children of working mothers, the lunch they get at the day-care center is the only hot meal of the day. Ms. Bell is determined to pack that meal with nutrients that growing bodies need. "To do this," she explains, "we have eliminated processed, empty-calorie foods. We are using more fresh fruit, mixed raw nuts, seeds and dried fruits, gelatin with fresh fruit and yogurt and homemade whole grain breads."

Vegetables are lightly steamed to preserve their flavors, textures, colors and nutrient values. They are cooked without salt; salt and pepper shakers are kept on each table, but many of the children prefer to eat their vegetables unseasoned. Leftover vegetables, instead of being reheated, are used in salads. This way more of the nutrient value is conserved, not to mention taste and texture.

Like Page Cullen at the Atlantis Center (mentioned in chapter 2), Sara has found that children will indeed eat unusual vegetables, grains and vegetarian dishes. A look at the center's menus shows that the children enjoy such out of the ordinary foods as spinach salad, granola souffle, soybeans, zucchini, barley soup, squash, broccoli souffle, assorted cheeses, beef and groundnut (peanut) stew, Brussels sprouts, millet dishes and carob brownies. (Some of Sara's menu plans are included in chapter 8.) Strange as it may seem, the kids really like these foods. Extra helpings are always available and most of the plates get cleaned. In fact, some of the children have been known to come back for thirds on liver. They call it steak.

The directors of the VOA center share Sara's concern that the children get the best possible meals, and also that they understand the importance of eating the right kinds of food. The staff hasn't tried to dupe the kids into thinking the food isn't different. Quite the contrary—the ingredients in new dishes are carefully explained by the teachers in an effort to make their young charges aware of basic nutritional principles. The educational approach has worked out so well that parents are asking for the recipes of the dishes their children are talking so much about at home.

Although the center no longer receives any government

commodities, Sara has managed to cut food bills by careful purchasing. Bulk foods such as grains, nuts and honey are ordered through two local health food stores, and the center gets them practically at cost. Some products have also been purchased through an area co-op, again with only a small markup. Fresh fruit is supplied by a fruit distributor, and vegetables come from the local farmers' market.

Her experience with the center has firmly convinced Ms. Bell of the merits of natural foods. "I always had a leaning toward the natural," she relates, "but I got a terrific boost and lots of guidelines when I attended a conference on 'The New Nutrition' at Rensselaerville, New York in 1975."

The conference alerted Sara to the dangers in food additives and preservatives and provided her with much valuable information on nutrition. She learned that natural and homemade foods actually cost less in the long run than canned and processed foods.

"Back at the day-care center, I found to my amazement that this is absolutely true. The fast-food purveyors are continually trying to sell us prepared stuffed cabbage rolls, fish sticks, lasagna, stuffed chicken rolls, and other pre-prepared, overprocessed foods. I turn them down flat and make everything myself. And, believe it or not, it takes no more time. Some people say that good food costs more. This is a myth. By using natural foods and making things myself, I have been able to stay under the proposed budget by $3,000 this year."

A School Lunch Program
To Be Proud Of
by Jean Farmer

Jean Farmer, a mother of four who lives in Bloomington, Indiana, took on a citizen's campaign to achieve victory over junk foods in school vending machines and lunch programs. In 1976, she was named to the nationwide "Terrific Ten" list by the Food Day organization, in recognition of her fight for better nutrition.

The ideal school lunch would feature wholesome natural foods: cold-pressed oils, whole grain breads and pastries, honeys, abundant salads and juicy fruits. Unfortunately, many schools are rapidly moving in the opposite direction—toward centrally processed and heated-up foods competing with vending machines laden with sodas and candy bars.

A few years ago, Milwaukee became the first major American city to reach the goal of serving hot lunches in all city schools (and banning vending machines). In 16 years as food director of the Milwaukee Public Schools, Thomas J. Farley has opened new kitchens at 101 schools.

Lunches at Milwaukee schools sell for 30 cents in elementary school, 35 cents in junior and senior high, and a new program makes the same meals available to senior citizens for 50 cents. Each day there is only one basic hot meal served at all 170 schools. Only the portions vary in size. By standardizing the menu, Farley saves enough money to add on the many extras that make the meals so enjoyable and beneficial.

Farley's meals delight the palate as well as the pocketbook. How about this student-planned meal: Western Meat Loaf with Ranch Gravy, Parslied Buttered Rice, Lettuce and Tomato Salad, Whole Wheat Pan Roll, Chilled Peach Slices? Every item was chosen by the students themselves!

The walls of Farley's office are studded with congratulatory letters, telegrams and awards. Not only has he been given the Silver Plate Award for the best school lunch, he has crowded out gourmet restaurants and hotels for the Gold Plate Award—the best food operation in the USA.

Is the Farley success story only charisma? Or is there a recipe, a "fabulous formula" that other systems can copy? Without spending a penny in consulting fees, you may learn Farley's three main success secrets. Like all great secrets, they are so simple few food systems have ever tried them—or even considered them. Yet the first secret will work even in your home kitchen.

Secret One: Discover what kids want, and then give it to them.

Democracy gone mad? How could it possibly work? Yet obviously, Farley makes it work.

"Kids love variety. They love juicy meat loaf, spicy lasagna, hearty bratwurst, Italian spaghetti with tossed green salad...." The words roll lovingly from Farley's tongue.

Judging from the menus, variety—extraordinary variety—is very much evident. Every kitchen bakes its own bread, its cookies, its pastry. The aroma from 43 varieties of bread, from crusty garlic loaves to poppy seed buns, must meet with enthusiastic response. Each day, over 90 percent of Milwaukee public school children enjoy food fresh from the ovens. Farley estimates that he saves up to 50 percent by baking his own goods. He is frankly puzzled why so few school systems seize this opportunity to cut costs and satisfy patrons.

As welcome as homemade goods are, they are only a small part of Farley's menu strategy. How does he find out what kids want to eat?

For nine years, Milwaukee students have elected representatives from junior and senior high schools for give-and-take sessions. Seven times a year, these representatives meet to taste and test brands of food and to discuss menu changes.

First, all foods are screened for quality. Farley insists upon USDA grading for all his meats. He buys only quality chuck for his burgers, with fat content limited to 15–18 percent and nitrate- and nitrite-free franks. He refuses to serve soy burgers, because the kids rejected them on the taste panel.

There is obviously powerful pressure for Farley to lower his standards to save money. But he insists, "We are not in the food business to make money." His goals are good nutrition, variety and customer satisfaction.

Pleasing the customer involves a lot of hard work. The student testing panel judges samples of new products from firms that have submitted bids. Items might include beef patties, breaded fish, mock chicken legs and perhaps a battery of brownies from the school kitchen. Each student tests each item and marks it for taste and texture. No brands are visible, but prices are.

The panel's decisions are always adhered to, and Farley contends that student testing saves him a lot of trouble with food sellers. If somebody complains that he didn't get a contract with a rock-bottom bid, Farley can simply tell him the kids just didn't like his product. What could anybody say to that?

Students even plan an entire menu. Farley maintains that they do it better than he can. And what do kids love to eat?

According to Farley, there are five basic vegetables, besides potatoes, that kids like to eat—at least in Milwaukee.

> Whole kernel corn
> Green beans
> Carrots
> Green peas
> Beets

The secret is that only top-quality, tender products are acceptable. The beans, for example, must be stringless, have good color and flavor; the carrots may have a whisper of brown sugar and butter; the beets are always diced and served with orange-flavored Harvard sauce.

Are the five vegetables monotonous?

Farley insists they are not, because he serves a fresh salad daily with crisp, raw vegetables. That's where the broccoli and spinach sneak in. And the Bibb lettuce, onion, cabbage and celery. Students select their own dressings from a separate service table, and the dressings, like everything else, are from scratch.

Although the Milwaukee lunch program is built around student choice, there is no a la carte service. Farley is staunchly opposed to the very idea of the profit-motivated a la carte system. The most obvious reason is cost. Bulk buying made possible by serving one menu to everyone naturally gives greater value.

Labor costs are another factor. In Milwaukee, labor costs are trimmed by serving the food quickly and efficiently.

113

Students appreciate swift service and voice their gratitude. The fastest lines employ a double belt system and serve 24 to 40 customers a minute. By contrast, a la carte might serve 5 to 7 a minute.

A la carte emerged, Farley believes, because the average school lunch was lackluster. As a result, for 85 cents or more, a child with money can buy a bunch of foods (not necessarily very nutritious ones) that he likes. The poor child who depends on a free school lunch for his noon meal is left with the tasteless, poorly prepared meal served on the regular meal line. To a dedicated food service director like Tom Farley, this kind of class distinction is inexcusable.

In Milwaukee the same fine food is served to everybody—preschoolers in Head Start, the grammar school set, teenagers in junior and senior high, the teachers, and senior citizens who come to the schools for lunch. This democratic leveling provides what Farley calls a "Bridge of Understanding" among teachers, students and Seniors.

Secret Two: Snack bars and vendors must not compete with school lunch.

"Snack bars and vendors" are fighting words to Farley. He testified before Congress that permitting vending machines in school cafeterias was like "allowing a typhoid carrier in a hospital." He insists that children in school are captive clientele, "obliged by law to be present." He feels that the machines which vend soft drinks, candy and chips are especially bad in disadvantaged areas, where parents know little or nothing about nutrition. It is illogical, says Farley, for Congress to vote over one billion dollars in lunch subsidies, and then allow vendors to subvert the very principle of school lunch: to provide the food children need for growth and development.

Many principals and school boards are also ignorant of the role of food in fueling alert brains. They welcome vending as an effortless cornucopia of funds for athletic uniforms, choir robes, dances, and band instruments. As vending takes hold, competition may make school lunch attendance sag.

Costs then rise, kitchen morale slips, and the spiral spins down and down. Sometimes whole lunch and breakfast programs collapse.

Secret Three: You must have professionals running the food service.

The Milwaukee Food Service Division is staffed by top-flight dietitians, armed with the latest equipment and production techniques. It is the only school service in the nation that offers a graduate program with a Registered Dietitian degree.

Farley insists that it is impossible to recruit a food service director from the local cafe or to promote a unit manager cook. "In this business," he says, "it takes a tough professional to stand up to school administrators, politicians and glib salesmen."

To achieve maximum output, Farley uses time-motion studies and the best equipment he can find. The right piece of equipment can save thousands of dollars in labor costs.

Critics of Farley's program may well protest that things that work well in a big city won't work in Bean Blossom Falls in a 90-year-old building. As usual, Farley has an answer for everything. He insists that a small operation enjoys great flexibility and often enviable labor rates. He hates central kitchens, because they cost a lot and don't really do the job.

"Think about it," says Farley tartly. "When you have central kitchens, who is in charge of the food? The truck drivers! What do they care about feeding kids?"

Farley obviously cares a lot. So strongly is he committed to his community, he requested his school board to allow him to feed senior citizens at their local schools. Permission was granted. He estimates he is now feeding a thousand elderly daily, without a penny of state or federal subsidy.

It is caring for people that makes the Milwaukee Food Service operation in a class by itself. It is this caring that puts tasty food into cheerful dishes or bright trays, not embalmed under plastic wrap. It is this caring that nourishes the heart, the head and the grateful belly.

The Lewis and Clark
Expedition into Natural Foods

by Conrad Wesselhoeft

Conrad Wesselhoeft has been a student at Lewis and Clark College, and a staff member of The Pioneer Log, *the student newspaper.*

"I am a platonic scholar and believe in the concept of a healthy mind in a healthy body," says John Howard, President of Lewis and Clark College in Portland, Oregon.

Prompted by President Howard, the college in fall of 1975 instituted a new food program for more than 1,000 students that emphasized natural and nutritious foods. The goals of the program were to teach students the fundamentals of nutrition and to replace poor eating habits with those that are nutritionally sound.

The challenge of implementing such an ambitious program fell to Thad Thomas, Saga Corporation's food service director at Lewis and Clark. Thomas's major concerns were the four problem areas in the American diet: too much sugar, too much saturated fat, too little roughage, and too many chemical additives.

The introduction of new and better foods required that old menus be completely overhauled. But the Lewis and Clark food service staff of 23 included no certified dietitians. Therefore, the responsibility for creating new and more nutritious recipes was assumed by the Saga Corporation's home office in Menlo Park, California. A large institutional food service firm, Saga regularly supplies meals to hundreds of colleges, universities, hospitals and industries in the United States. But the innovative program Lewis and Clark was proposing was a singular experiment. Meal planners had to literally start from scratch. While creating the new recipes, Saga dietitians frequently referred to such contemporary books on nutrition as Frances Moore Lappé's *Diet for a Small Planet*.

116

Once the new menus were devised and a local natural foods wholesaler lined up, the program was ready to roll. But there was much frustration at first. The cooks at Lewis and Clark were unfamiliar with many of the new recipes. Thomas's daily meetings with them became more complicated and detailed. He would announce to the cooks, for example, "Today, we're going to have buckwheat groats."

"What are buckwheat groats?" they would say. "We've never heard of them. How do we cook them?"

"I had never seen buckwheat groats, myself," says Thomas. "I didn't know how to answer them. 'We'll just have to go back into the kitchen and try,' I told them. Through this process and open-mindedness, we and the cooks educated ourselves."

One of the first things Thomas did was remove all soft drink vending machines from the dining hall. Then, the following foods were virtually eliminated from his menus: luncheon meats, colored gelatin, hot dogs, bacon, all cakes, breads and doughnuts made from mixes, imitation dairy products, potato chips, presweetened dry breakfast cereals and sherbet. Whole wheat flour was substituted for white flour whenever possible. (The use of white flour was of particular concern to President Howard.)

Corned beef, ham and fried foods were served with less frequency.

While playing down the less nutritious foods, Thomas began introducing several new foods, including toasted wheat germ, granola, yogurt, more nutritious cakes and cookies utilizing whole grains, new meatless entrées, a wider variety of vegetables and cooked grains, honey, and polyunsaturated oils for cooking.

While introducing the new items, Thomas and the Saga dietitians were careful to see that the Recommended Dietary Allowances for important nutrients were either met or *exceeded*.

In the beginning, Thomas admits, he was skeptical of the whole idea: "I wasn't totally convinced that it was a good thing or a bad thing; I was in the middle."

But President Howard strongly opposed the old food program, saying, "I see no reason to surrender to general forces or bad habits in society. The old canard about colleges—that they are always the last to practice what they teach—I've always deplored that. It seems to me the college has a moral and professional obligation to apply something when we know it is right."

His skeptical stand at the outset notwithstanding, Thomas resolved to make the nutritional program succeed despite major obstacles. First he had to contend with the lifelong poor eating habits of students as manifested in their preference for "junk" foods. Many of them, raised on hot dogs, potato chips, cookies and soft drinks, were likely to rebel against a program that would eliminate these.

Thomas decided to introduce the new foods gradually, or "phase them in," as opposed to an abrupt shift. Thus, he did not totally eliminate "junk" foods. Occasionally old favorites like brownies, hot dogs, doughnuts or fried foods were still served to please the students. This reflects his theory that "the most important factor influencing any person's state of nutrition is the nutritive value of what she or he eats most of the time rather than occasional deviations."

During the fall semester 1975, Thomas was able to realize about 85 percent of the necessary changes. But reeducating people's palates takes time. He conceded that it could take up to three years before all the old foods were phased out 100 percent.

The gradual "phasing in" seemed effective. One student commented, "If I hadn't been told they'd changed, I'm not sure I would have noticed the shift to health foods."

But the new program encompassed more than simply a series of menu changes. It aimed to provide students with nutritional information in the forms of charts, posters and other visual aids. These list the calorie and vitamin contents of many kinds of food, as well as convey sound principles of nutrition. Thomas collected pamphlets and books in an effort to open a small nutrition library, available to all students. He proposed that a class on nutrition be added to the general curriculum.

A bulletin board was provided as a handy medium for communication between students and their dining service. Here students voiced their complaints about foods or recommended changes. Thomas replied in writing to each note on the board. "The suggestion board," he said, "is my greatest measure of student likes and dislikes regarding food."

Glancing through Lewis and Clark's menus for a typical week (see chapter 8), one notes little that is exotic or "far-out" about the foods. Instead, the emphasis is on fresh, wholesome foods, prepared as simply as possible.

A typical breakfast might include fresh fruit, a cooked whole grain cereal or dry granola, eggs, whole wheat bread and perhaps a potato. At lunchtime, students looked forward to homemade soup, a fresh vegetable salad bar, flavored yogurt and choice of entrées (including one meatless item daily). The avocado, egg, tomato and alfalfa sprout sandwich on whole grain bread was a popular selection. Dessert might be delicious homemade sesame seed or peanut butter cookies or cake, sweetened with honey instead of white sugar. For dinner, there was fresh soup and salad again, choice of three entrées (including a meatless main dish), vegetables and homemade pudding, fresh fruit or other dessert.

Entrées ran the gamut from spinach and cheese casseroles and hot roast beef sandwiches (on whole wheat) to a tempting dish Thomas called "Healthy Chop Suey." It features soybean sprouts over a bed of natural brown rice.

Whole grain bread pudding and brown rice pudding with raisins are two pleasantly healthful ways to close out the meal.

Beverages included low-fat or skim milk, fruit and vegetable juices, coffee, tea and herb teas. Absolutely no colas or other soft drinks were served.

The cost of the new program was greater than that of the old. The reason for the cost hike, Thomas said, was "partly due to inflation, but mostly to an upgrade in the quality of the foods."

Thomas summed up the economics of the new program this way: "We desire to achieve maximum nutrition benefits for the food dollar." He paraphrased the views of President Howard: "If we're going to spend x amount of dollars on food, then I want my money to go towards nutritious food, not garbage food. I want those foods to be A-1 in quality and nutritive value."

What was the students' reaction? Did the food taste good? Was there an adequate selection? Were students pleased with the new look of their food service?

Thomas conducted a survey in which these and other questions were asked. Of the 1,048 students using the dining facilities, approximately one-third participated in the survey. The results? More than 76 percent favored the new program!

There were dissidents, of course. Some students still longed for the return of soft drinks, rich desserts, potato chips and similar "junk" foods.

Generally, however, the students responded positively to the Lewis and Clark program. In particular, they extolled the salad bar, with its varied offering of fresh, raw vegetables, and the homemade wheat bread and rolls.

One student told Thomas that, though he was ordinarily sick quite often, he had not been sick once since the nutrition program started. He also mentioned that his complexion had improved, due largely in his opinion to the dearth of fried and sugary foods. Another student commented, "It's not Mom's cooking. How can it be? But it's not second-rate food either. I think it's very good, and certainly the good intention is evident."

Best of all, the program successfully tackled the four problem areas characteristic of most college food:

1. Too much sugar. Sugar purchases were down 40 percent at Lewis and Clark compared to a year earlier.
2. Too much saturated fat. Deep-fried foods were offered only once all term, and vegetable oils were used exclusively in the limited frying that was still done.

3. Too little roughage. Students ate more whole grain breads and fresh, coarse vegetables such as broccoli, cauliflower and kale. (All vegetables were "undercooked" rather than overcooked.) High-fiber whole grain cereals were served at every meal.

4. Too many chemical additives. The swing to natural foods reduced the intake of preservatives, flavorings and many other chemicals. In an effort to avoid sodium nitrate and nitrite, for example, processed meats were drastically curtailed. Instant mashed potatoes were used only in an emergency. Whole wheat and/or vegetable noodles were used.

At first dubious of the experimental program's objectives, Thomas whole-heartedly agreed that the change was for the better. "I now see the merit and need of this program," he said. "I think it will continue." In this age of factory foods and dwindling resources, "we all must become aware of what we eat," he added.

That's the kind of education desperately needed by many young people who up until now, perhaps, haven't thought to question their own eating habits. In a small but promising way, Lewis and Clark College helped to get across the message that sound nutrition can help build sound bodies and sound minds.

"In this experiment," President Howard said, "we have hoped to experience and learn. Perhaps we can make contributions to food services elsewhere."

A Natural Food Service for Meadowbrook Hospital
by Helen Rose McDowell

Helen Rose McDowell currently lives in Las Vegas where she maintains an office as a licensed nutrition consultant. In addition to her private practice, she works on a referral and consulting basis for local M.D.'s and dentists. She writes a weekly nutrition column for the Las Vegas Sun.

In August of 1974 I was asked by Ray Evers, M.D., and his staff to convert the Meadowbrook Hospital kitchen from its catering institution-style food service to a natural foods kitchen. Dr. Evers had recently moved to New Orleans from Alabama and opened Meadowbrook Hospital as a facility for degenerative diseases, utilizing the techniques of preventive medicine. Up to this point he had been unable to find someone who understood natural foods and how to prepare and serve them in an institutional setting.

To say the least, it was a challenge. First, there was the matter of a smooth transfer. To make such a drastic change while serving three meals a day and snacks seven days a week takes timing and perseverance!

I began with a staff that had been hired and trained by the caterer. The caterer furnished the staff, a consulting dietitian, food and other supplies. The greatest problem in making the change was the kitchen staff's inability to understand the new approach to natural foods that Dr. Evers wanted. It was like a foreign language to them. It was an educational process to change their way of food preparation. They had been trained to use the convenience foods, prepared and portioned for them. The recipes were all standardized to use the company's products. Their gravy mixes, cake mixes, frosting, pancake mixes, etc., were all part of the program. In most cases, their canned products were used in place of fresh or frozen fruits and vegetables.

The kitchen staff was puzzled by the change. They had worked in hospitals for many years and everyone else was serving this kind of food. Why wasn't it good enough for Dr. Evers and his patients? A valid question, which I tried to answer. As we made the change, the cooks began to see for themselves the difference in the quality of the food. They had just never baked and eaten whole wheat bread. As they became more familiar with natural foods, the reasons for the change began to make sense to them.

Because the hospital was already in operation, it was impossible to shut the kitchen down, regroup and start all over. Three meals a day had to go out, so I began by simply telling everyone what to do with a minimum of explanation. That had to come later—as we worked the details out.

I began to put together menus, recipes and therapeutic diets. The diets had to be changed to natural foods. For some of the patients this was a new experience. Time had to be spent explaining to them why they were to eat certain foods. But some of the patients were well versed in their knowledge of natural foods, and this was a big help, as they helped give support and encouragement needed to accomplish the job.

Dr. Evers gave me carte blanche with the staff. However, I did consult with him regularly. It was soon evident that we did not need the caterer and his management staff, and the natural food service would have to be developed internally. The cooks, however, were very encouraging. They were willing to learn and make the necessary changes. They soon learned to make delicious bread, use carob, cook millet and brown rice, steam vegetables, etc. But not without some experience first!

The hospital is 50-bed capacity, and required a consulting dietitian one day a month. Her responsibilities were to consult with the Dietary Department Supervisor, check the physician's dietary orders (to insure they were being carried out properly), check the menus, visit with the patients and be sure they were being fed properly, were happy with their meals and understood their diets.

Of course, one day a month was hardly enough time to accomplish much, but in our case, since we were not operating under the standard diets and procedures, but under Dr. Evers's and other physicians' dietary orders, we really did not need one day a month. Had the dietitian been cooperative and knowledgeable in the area of natural foods and diet-disease relationships, she could have been a vital, active part of Meadowbrook Hospital.

Dietitians considered our change at the hospital an insult to them. The caterer's dietitian avoided me. She never came on the assigned days, and I could never get her to make a definite appointment with me. In fact, I never even met her personally. The catering company was soon terminated and we had to find another dietitian.

It soon became clear that finding another dietitian would not be an easy job. As I explained our approach to nutrition and diet, I would get the response that they did not feel they could agree with us nor work with us. They could not tell patients, should they ask, that our kitchen-baked whole wheat bread was a more nutritious product than commercial white bread—or that any of our food, for that matter, was better than the standard institutional portion-controlled foods.

They did not agree with Dr. Evers's preventive medicine approach, nor the use of supplements. Not only did they know very little about it, they were unwilling to learn. They were satisfied with what they already knew and saw no need for change.

A bright spot appeared at this time. I found someone to manage the kitchen who understood our aims and goals. Genia Lee Roper, who had served in a management capacity at a large New Orleans hospital, was hired to serve as dietary supervisor. She was required to return to school sponsored by the local health department. Her instructor, a dietitian, was willing to help us by serving as consultant to the hospital.

With the dietitian problem at least temporarily resolved, we worked (with Dr. Evers's backing) to teach our staff the art of cooking for health's sake. And we almost made believers out of some of them! It is difficult to retrain personnel in a working situation, especially employees such as cooks, who aren't very well paid and have one of the hardest jobs in the hospital. Cooks get little respect and lots of complaints, and the cooks at Meadowbrook found the new program a challenge they were not accustomed to.

When a cook is accustomed to the instant quick cooking process, it is difficult to get the timing down for cooking such foods as millet, brown rice or fresh vegetables—especially when you don't know what millet looks like when it is done! It's difficult also to avoid the temptation to stir something that cooks as long as brown rice. We even have had to help our cooks find foods in the storage room, because they didn't know what some of the foods looked like or how they were packaged.

But as they began to make carob brownies with sunflower seeds, to cook fresh vegetables and make delicious, attractive salads, the cooks began to enjoy the change. Now they could begin to be creative and inventive. They could use some of their own ideas. They began to really take an interest in doing a fine job, and they especially enjoyed compliments from Dr. Evers and the patients.

We found it was not necessary to have a large number of recipes. There should be good basic recipes with a minimum of casseroles and concoctions. Vegetables should be lightly steamed, using fresh or frozen ones when necessary. Large green salads should be served generously along with fresh fruits. It is a very simple and basic way to cook and prepare foods.

But you must have good quality to begin with, and that requires good vendors. I spent much of my time searching out good vendors and market areas. Fresh meats and poultry as well as fish can be a problem, since most institutions use them portion controlled. Fresh meats in the needed quantity and quality required some scouting.

Good produce also required some searching. For example, head lettuce is not the most desirable green for salads. The other greens, such as romaine, Bibb, bronze, endive, etc., should also be used, but must be used fresh. I had to find a reputable produce house that bought good quality produce and delivered it fresh.

I found that most things can be found for the person willing to look. Preserves without sugar are available, and honey can be obtained in serving packets just like granulated sugar. There are also large vendors who service health food stores and institutions. They make deliveries to outlying areas, and we made use of several of them for needed items.

I lived in East Texas and made the trip to New Orleans

each month for about ten days. During that time I worked with the staff, smoothing out the rough edges of the program.

What was accomplished at Meadowbrook Hospital can be accomplished anywhere with an administration that recognizes the problems and is willing to make the change. Too often people become comfortable in their rut and are unwilling to change.

Therapeutic diets don't have to create a problem when natural foods are used. On the contrary, we found that the accepted diets in most institutions are outmoded when compared with current research. The patient diet program at Meadowbrook Hospital was greatly enhanced by the supplement program which increased the patients' ability to properly utilize the foods in their diets.

Special requirements made of Meadowbrook Hospital by regulatory agencies were more in the light of punishment for not conforming to the "established" ways of hospitals. We were to be given no freedom of choice. But we persevered, and Meadowbrook Hospital is open today, treating and caring for those stricken with degenerative diseases. Many who have been given no hope by "orthodox" medicine are finding that hope in the concepts of preventive medicine practiced by Dr. Ray Evers and his staff at Meadowbrook Hospital, New Orleans, Louisiana.

Chapter 5

Equipment For The Natural Foods Kitchen

Our discussions of equipment and appliances, storage costs and staff are not intended as a complete manual on how to set up a kitchen for natural food service. Rather, we are offering a collection of suggestions that have proven helpful to various people already working in natural foods-oriented quantity cooking. Much of the information for this section came from the staff of the Fitness House kitchen here at Rodale Press. Additional ideas were supplied by the various people mentioned throughout the book, and from other professionals in the food service field.

We're all familiar with the way convenience in the kitchen has become an end in itself in the food service system; it has produced a TV dinner syndrome on a grand scale. What we're looking for in equipment is not simply convenience, but convenience harnessed to the goal of good eating—tools that can help you serve fresher, tastier and more nutritious foods to large numbers of people.

By now it is probably obvious that food preparation procedures and cooking methods for natural foods differ substantially from the techniques employed in the standard convenience-foods kitchen, and some different pieces of equipment are needed. Converting a conventional food service will, of course, mean some new equipment will have to be purchased. But it might also mean that some items will no longer be needed, and could be traded in or sold. You might, for example, decide not to fry foods any longer (fried foods are high in calories and hard to digest), and trade in your deep fryer to offset part of the cost of purchasing a new piece of equipment.

Don't discount the possibility of buying some second-hand equipment—it is usually quite a bit cheaper, and can sometimes be a really good buy. If you make sure you get a written guarantee with it, all faulty parts, even the most expensive ones, must be replaced for free within the time specified.

First, a word about various cookware materials. Much institutional equipment is made of stainless steel, which is probably the best material for quantity cookware. Although stainless steel is not the best heat conductor, it seems to be the safest thing to use because it has none of the drawbacks associated with various other materials. Aluminum, the other metal most often used for quantity cooking equipment, is an excellent heat conductor, but reacts with the acids in foods to alter taste and color. Cast iron is also not recommended for acid foods.

Conservation of nutrient value becomes terribly important to the food service using whole foods instead of convenience items. Cooking methods play an important role in determining whether vitamins and minerals are preserved or destroyed, especially where vegetables are concerned. Steaming vegetables instead of boiling them can immensely improve the quality of vegetables dished out in institutional settings. A full explanation of the merits of steam cooking as opposed to boiling can be found under "Why Steaming Is Best" in chapter 8, but basically, steaming conserves nutrients and takes only a few minutes. This means that vegetables can be cooked in small batches as needed (instead of one huge batch that stands around throughout the entire serving period), brought to the steam table and served with less delay. In fact, there is a growing trend in quantity food service toward small-batch, made-to-order cooking.

Many different kinds of steam cookers are on the market to fill a variety of food service needs. Steamers range in size from small pressurized models that hold from one to three tray pans, all the way up to mammoth steam-jacketed kettles that hold 20, 40 or even more gallons. Of course, if your goal is to cook in smaller batches to reduce holding time, you'll be interested in the small steamers.

Unless you are planning to install a special boiler system for your steam cooker, choose one that makes its own steam rather than one that does not. Although steamers can sometimes be hooked into the central heating system, the steam produced for heating purposes is polluted by the solvents that are used in heating boilers. You wouldn't want to cook food in this steam.

Steam equipment is expensive, and if your budget will absolutely not allow for the purchase of a steam cooker, it doesn't mean you have to keep on boiling your vegetables. A colander or rack that fits inside a conventional stockpot will make a perfectly serviceable steamer. If you don't have anything that fits, shop around and see if you can find the right size rack or colander—it's a lot cheaper than investing in a steamer. If all else fails, cooking vegetables in only a small amount of water in a tightly covered pot is still better than boiling them in large amounts of water.

Steaming vegetables doesn't mean there will no longer be any need for stockpots. They can now be put to good use making soups. It's a good idea to keep a stockpot simmering on the stove every day. That way, vegetable scraps and meat bones can be tossed in as they accumulate. Making your own soup stock is economical and efficient as well as nutritious and flavorful—you get all the nutrient value and flavor from your foods without any waste.

If you decide to do some or all of your own baking, you will probably need additional loaf pans and baking sheets.

The right oven can be important, too. Convection ovens are becoming quite popular in food service kitchens, and are

Better Food for Public Places

recommended both by equipment distributors and also by cooking authorities such as the authors of *The Cook's Catalogue*, a highly respected directory of the best cooking tools and appliances available (by James Beard, Milton Glaser and Burton Wolf). Convection ovens work by circulating hot air around the food, with the result that food cooks faster and at lower temperatures than in the standard deck oven. Using the more energy-efficient convection oven can help reduce operating costs on a long term basis. In addition, convection ovens take up less space than deck ovens.

The chief purpose of the microwave oven in institutional feeding is to heat up precooked frozen entrées and meal packs; as such, the natural food service would have little use for one. But as microwave ovens are becoming more and more popular in food service operations, it might be worthwhile to take a look at their properties.

Microwaves are high-frequency energy waves, a lot like radio waves. In the oven, electrical energy is converted to microwaves by something called a magnetron tube. The microwaves are absorbed by food and cause the molecules of liquid in the food to vibrate very quickly, producing friction. The friction in turn creates heat which is conducted throughout the food. This means the food in effect cooks itself. You may be wondering why only the food gets hot. The answer is that microwaves are reflected off the metal sides of the oven and transmitted through the glass door (and out into the kitchen where you are); only the food absorbs the energy.

Microwave cooking is fast, no doubt about it. But there are several formidable drawbacks to the method that aren't often mentioned by its proponents. You can't bake bread or pie crusts, or brown *anything* in a microwave oven. And despite manufacturers' claims, the ovens do tend to dry out foods.

The biggest problem with the microwave, however, is that cooking time increases in direct proportion with the mass of the foods being cooked. Two potatoes take twice as long as one potato. Bulky foods cook slower than less dense foods of the same weight.

130

No metal containers can be used in a microwave or the energy will just bounce off and never reach the food. So pre-plated meals are packaged in disposable containers, creating extra packaging expense and shameful amounts of waste.

It seems like a much better idea to avoid the exposure to radiation and all the drawbacks of microwave cooking and just stick to conventional methods of food preparation.

With a little ingenuity, most of the equipment used in the standard food service kitchen can be employed in the preparation of natural foods. Steam table pans, for instance, can be used for casseroles, to store fresh greens and to grow sprouts.

An electric roaster is good to have if your oven space is very limited. The roaster can be used for cooking stews and poultry, baking potatoes and cakes, and can prove a welcome addition to cramped and inadequate facilities.

Special Equipment

Beyond the bare essentials, there are additional appliances especially well suited to the natural foods kitchen. A blender is one item that most natural foods cooks find indispensable for whipping up salad dressings and drinks, pureeing foods for cream soups and fruit whips, chopping nuts and other tasks. Osterizer and Sunbeam are two good brands of small blenders. Take note that glass or stainless steel containers are better for blenders than plastic. The plastic containers can retain bacteria, and, believe it or not, they break more easily. For food service use, a commercial-size blender is probably better suited, especially if 100 or more people are being served. These larger blenders have a one-gallon capacity; the containers are made of stainless steel and have clamp-on lids. The Waring commercial-size blender has an excellent reputation among cooks who use it and equipment men who sell it.

Fresh vegetable preparation is easier with a slicing/chopping/shredding machine, particularly in large-volume kitchens. Hobart makes an all-purpose vertical cutter-mixer in 25-, 40-, 60-, 80- and 130-gallon sizes that purees foods, shreds vegetables or cheese, grinds meats and nuts, kneads dough and does all the jobs a mixer does. In short, it combines the features of a mixer, blender and grater. Of course, only a large volume of food would justify the expense of such a sophisticated machine, but for the large feeding operation it could be a big time saver. Some caterers who preprocess vegetables for shipment to client kitchens, and firms that market salad products, use machines like this one. Doing this sort of preparation in-house would insure fresher salad vegetables and eliminate the need for all those preservatives the outside caterer must use to keep prechopped vegetables fresh during shipping and storage. Of course, this kind of machinery is expensive, costing up to $3,000. Some food services will find it worth the expense; others will not.

For smaller scale food services a smaller food cutting machine that does many of the same jobs would be more suitable. Basically, what's needed is a power source with which various interchangeable attachments can be used, instead of separate machines for each task. The Hobart line, for example, includes a group of standardized attachments that can use either a mixer or a food cutter as the power source. Every institutional kitchen has a mixer, so the natural place to start is with attachments for that. If grating cheese and chopping vegetables ties up the mixer when it is needed for cake batter or something else, the purchase of a food cutter which uses the same attachments may be warranted.

If you already have an electric slicing machine, chances are it can be adapted to shred lettuce and cabbage, and maybe for other operations as well.

A smaller all-purpose machine along the same lines as the vertical cutter-mixer might also fill the needs of the average size in-house food service. Such a machine is the Robot Coupe, which has been used in European restaurants for many years. It slices, shreds, chops nuts, cuts, grates, grinds, mixes and kneads, and has a capacity of 2½ quarts. The Cuisinarts food processing machine which has been so popular over the past year is a simplified home version of the Robot Coupe.

This appliance has some very nice features. Its heavy-duty motor is equipped with a circuit breaker which turns it off before it overheats. In addition, the machine will not start up until the cover is locked in place. The Robot Coupe costs around $350.

If you don't do really large volume feeding, hand-operated tools could still save lots of time, at a fraction of the cost of an electric machine. For grating up to 50 pounds of food a day, a Gricer grater can be indispensable. This small, metal, hand-cranked grater clamps right on the edge of a counter or table. It comes with assorted sizes of cones to grate fine or coarse, and grates everything from cheese to vegetables and chops nuts as well. The whole unit unclamps from the counter and goes into the dishwasher for cleanup. The beauty of this appliance is that it is dependable, simple and sanitary to use.

The food service planning to do all its own baking with whole grain flours might consider purchasing a grain grinder. Of course, grinding your own flour will require a little extra time. But let's look at some of the advantages of having a grinder of your own. First, you will be sure that the flour is fresh and you will know that it contains no preservatives or other additives. Storage difficulties will be eased as well. Whole grain flours must be refrigerated to stay fresh, and since many mills only sell the flours in 100-pound bags, refrigerator space can present a decided problem. Whole unground grains, on the other hand, may be stored differently (see the next chapter), and allow you to grind only as much flour as you need at a time.

Another advantage to owning your own grain mill is the variety of jobs it can perform. A grinder is a versatile machine, grinding nuts and seeds as well as a variety of grains including corn, rye, millet, sorghum, oats and rice, in addition to wheat. It allows you to control the texture of the flour produced—coarser for breads, finer for pastries and other lighter products. The home grinder gives you the ability to experiment and try different combinations of flours for new taste sensations.

When discussing grain grinders, essentially we are dealing with three basic levels of price and complexity. At the top is a large, completely electric machine which is capable of turning wheat berries into a fine, stone-ground flour similar to the type available from natural foods stores and distributors.

These grinders, which cost as much as $250, are easily the most desirable kind to own, and probably the best suited for institutional use. They produce virtually any kind of flour you could want. You can grind coarse, medium or fine. Even cornmeal is easy to make. It takes nothing more than a turn of a knob and a flick of the finger and it's done. In the institutional kitchen where baking is done on the premises, such a fully automatic grain grinder, capable of producing pound after pound of high-quality flour, might well pay for itself in the long run.

For all its convenience and efficiency, though, a large electric grinder does have one drawback compared to smaller, less expensive models. You can't use it to grind sunflower and sesame seeds, peanuts, soybeans or other foods with a high oil content. The resulting oily residue on the stone cutting surfaces tends to clog the machine and is quite difficult to clean.

Smaller, simpler mills don't carry this limitation. For the smaller kitchen with an especially tight budget, a smaller model might prove more suitable in many ways. This type of mill attaches to another piece of equipment which acts as the power source, like the slicing and shredding attachments available for Hobart mixers.

The flour produced by this type of grinder, although not quite on a par with flour ground in the automatic mill, is still more than adequate. Grinding wheat berries in this sort of attachment, which costs about $45, takes several minutes, as the berries must be fed gradually into the grinding mechanism. This is much slower than using the automatic machine, but still faster and much more effortless than a hand-powered grinder.

Flour made with an attachment-type grinder is usually rather coarse, and must be put through the mill a second time in order to be fine enough to use in most recipes.

The third type of grinder, the hand-operated variety, is so laborious and time-consuming to use that it would be of little value in a quantity kitchen.

When fruit juices are served instead of soft drinks or drinks made from powdered mixes, a juicing machine can save lots of time and effort. It enables you to make your own fresh fruit juices with a minimum of bother. All-purpose machines, such as Acme and Braun juicers, are the most versatile and can be used to juice most fruits and vegetables. One very simple Braun juicer, for example, is hand-operated and costs about $75. It crushes stems and all, and works best if the fruits or vegetables are whole or in large pieces. The juice is expressed through a rotary basket, in which a filter can be placed if you prefer clear juice. This kind of juicer could be useful in a small volume food service, or in a system like Meadowbrook Hospital's, where patients can request a glass of freshly squeezed juice any time. In addition to the all-purpose juicers, there are also several good specialty machines on the market.

Another kind of machine takes 350 servings of frozen pure juice, mixes it and dispenses it into sealed cups every seven seconds. This machine is popular among Florida schools. At a few thousand dollars, it may sound like a tremendous expense, but consider its total value. You pay up to 25 or even 35 cents for single-serving canned juices of poor quality. Your own juice machine would enable you to produce fresh, high-quality juice for 10 to 15 cents a cup. Juice dispensers would be especially helpful to institutions where breakfast is served.

The customer participation approach to serving juice is typified by the Rotary Orange Juicer available from the Roto-Rico Company in California.* This machine takes an orange,

*Addresses of juice machine companies are supplied in the Appendix.

slices it, reams out the juice and discards the peel. It would require supervision to be used by young children, but older students and adults generally get a kick out of dropping the oranges in the machine and making their own glass of juice.

The key to successful food service is making do with whatever equipment you are able to have. Few kitchens come equipped with the ideal assortment of machines and appliances. More often than not, facilities are terribly limited. At the Distribution Center here at Rodale Press, a soup/sandwich/salad lunch is prepared for 100 people each day in a makeshift kitchen set up at one end of the employee's lounge.

The staff of three (one of whom is part-time) has at their disposal one rather small refrigerator, one chest freezer, a six-burner stove with oven underneath, a meat and vegetable slicer, a counter-top mixer with grater/shredder attachments, an electric roaster and a large blender. That's all they have—not the very latest in sophisticated equipment. But they are able to manage well with the equipment they have, and turn out fresh, delicious lunches every day.

Chapter 6

Where To Store Natural Foods

The most important rule to remember in storing natural foods is that rapid rotation of stock is vital. Because they don't contain artificial preservatives, most natural foods have a shorter shelf life than their more processed counterparts. It may mean buying smaller quantities at slightly higher prices to avoid waste through spoilage. But buying 500 pounds of whole wheat flour at a good price is no bargain if 100 pounds of it spoil before it can be used.

Another point to consider is that prolonged storage allows vitamin depletion. Exposure to light and air also destroys vitamins, so all storage containers should be opaque and have tightly fitting covers.

The absence of artificial preservatives makes it necessary to refrigerate or freeze many natural foods. The ideal storage setup would include ample freezer space, one refrigerator for semiperishable foods such as cold-pressed or additive-free cooking oils, and another refrigerator for day-to-day perishables such as dairy products.

In a natural foods kitchen, a nice, big freezer can easily become indispensable. At Fitness House, the freezer always seems to be overflowing. Various items, in addition to some meats, fish fillets and vegetables, lend themselves to freezer storage. Nitrate- and nitrite-free hot dogs, sausages, bacon and luncheon meats are almost always received frozen because their lack of artificial preservatives makes them highly perishable and next to impossible to ship in any other form. If you purchase nitrate- and nitrite-free meats from a local butcher, you may get them unfrozen, but if they are not going to be used within a day they should go right into the freezer.

Fresh vegetables purchased locally in season, when quality is highest and prices are lowest, can be frozen to be used later on in the year. Extra soup stock and some leftover foods can also be frozen. But it hardly needs to be said that freezing all these foods is a waste of time if they don't get used. Frozen food stores have to be rotated just like other stock—it's too easy to forget about something you wrapped up and stuck in the freezer a week or two ago.

As we noted before, it's a good idea to have two refrigerators if possible. Day-to-day perishables including milk, eggs, butter, cheeses, fresh vegetables and fresh fruits can all be kept together. Fresh greens such as parsley and watercress keep longer if you stand them upright in a covered pan of water before refrigerating. They can also be kept in gallon-size glass jars if kept dry and airtight. Semiperishable items such as whole grain flours and meals, dry beans, nuts, dried fruits and soybeans all require refrigeration and could be stored in a second refrigerator.

It's important to note that natural cooking oils must be refrigerated or they will become rancid. The same applies to whole grain flours. Commercial white and unbleached flours, in addition to containing preservatives, are made from only the starchy middle portion of the wheat kernel. The bran and the germ, which contains oil, have been removed from the wheat before it is milled. But in whole wheat flour, the whole kernel is ground, so although it may not seem like it, there is oil present in the flour. If the flour isn't refrigerated, the oil will go rancid and the flour will develop a stale, "off" flavor. It is also necessary to keep flour in a closed or tightly covered container. Left uncovered it will absorb odors, just as butter does.

In kitchens where semiperishables are kept in a walk-in cooler, large metal or plastic trash cans mounted on dollies can make it easier to use and store bulk goods. These containers have the advantages of a fairly large volume and tightly fitting covers. Mounting the cans on dollies makes them easy to wheel around to wherever the food is needed, and also means the cans won't have to sit right on the floor.

One final note about bulk foods like grains and beans: if these foods were handled carelessly during shipping or storage, freezing them for a few weeks will kill any bacteria that might have developed in the foods.

Storing Whole Grains

To people who have always worked with convenience-type foods, whole grains are going to be an entirely new food experience. Cooks will have to learn how to prepare them, and storage people will have to learn how to store them. Generally speaking, grains should be stored in tightly sealed containers in a cool, dark, dry place. They may also be refrigerated. Most grains, including brown rice, bulgur, buckwheat and millet will keep for several months if stored properly. Wheat berries may be stored up to a year, and sometimes even longer.

Perhaps the biggest problem created by keeping large quantities of grains on hand is the possibility of mold growth or insect invasion. Beetles and moths can infest other dry foods as well. You might find them in flour, meal, cereals, crackers, spices, spaghetti, shelled nuts or dried fruits. The presence of insects doesn't necessarily mean the food has to be thrown out. There are various methods of treatment, which we'll discuss later, that can destroy the invaders and reclaim the food.

First, it is necessary to learn how to recognize insect damage, and to be aware of how pests can get into your grain products in the first place.

Determining how grain becomes infested is like asking whether the chicken or the egg came first. In many grain-growing regions, infestation begins in the field, when insects lay their eggs in the grain before it is harvested. The eggs get harvested along with the grain and hatch in your storage container. In some cases, the eggs will be in your storage container before you put in the grain. In other cases, mature insects may find their way into the container.

The eggs of the most common kinds of flour and grain insects are rarely seen. They are usually white in color and are often covered with a sticky substance that makes particles of flour or bits of grain adhere to them to make them practically indistinguishable from the food itself. Matters are complicated by the minute size of many eggs. The eggs of the flat grain beetle, for example, are so tiny (if placed side by side, 150 would fit in an inch) that they can easily pass through the silk bolting cloth used to sift commercially marketed flours before they are packaged.

The trucks and railroad cars used to transport food products are known to be the sources of much infestation. Warehouses already containing infested foods cause the contamination of uninfested products stored there. Unsanitary conditions in processing and packaging plants are additional sources of infestation. The complex systems of distribution and storage points foods may pass through before you receive them increase the chances for insect invasion. The moral of the story, then, is to buy your grain as directly as possible from the grower.

Even when you buy your grain directly, take a few precautions to guard against insect invasion:

- Store all foods in tight, clean, metal or glass insect-proof containers that have tightly fitting lids.
- Keep foods off the floor and away from damp areas.
- Storage areas should be clean, cool and dry.
- Never store food in open containers on shelves.
- Keep food storage areas free of spilled food and food particles.
- Good housekeeping helps prevent insect infestation.

There are a few more elaborate ways to "treat" the grain to prevent insect attacks. One such treatment involves the use of dry ice. For grains, cereals and similar foodstuffs stored in large containers, dry ice, which vaporizes into carbon dioxide, is effective in eliminating possible insect infestation. Here's an example of how wheat may be treated this way:

Spread two ounces of crushed dry ice over the bottom of a five-gallon can and put the wheat immediately over the top of the dry ice. Allow sufficient time for the dry ice to evaporate before placing the lid on the can (about 30 minutes ought to do it). If pressure develops in the can, it will begin to bulge. If this happens, remove the lid cautiously and leave it off for about two minutes before replacing it.

Another way to keep insects out of your grain is to mix it with diatomaceous earth. This material, which is available from a number of commercial sources, is an extremely abrasive powder which scratches or penetrates the waxy outer surface of the insects and allows them to dehydrate. It is, however, harmless and tasteless to humans. To 25 pounds of grain you add one cup of diatomaceous earth and mix the two thoroughly. It is important to make sure each kernel of grain is coated with a light layer of the powder. For maximum effectiveness, the moisture content of the grain should not exceed 12 percent.

Remember, the presence of insects does *not* always mean that the food is unfit for use. The only health hazard of which we are aware is the possible spreading of salmonella by insects in dry milk powder. With the exception of dry milk powder, most foods may be used if treated properly to destroy the pests.

Lightly infested raisins, dried prunes and home-dried fruit may be placed in boiling water for five to ten seconds to destroy any insects present. Sift or strain through a coarse screen, retaining the fruit. Following this treatment, the fruit should be thoroughly dried, then stored in insect-proof containers.

When packaged goods such as flour, beans, cereals, whole grains, nut meats and similar dry foods become infested, they may be "sterilized" by heating in an oven at a temperature of 140°F. for half an hour, or by freezing in a home freezer held at 0°F. for three or four days. The contents of large packages should be spread (not more than ¾ of an inch deep) in cake pans or pie pans so that the heat can penetrate easily. Leave the oven door slightly open to avoid overheating. Both the heating and freezing treatments will destroy all growth stages of the insect. After treating flours and meals, they should be sifted through a flour sifter or a fine-mesh screen. Beans, whole grains and nuts should be placed on a screen fine enough to retain the food but allow the insects to fall through. The foods should then be re-stored in clean, insect-proof containers.

These practices should, in most cases, suffice to make the food edible. However, if there are a lot of insects in the food, or if the food is damaged as in the cases of the rice weevil or the lesser grain borer, throw the food out and take precautions to protect the other foods in the storeroom from infestation.

Molds are the other major cause of spoilage in stored grains and seeds, ranking second only to insects as a cause of deterioration and loss in all kinds of stored products. Their rapid growth under warm, moist conditions makes it nearly impossible to save products once they have become infected.

Where do these molds come from? There are probably close to a hundred thousand different kinds, growing on all conceivable things. They are truly omnipresent. Many molds, including those that cause deterioration of stored seeds and grain, produce spores in astronomical numbers, and these are carried everywhere by air currents. Whenever the right combination of environmental conditions are present, molds will grow.

The only way to control molds is to keep the moisture level of grain between 12 and 15 percent. Moisture levels in grain can be reduced by air-drying in the sun or in a well-ventilated facility. Grain can also be dried by forcing hot air through it.

In addition, storing grains and grain products in airtight containers in a cool, dry place (45–50°F.) will help prevent mold growth.

Chapter 7

Costs And Staff In Natural Food Service

Can You Really Save Money with Natural Foods?

On a strictly item per item basis, it cannot really be proven that natural foods are cheaper than convenience foods. In fact, when you take into account the additional labor costs incurred by cooking from scratch, using natural foods can get to be an expensive proposition.

But there *are* ways to hold costs down. A natural food service *can* be run on a budget comparable to conventional food service. Some people have found they were able to operate on a smaller budget as soon as they began to serve natural foods; others found they had to introduce the new foods on a gradual basis to stay within economic boundaries.

As we saw in chapter 2, the State University of New York (Purchase campus) food service cut costs by 10 percent when they served natural foods. This meant a substantial saving of $700 a week. At the Atlantis Day-Care Center, Page Cullen fed 60 children on $60 a week. When Yale University introduced natural foods in 1971, costs initially soared, but leveled off after a few months to a very reasonable level.

There are several basic money-saving techniques that all these people used, and that can help anyone save money.

The single most important factor in serving high-quality foods within a reasonable budget is conscientious and prudent management. There is more potential for waste with whole foods, so cost control requires careful menu planning, sensible food purchasing and proper storage and handling to reduce waste and spoilage to a minimum.

As we have seen, cooking with whole foods produces more "food waste" than cooking with processed, portion-controlled products, which create mostly "package waste." But food waste doesn't have to be a liability—good management can turn it into a money-saving asset, for much of what is considered "waste" contains good food value and should be recycled. Meat bones and vegetable scraps, as we said before, belong in the stockpot and not in the trash. If you have a garden, vegetable cores, seeds and peelings can go on the compost pile to enrich the soil. The garden itself can help cut costs by providing high quality produce to be used fresh from the garden or frozen for wintertime use.

Serving occasional vegetarian meals, or offering a vegetarian alternative at every meal, is another tried and proven money saver. Meat is the single most expensive item on everyone's shopping list, and cutting back meat purchases lowers overall costs. Putting some meatless meals on the menu at Purchase reduced meat expenditures from 13 percent to 10 percent of the total budget, resulting in an overall saving for the food service. The Purchase food service learned that beans, grains, nuts and dairy products can be combined in many different patterns to supply as much protein as sirloin steak at a fraction of the price. For more information on vegetarian meals, see "High-Protein Meals without Meat" in chapter 8.

Another point to consider is that soup/sandwich/salad lunches and nutritious casserole dishes make it easier to save money with natural foods.

Where you buy the food can be as important as what you buy when you're trying to stick to a limited budget. The Fitness House staff has found they have the most success in cutting prices by buying as directly from the producer as possible. They go to local farmers whenever possible for produce, eggs and especially meats. Prepared meats, such as sausage, are made to order without nitrates or nitrites or sugar by an area butcher. Buying as directly from growers as possible also reduces the chances that foods will be spoiled or infested with insects. This is particularly true of grain products, for as we learned in the last chapter, every shipping and storage point a load of grain must pass through presents another opportunity for insects to invade.

By all means investigate the possibility of joining a co-op to purchase foods. Co-ops are able to purchase foods in larger quantities for lower prices than the individual food service can get. Co-ops are generally regarded as organizations of individuals, designed to help individuals purchase food at lower prices. But co-ops can also work at the institutional level.

In Los Angeles, the Hospital Council of Southern California set up a co-op to buy food for area hospitals.[1] By the summer of 1975, the Council was buying for 50 hospitals and had 200 more on their waiting list. The savings have been impressive—about 10 percent for larger hospitals and up to 20 percent for smaller facilities.

The Hospital Council's co-op is organized so that an independent organization does the actual purchasing of food. A central Dietary Committee made up of representatives from member hospitals decides what foods should be bought, and the purchasing organization buys them after shopping around for the best price. All new products are sampled by the committee before they are bought.

Special training programs have been set up to teach proper storage and handling techniques to food service employees who receive perishables into hospital kitchens.

The Hospital Council's co-op works because of the professionalism of the Dietary Committee's efforts and the cooperation between the committee and the purchasing firm.

Staffing the Natural Foods Kitchen

A competent, dedicated staff can be the key factor in turning out meals of consistently high quality while still keeping the lid on costs. It may seem that responsible staff are hard to find even to prepare convenience foods which require little work or skill. But the important point to keep in mind is that these products are really totally uninspiring to work with. This leads to disinterest and apathy among personnel, which in turn leads to a poor quality product.

Quality food begins with the food service staff. If they are to feel like more than factory workers, they must be able to have a real sense of working with foods—foods which challenge their creativity. Artists aren't inspired by paint-by-number sets, and real cooks and chefs are not attracted to finishing kitchens. Responsible management and an atmosphere of respect for high nutritional standards and a top quality product will naturally help to attract or develop a top-notch staff.

Training programs too have proven their worth. In many places, staff members have responded to training programs with increased enthusiasm and new capability. At Syracuse University, showing a film on vegetable cooking resulted in increased productivity among personnel and higher quality vegetable dishes.[2] More and more food services are finding that extra time and money spent teaching proper preparation and handling techniques are good investments. In most cases, after training programs have been instituted, more care is taken in working with food, productivity increases, and the rate of employee turnover drops. The kitchen staff begin to feel their jobs are truly important and can start to take more pride in their work.

Educational programs are especially needed when the food service switches over to or begins to incorporate more whole, natural foods in the menus. Natural quantity cookery is a new field. Many of the foods are unfamiliar to a lot of people, and they must be prepared, stored and handled differently than preportioned products. People who have spent many years in convenience-oriented food service cannot be expected to reverse their habits overnight. To the person whose background is in convenience foods, converting to a more natural kind of cookery poses a threat to all his or her knowledge of food service techniques. It is only natural for people to resist a change that makes them feel insecure in their work, and the food service manager must always bear that in mind when working with the staff.

In spite of the difficulties, the right combination of educational techniques and gradual changeover can bring even less-than-inspired cooks and assistants to competence in natural foods preparation. Often the manager and staff must learn together about the new foods, and this kind of shared experience can help build a mutual dependence and respect that makes for smoother operations. Thad Thomas, food service manager at Lewis and Clark College (see the success stories in chapter 4) explained that when foods such as buckwheat groats first appeared on the menu, the cooks came to him for advice on how to cook them. Since Thomas had never seen buckwheat groats himself, he couldn't answer the cooks, except to say they'd all just have to go back to the kitchen and try. Through this kind of open-minded approach, the management and staff learned about natural foods together, and the result was a successful food service program.

At Meadowbrook Hospital, the nutritionist and food service manager were already knowledgeable in the area of natural foods. By conducting classes, they taught their staff how to prepare the new foods, and all the cooks came to understand why they are asked to prepare foods the way they do. Initially, the management was surprised and delighted to find that the staff were very eager to learn, and readily accepted their new challenge. Most of the cooks that were at Meadowbrook before the change to natural foods stayed on even though it meant they had to change their habits and methods of cooking. Today the kitchen runs smoothly; the capable staff turns out fine quality meals and snacks for all patients.

After the staff has accepted the change to natural foods, there still remains the problem of all the new jobs that must somehow get done. Additional help may be needed to clean, trim and chop or cut fresh vegetables and meats for cooking. There are various ways the gap might be filled without hiring more full-time employees.

Perhaps a part-time worker could do the job. Retired persons wishing to supplement social security incomes might enjoy helping out in the kitchen a few hours a day. A retired person is allowed by law to work only a limited number of hours without losing social security benefits, and jobs without too many hours are often hard to find. But time can hang heavy on the hands of the retired, and working a couple of hours a day would be a welcome diversion for many.

If you serve children in an environment such as a day-care or Head Start center, you may have the perfect opportunity to bring children into the kitchen to help out. As we saw in chapter 2, children usually love to help in the kitchen. They can do some of the simpler jobs, like washing off fruit, scraping vegetables or watching the soup pot, and at the same time receive a valuable lesson in nutrition and how foods are cooked.

Wise menu planning can go a long way to keep new preparation procedures within the capacity of the present staff. But if extra help is needed, explore the alternatives that might be available before you hire more full-time help.

Chapter 8

Foods And Their Preparation

Working with natural foods will be a new experience for those accustomed to convenience products. Some of the foods may be unfamiliar, and preparation and handling techniques may have to be learned. In this chapter, we have tried to provide basic information on the kinds of foods that can be used and why, techniques for handling and preparing these foods, cooking instructions, and menu and recipe suggestions to help you serve them.

Foods to Use in Natural Food Service

Dried beans, peas and lentils—These versatile, inexpensive foods are an essential part of many meatless entrées, and lend themselves to soups, casseroles and side dishes as well. Dried legumes are good sources of protein, iron and other minerals, fiber and B vitamins.

Brown rice—By all means use brown rice instead of instant or converted or any other kind of white rice. White rice is simply brown rice with the brown outer hull polished off.

149

Unfortunately, most of the nutrients are polished off along with the hull, leaving the starchy white interior. Brown rice supplies more protein, B vitamins, calcium, phosphorus and other minerals than its polished counterpart.

Brown rice is one food that's universally popular in institutions where natural foods are served. Everyone, from preschoolers to Seniors, seems to like it. Many people actually come to *prefer* the rich, nutty flavor and chewy texture of brown rice. White rice seems mushy and bland by comparison. If you are in a situation where you must use white rice, under the government commodities program for instance, you might try sprinkling it with rice polish just before it is served. Rice polish, as the name implies, is the nutrient-rich hull which is removed from white rice and is used as a supplement to food. It is available from health food stores and natural foods distributors.

Buckwheat—Buckwheat's greatest claim to fame is that it "stays with you." It has been said that six buckwheat pancakes will fill you for six hours. This grain, currently enjoying a comeback in the U.S. in the form of kasha, or cooked buckwheat groats, has long been a favorite in Russia and Eastern Europe. The groats can be cooked with egg stock and seasonings to make kasha, or cooked in water and served as a breakfast cereal with raisins and dates. When cooked, buckwheat groats take on a light, fluffy appearance.

Nutritionally speaking, buckwheat compares very favorably with the hard, red wheat commonly used for flour and cereal products. Buckwheat has almost as much protein, iron and phosphorus, and more fiber, calcium and B vitamins. Buckwheat flour is relatively low in calories and cost, and can be used for pancakes. It cannot substitute for whole wheat flour, however. Buckwheat flour contains no gluten and can't be used to bake bread or other yeast products because it will not rise properly.

Bulgur—This form of precooked, cracked wheat closely resembles brown rice and can be used in many of the same ways that rice is used. Pleasant, nutty-tasting bulgur requires very little cooking. It can be used in pilafs, soups, casseroles and special salads, such as the tangy Middle Eastern favorite, tabbouli. Try serving bulgur as an occasional change from potatoes.

Like other forms of wheat, bulgur contains protein, fiber, calcium, phosphorus, iron, potassium and B vitamins. It's true that some of the B vitamins are lost in the processing of bulgur, but this loss is to a degree countered by the increased availability of its protein.

Cornmeal—Whole ground cornmeal can be used to make hearty foods like grits, cornbread, cornpones, hush puppies, spoon bread and mush. Polenta, a type of cornmeal mush, is especially good with Italian meat sauce, beef stroganoff or stew.

Be sure to use whole ground cornmeal if at all possible. Most commercial brands have had the germ removed and are considerably less nutritious. Degermed cornmeal contains substantially smaller amounts of protein, fiber, calcium, phosphorus, iron, vitamin A and B vitamins than whole ground cornmeal. Although many commercial cornmeals are enriched, why pay for some added synthetic vitamins when using whole ground meal supplies all the nutrients present in the original corn kernel?

Dried fruits—Dried apricots, peaches, pears, apples, dates, prunes and raisins have all the natural sweetness of the fresh fruits without the water. All contain lots of minerals, and apricots, peaches and prunes are rich in vitamin A.

Serve dried fruits plain, in combination with nuts and seeds, or in granola. They are also good stewed, and served with yogurt or used in dessert sauces. Try to get fruit that has not been treated with sulfur dioxide. Unsulfured fruits don't retain their color as well as those treated with sulfur, but most people seem to like them just as well as dried fruits of bright but chemically preserved colors.

Fresh fruits—A piece of fresh, juicy fruit is a welcome treat on a hot day, or in the middle of winter. By all means serve raw, fresh fruit in season, leaving the skins on whenever possible. If the fruit is organically grown, it shouldn't need to be peeled before serving. Fruits frozen without syrup are also acceptable substitutes when fresh fruit is not available, but try to avoid canned fruit unless it is packed in water or its own juice. If you must use syrup-packed fruit, drain off all or at least some of the syrup before serving.

Fresh vegetables—Purchased locally in season, fresh vegetables are relatively inexpensive and high in nutritional quality. Properly prepared and imaginatively presented, vegetables add a wide variety of colors, textures and flavors to a meal, in addition to supplying an assortment of many vitamins and minerals. Raw vegetables are especially valuable because none of their nutrients have been destroyed by cooking. Some nutrients are lost even when vegetables are carefully steamed, so raw vegetables should be an important part of any food service. They can be included in salads or sandwiches, or just served plain or with dips. And the selection need not be limited to the usual carrot and celery sticks. Salads can be made of lots more than iceberg lettuce and tomatoes. Many vegetables are delicious served raw; you might experiment with escarole, endive, romaine, spinach, cauliflower, broccoli, shredded cabbage, radishes, cucumber, green beans, sugar peas, green and red peppers and, by all means, sprouts. Vegetables offer a splendid opportunity for creativity.

Preparation should be carefully planned to minimize waste and storage time.

Organically grown vegetables can generally be served with skins intact. Most of the nutrients in vegetables like carrots and potatoes lie just under the skin and are lost through peeling. (Basically, organically grown vegetables are those that are grown without the use of artificial fertilizers or chemical pesticides. Manure, compost and other natural substances are used to enrich the soil; biological controls, companion planting and similar means are employed to keep pests away.)

Gelatin desserts—These have become real fixtures in institutional food service. Instead of making them from presweetened powders containing sugar and artificial colors and flavors, these treats can be made with unflavored gelatin and fresh fruits or canned fruits minus their syrup, and sweetened with honey.

Honey—This natural sweetener should replace sugar as much as possible. White sugar is a highly processed food which contributes absolutely nothing to the human body but pure carbohydrate, in other words, empty calories. Honey is better because it contains minerals and because it is a more powerful sweetener and may therefore be used in smaller amounts. Brown sugar contains minerals if it is not as heavily processed as white sugar, but sometimes brown sugar is produced by adding coloring agents to white sugar, in which case it's no improvement.

As a general rule, use half as much honey as the amount of sugar called for in a recipe. Because it is a liquid, honey is difficult to substitute for sugar in recipes where the proportions of ingredients are crucial, such as in cakes. In such cases, dry ingredients will probably need some adjustment to compensate for the extra liquid.

Molasses and maple syrup can also be used as sugar substitutes, but their pronounced flavors make them best suited for certain baked goods and special dishes such as candied sweet potatoes.

Nitrate- and nitrite-free meats—These products are available from several nationwide distributors. It is usually cheaper, however, to contract with a local butcher to prepare nitrate- and nitrite-free meats to your specifications. The nitrates and nitrites used to preserve and impart a red color to most commercially processed bacon, ham, hot dogs and luncheon meats are believed to combine with other substances inside

153

the body to form carcinogenic (cancer-causing) substances called nitrosamines. For this reason it's a good idea to replace these meats with nitrate- and nitrite-free products. Nitrate- and nitrite-free meats are not the familiar red hue of other processed meat products; instead they are a more brownish color. They taste somewhat different too, but most people find them quite delicious.

Noninstant powdered skim milk—Dried skim milk can be reconstituted and used in cooking instead of whole milk. Not only does it cost less and have less fat than whole milk, powdered skim milk is easier to use and is also available under the government commodities program for use in the school lunch program and Head Start.

Although dried skim milk has no vitamin A unless it is fortified, it contains more protein, calcium and phosphorus than whole milk. Using powdered skim milk instead of whole milk in cooking is a good way to help cut costs.

Nuts—Untoasted peanuts, almonds, walnuts, cashews, filberts, Brazil nuts and all the rest are good sources of protein, B vitamins and minerals. Nuts make popular snack foods, whether served alone or mixed with seeds, raisins or an assortment of dried fruits. A tremendously versatile and too often overlooked food, nuts can be used in a broad array of dishes from breakfast cereals to vegetarian entrées to desserts.

Peanut butter—A nutritious food with lots of protein, calcium, phosphorus, iron and B vitamins, peanut butter appeals to adult as well as younger taste buds. Unfortunately, some brands of peanut butter are made with unnecessary sugar and various artificial flavorings and texturizers. However, it is inexpensive and fairly easy to make your own fresh, additive-free peanut butter in a blender. Use an eight to one proportion of peanuts to oil; for a thicker spread, eliminate the oil entirely.

Rolled oats—Old-fashioned rolled oats contain B vitamins, protein, fiber, calcium, iron and phosphorus. Rolled oats are available from most commercial sources and can be used for a lot more than hot cereal. They're an essential part of granola, Swiss muesli, oatmeal bread and oatmeal cookies, and also work well in meat loaf and in dessert toppings for streusels and fruit crisps.

Seeds—Raw sunflower, sesame and pumpkin seeds pack a lot of nutrition in a small package. They are fine sources of B vitamins, protein, fiber, vitamin A, calcium, phosphorus, iron and essential fatty acids. Seeds make fine snack foods, and can be used in many of the same ways nuts are used.

Soybeans—Probably the most talked about source of nonmeat protein, soybeans can be combined with grains, nuts and seeds, other kinds of beans and dairy products to make complete protein, meatless main dishes. (For more information on complete proteins, see "High-Protein Meals without Meat" later in this chapter.) Soybeans can also be prepared in various ways to be served as a vegetable, ground into flour for a high-protein supplement to use in baking breads and cakes, or made into soy grits (partially cooked, cracked beans) to use in hot breakfast cereals and casseroles. Soybeans are often made into tofu, or bean curd, a substance used extensively in Oriental cookery and served in many vegetarian and natural foods restaurants.

Meat extenders and substitutes made from soybean protein or textured vegetable protein (TVP) should not be confused with whole soybeans. Soybeans undergo an involved fractionating process when TVP is manufactured, and the final product, to which synthetic colors and flavors have been added, bears almost no resemblance to whole soybeans.

Sprouts—Fresh sprouts belong in every kitchen. Offering substantial quantities of minerals, including iron, and vitamins A, B and C, sprouts are a versatile, inexpensive vegetable you can have fresh all year 'round. They are readily adaptable for use in soups, salads, sandwiches, casseroles, omelets and many other dishes.

Mung beans and soybeans are most popular for sprouting, but alfalfa seeds, lentils and most other dried beans can be sprouted, too. You can purchase sprouts, but in the interests of freshness and nutrient value, it's better to grow your own (see "Grow Your Own Sprouts" later in this chapter). Sprouts are the most economical of vegetables. A pound of mung beans makes about three gallons of sprouts. At about 58 cents a pound for the beans, that's good value.

Unsaturated oils—We've all heard the term "polyunsaturated fats," and they are the reason why oil is better to use for cooking and sautéing than margarine, lard or other solid shortenings. Saturated fats are now believed to play an important role in causing heart disease and circulatory disorders. Saturated fats are those which are solid at room temperature, like the fat found in meats. Lard, which is made from hog fat, and butter are both saturated fats. Solid shortenings made from vegetable oils are artificially saturated by undergoing a rather complicated process known as hydrogenation, to turn the liquid oil into solid, saturated fat. The hydrogenation process involves high heat, which destroys vitamins. The soft, tub-style margarines made with safflower, sunflower and corn oils are somewhat better to use than stick shortenings, but pure liquid oils are still the most desirable.

Safflower, peanut, corn and soy oils are highest in polyunsaturates; safflower is most unsaturated of all, and has the mildest flavor. Sesame and olive oils are available cold-pressed, and thus contain the most nutrient value. All other oils are refined to some degree; heat must be used to express the oils from peanuts, corn kernels, soybeans and other foods, and some of the vitamins are therefore destroyed. It is a good idea to avoid vegetable oils that are part cottonseed oil. Cotton is one of the more heavily sprayed crops grown in this country, and there is a chance that some pesticide residues may remain in the oil.

Wheat bran—The outer hull of the wheat kernel, which is removed in the milling of white flour, bran is a valuable source of the dietary fiber we need to maintain intestinal health. Unprocessed bran is available in quantity for a nominal cost (although the current fiber craze has caused the price of bran to increase) from national distributors of natural foods and sometimes from millers. Bran can be used with bread crumbs, in dessert toppings, meat loaf, breads, muffins, cookies, granola and casseroles.

Wheat germ—The germ is the heart of the wheat kernel, which is also removed when white flour is milled. Wheat germ is an especially rich source of vitamin E and also contains protein, minerals and vitamins A and B. Wheat germ can be used in most of the same ways bran is used, and it can also stand alone as a nutty flavored topping for vegetable casseroles, fruit desserts and yogurt.

Whole grain flours—These flours contain all parts of the grain kernels from which they are ground and are therefore more nutritious than the more refined types. All-purpose white flour is ground from only the starchy middle portion of the wheat kernel; the nutritious germ and fiber-rich bran have been discarded. If you are now using white flour and are unable to purchase whole wheat flour, try supplementing it with some wheat germ and unprocessed bran whenever possible. Whole wheat pastry flour, which is ground from soft wheat, makes excellent pie crusts, popovers and similar products. Don't try to use pastry flour for bread, though—it has too little gluten and will not rise. For delicate foods, such as light cakes, unbleached flour will work better than whole wheat. Although it is lacking in nutrients, unbleached flour is still a notch above white flour, because bleaching alters protein and destroys vitamin E.

In addition to whole wheat flour, whole grain rye, buckwheat, brown rice, oat and barley flours are available

157

commercially or can be ground in a flour mill. Oily foods such as peanuts and cooked soybeans will clog most mills and should be ground in a blender.

There are several points to bear in mind when working with whole grain flours, especially when grinding your own or buying directly from an individual miller. First, remember that the degree of fineness or coarseness of flours varies somewhat from one mill to another. The kind of grain used also influences the final product. Don't be upset if you find that the same recipe doesn't come out exactly the same every time—the difference in flours is not enough to make it fail.

Now that your flour is stored in the refrigerator, don't be tempted to use it cold to make yeast breads. Warm the flour in an oven or allow it to reach room temperature before using, to avoid retarding the action of the yeast.

Finally, when converting recipes from white flour to whole grain flour, substitutions will not always be exact if you use a coarsely ground flour. For coarser flours, use approximately ¾ cup for every cup of white flour called for. Whole grain flours may also require slightly less shortening, more baking powder, and more liquid.

Whole wheat pasta products—Macaroni, spaghetti and noodles made from whole wheat flour are more nutritious than their white enriched counterparts and can provide an important source of protein in meatless meals.

Whole wheat pasta products are available from several national distributors and can be substituted for white flour pasta products in any recipe.

Some Tips for Cooking Natural Foods

These tips are not meant to serve as recipes; they are simply guidelines to basic, nutrition-wise preparation methods for foods in the natural kitchen. Cooking times and amounts of water will vary, and a cookbook or recipe file should be consulted for specifics. Also bear in mind that as cooks gain experience with new foods, preparation becomes easier and results are better.

Dried Beans[1]

The same general procedure may be followed when cooking any kind of dried beans. First wash the beans and add them to boiling, salted water (100 servings of beans requires about ¼ cup of salt). Boil the beans for two minutes, then remove from the heat, cover the pot and let the beans soak for one to two hours at room temperature, or overnight in the refrigerator. Then cook the beans in their soaking water for the amount of time specified. You might also try pressure cooking beans, but times and amounts of pressure will vary.

Black-eyed peas—for 100 servings, use 21 cups of peas and 3¾ gallons of water; cook for about 30 minutes.

Pinto and red kidney beans—for 100 servings, use 21 cups of beans and 3¾ gallons of water; cook for about two hours.

Small lima and Great Northern beans—for 100 servings, use 21 cups of beans and 3¾ gallons of water; cook for one to 1½ hours.

Large lima beans—for 100 servings use 24 cups of beans and 3¾ gallons of water; cook for about an hour.

Pea beans—for 100 servings, use 21 cups of beans and 3¾ gallons of water; cook for two to 2½ hours.

Garbanzo beans (chick-peas)

Chick-peas are cooked the same way as dried beans. Garbanzos need three to four times their volume of water to cook properly and take about four hours to cook.

Soybeans

Here's where pressure cooking becomes quite advantageous. Prepared by regular methods, soybeans need at least eight hours of soaking and must be cooked for two to three hours.

Brown rice

For short grain rice, use two parts water to one part rice;

long grain varieties require 2½ parts water. Brown rice makes the same number of servings as the same amount of white or parboiled rice. Cooking time varies between 35 and 40 minutes, depending on the type of rice used. After the first few times, cooking brown rice will become a familiar procedure. One important reminder: do not stir brown rice as it cooks, or it will stick together.

Dried corn

Dried corn is usually ground before cooking, and is used for cornmeal mush, grits or baked goods. Ground corn requires roughly four cups of water for each 1½ cups of corn used.

Millet

To cook millet, use three parts water for each part grain, and cook for 30–45 minutes, until all the liquid is absorbed. Millet may also be substituted for rice in casseroles and similar recipes, to add variety.

Fish

Fresh or frozen whole fish, fillets or steaks should be broiled or baked rather than pan-fried or deep-fried. Frying adds calories and makes foods harder to digest. Cook fish only until it flakes—about five to ten minutes for fillets and no more than 30 minutes for whole fish.

Meats and Poultry

Again, baking and broiling are the preferred methods of cooking. Meats and poultry must be carefully handled and thoroughly cooked to prevent any possibility of bacterial infection. When using frozen meats, either allow enough time to defrost them (covered) in the refrigerator, or cook them while still frozen, adjusting cooking time accordingly. Frozen meats should never be thawed at room temperature; fresh meats should not be removed from the refrigerator until you are ready to use them. Leftover meats should be covered and refrigerated immediately.

Vegetables

As we said earlier, vegetables should be served raw far more often than they are. The nutritional quality of raw, fresh vegetables is hard to beat. When you do cook fresh or frozen vegetables, steam, sauté, stir-fry or bake them only until they are fork tender. If you must boil vegetables, use only a small amount of water so they can cook primarily in their own juices. Cover tightly and cook on medium-high heat for as short a time as possible.

Generally speaking, it is much better to undercook vegetables than to overcook them, as is the tendency in most institutional kitchens. Properly cooked vegetables are crisp and juicy—never mushy—and retain their brightest colors. Once again, tight management is the key to success. Production schedules should be drawn up so that vegetables are ready just as they are needed and not before. In a serving line situation, steaming vegetables in smaller batches and bringing them to the serving line at more frequent intervals reduces overcooking caused by holding in steam tables.

Why Steaming Is Best

Steam offers six times as much heat as boiling water, because additional energy is needed to change water from its liquid to its gaseous state. The resulting shorter cooking time eliminates the need to precook and reheat vegetables—they can now be cooked in smaller batches and served promptly. Steaming means less food waste (and more for your dollar) because you won't be throwing away food that has dried out from being held too long in a steam table. Most important of all, steaming vegetables preserves, on the average, 50 percent more of their nutrient value than boiling.

How to Prepare Some
Common Fresh Vegetables[2]

Sort fresh vegetables carefully to remove damaged or spoiled pieces. Steaming times listed below are approximate; they will vary with freshness and size of vegetables, amounts being cooked, etc. The best guide until you gain experience with steaming vegetables is to be aware of the qualities of properly cooked vegetables and to keep checking the vegetables you are steaming until you see they are ready. After a few experiments you'll be able to estimate steaming times more accurately.

Vegetable	To Clean	Steam For
Asparagus	Break off tough ends of stalks; check carefully for dirt under scales.	5–10 minutes
Beans, lima	Shell beans and rinse thoroughly.	15–20 minutes
Beans, snap	Wash; snap off ends; break into inch-long pieces.	15–20 minutes
Beets	Remove tops, leaving about 2 inches of stem; wash thoroughly; do not peel or cut off roots and stem until after cooking.	30–40 minutes
Beet greens	Remove tough stems; wash well.	5–10 minutes
Broccoli	Cut off tough ends of stalks; do not peel; wash well.	7–10 minutes
Brussels sprouts	Remove any discolored outer leaves; wash.	5–10 minutes
Cabbage	Remove outer leaves only if damaged; wash whole head; cut in quarters and remove core; shred or cut in wedges.	10–15 minutes 5 minutes if shredded
Carrots	Cut off tops; scrub well; do not peel if organically grown; cut to desired size.	10–15 minutes
Cauliflower	Remove outer leaves and stalk; separate into florets and wash.	7–10 minutes
Celery	Scrub well; cut off tough ends of stalks and any spoiled leaves.	10–15 minutes
Chard	Discard tough stems; wash well.	10–20 minutes
Collards	Remove leaves from tough stems; wash well.	10–20 minutes

Corn	Husk; remove silk; rinse quickly.	5–8 minutes
Eggplant	Wash; peel and slice.	7–12 minutes
Kale	Wash well; remove leaves from tough stems before cooking.	10–20 minutes
Mustard greens	Wash well; discard tough stems.	10–20 minutes
Okra	Wash; remove stem ends.	7–12 minutes
Parsnips	Wash; peel and cut to desired size.	10–15 minutes
Peas	Shell; rinse thoroughly.	10–15 minutes
Potatoes	Scrub well; remove eyes; leave skins on whenever possible.	20–40 minutes
Pumpkin	Wash; cut in half and scoop out seeds and fibers; peel; cut in pieces.	10–15 minutes
Rutabagas	Wash; peel; cut in pieces.	10–25 minutes
Spinach	Wash carefully; cut off any tough stem ends.	5–7 minutes
Squash, summer	Wash; trim off stem ends; slice or cut as desired.	8–15 minutes
Squash, winter	Wash; cut in half and scoop out seeds and fibers; peel; cut to desired size.	10–20 minutes
Sweet potatoes	Scrub well; cook in skins.	15–30 minutes
Turnips	Cut off tops; wash; peel; cut as desired.	8–12 minutes

Fifteen Helpful Hints

Here are some miscellaneous suggestions for the novice natural foods cook or food service manager:

1. Bread—whole grain breads are more likely to stick to the pan than white bread, so pans must be oiled generously.
2. Nuts and seeds—make a tasty (and nutritious) addition

163

to salads, fruit cups and vegetable dishes.

3. Seasonings—caraway, dill, celery and mustard seeds make interesting seasoning substitutes for salt. There are also several commercial vegetable seasoning mixtures available. These seasonings offer a viable way to cut down on salt without losing flavor and are especially beneficial to people on low-salt diets.

4. Soups—when making minestrone and vegetable soups that will simmer for a long time, sautéing vegetables briefly before adding them to the soup seals in flavor and keeps them firm. This method would not be used for bean soups or cream soups.

5. Soups—leftover rice, bulgur and kasha will add body and flavor to many soups.

6. Soups—cream soups can be made with skim milk powder instead of whole milk. Just be sure to mix the milk powder and water with a wire whisk instead of a blender to prevent curdling.

7. Soybeans—freezing soybeans after soaking them decreases the amount of cooking time necessary.

8. Sweeteners—honey keeps indefinitely; if it becomes "grainy," don't throw it out. Just set the jar in a pan of hot water and stir the honey occasionally until the crystals dissolve.

9. Vegetables—save the cooking water from vegetables to use in making stocks, soups and sauces.

10. Vegetables—organically grown vegetables don't have to be peeled; a good scrubbing should be sufficient. Much of the nutrient value of such vegetables as carrots and potatoes lies just beneath their skins and is easily lost when they are peeled before cooking. If you grow some of your own vegetables on the premises, you can be sure they are free of pesticide residues and chemical fertilizers.

11. Vegetables—some vitamins (B-complex and C) are water soluble and can leach out of vegetables during prolonged submersion in water. Never soak your vegetables; instead, wash them quickly and chop or slice them right before cooking. Washing vegetables after they are chopped

will also remove water soluble vitamins.

12. Vegetables—exposure to air also depletes vitamins, and vegetables should not be allowed to stand uncovered before cooking and serving.

13. Vegetables—it's a good idea to salt vegetables after, not before cooking, because salt tends to draw out the natural juices.

14. Vegetables—instead of reheating leftover vegetables, serve them in salads. Reheating destroys much of the nutrient value remaining in cooked vegetables. Try chopping up leftover beans, carrots, broccoli, cauliflower and other vegetables and adding them to tossed salads or finger salads.

15. Yogurt—makes a good substitute for sour cream, although it is not recommended in cases when prolonged cooking is required. Yogurt has more protein and less fat than its more expensive counterpart and is actually a valuable aid to digestion.

Supplement	Supplies	Add to
Bran	dietary fiber	cereals casseroles breads bread crumb mixtures white flour dessert toppings
Brewer's yeast	B vitamins protein minerals	soups casseroles breads beverages
Kelp or other powdered seaweed (as a partial salt substitute)	iodide	soups sandwiches casseroles meat dishes
Rice polish	B vitamins	white rice breads cookies
Soy powder or soy grits	protein	stews meat loaf breads cookies

Supplement	Supplies	Add to
Wheat germ	vitamin E B vitamins	cereals casseroles breads bread crumb mixtures white flour cakes cookies dessert toppings

Grow Your Own Sprouts

One fresh vegetable no institutional kitchen should be without is sprouts. Sprouts are inexpensive, easy to grow and don't require any special equipment or a lot of attention. You can use a large jar or even a tray pan, wire basket, colander—any kind of container you can spare for a few days. Lentils, alfalfa seeds, mung beans, soybeans and most kinds of dried beans can be sprouted.

One word of caution before you set out to grow your own sprouts. Make sure that the seeds or beans you use are the kind intended for eating and cooking, not those intended for planting, which are sometimes treated with fungicides and insecticides. Beans and seeds can be purchased from natural foods distributors, health food stores and grocery stores.

Gena Larson, whose successful innovations in school food service were discussed in chapter 2, used the following method to sprout lentils and mung beans.

Soak one quart of beans or lentils in warm water for eight hours. Then dump them into a large colander and rinse under warm tap water. Set the colander over a bowl and cover with a warm, damp tea towel, then a dry towel. Keep the container in a warm, dark place overnight, such as near the pilot light on your stove (if you have a gas stove). The next day, rinse the sprouts again and cover.

If you grow your sprouts in a jar instead of a colander, cover the mouth with cheesecloth and turn the jar upside down so any remaining moisture can escape. If you're using a pan, be sure it is well drained after each rinsing. Keep the beans warm and damp and rinse them daily until the sprouts are an inch or two long—about three or four days. Then give the sprouts a final rinse and store them in covered gallon jars in the refrigerator not longer than a day or two before using. One pound of beans will produce about two gallons of sprouts.

Rinsing the sprouts is most important to prevent mold from growing. In fact, it would probably be best to rinse your sprouts two to three times a day instead of only once. Soaking beans or seeds in the very hottest tap water (about 150°F.) will also help to discourage mold growth.

High-Protein Meals
without Meat

As we have learned, vegetarian meals are both popular and economical. They should certainly become a regular feature of the menu in any institution concerned with upgrading the quality of food it serves. The first requirement for planning nutritionally sound vegetarian meals is an understanding of complementary proteins, and the best place to begin is with a discussion of basic body chemistry.

Our bodies are made of protein, and to be healthy we must provide them with sufficient protein to keep cells and tissues in good repair. The building blocks of protein are amino acids, which our bodies put together into protein molecules to build new cells and tissues. Some of these amino acids are manufactured inside the body, but some must be obtained from food. These are called "essential amino acids," for it is essential that they be present in our food since our bodies cannot manufacture them.

Foods which contain all eight of the essential amino acids in the proportion our bodies need are called "complete proteins." The only complete protein foods are meats, fish and poultry, but many other foods contain some of the essential amino acids in varying combinations.

Nonmeat protein foods can be classified into four categories: grains, legumes (beans), dairy products and nuts and seeds. Foods from these four groups can be combined in various ways so that the amino acids missing from one food are supplied by another. This is what is meant by the term "complementary proteins." One important point to remember about complementary proteins is that they must all be supplied in the same meal. You can't make up at dinner what you missed at lunch.

The four groups of protein foods can be combined in many ways, but there are three basic combinations which can be memorized and used as a foundation on which to begin building a more thorough knowledge of vegetarian cookery:

1. Grains + legumes (includes such familiar dishes as rice and beans).
2. Grains + dairy products (such as whole wheat macaroni and cheese).
3. Seeds + legumes (for example, the Middle Eastern classic, chick-peas with sesame).

For a thorough discussion of complementary proteins and many valuable recipe ideas, two excellent books, *Diet for a Small Planet* and *Recipes for a Small Planet* are indispensable (see the Appendix). A group of complete protein casserole dishes is provided in the Recipes chapter.

Some Points to Consider
When Planning Menus

1. Plan the day's three menus together, bearing in mind that foods should not be repeated—if eggs are planned for lunch or supper, they should not be on the breakfast menu; if corn is part of the menu for lunch, corn chowder should not be planned for supper; if fresh apples are the dessert at lunch, applesauce is not a good choice for the supper menu.

2. Strive for a good balance between starch roughage and protein to avoid overly heavy meals. A meal containing more than one or two of the following—potatoes, beans, corn, cream sauces, cakes, pasta, bread—is too heavy.

3. Space meat and meatless entrées throughout the week.

4. When planning luncheon menus, take advantage of the fact that soup-sandwich-salad meals are universally popular.

5. Ethnic and regional dishes can broaden cultural experience while bringing welcome variety to menus.

6. Plan carefully for the preparation time required for each dish and any preparation that may be done in advance. Take into account space needed on counters, range and in oven, and for manpower needed.

7. Desserts can be an important part of the meal and should supply nutrients, not just calories and sugar. Plan to serve sweet desserts only occasionally, and only when raw fruits and vegetables are also part of the meal.

8. Try to include a raw vegetable or fruit at every meal, if at all possible.

9. Beverages need not be limited to milk and fruit juice; apple cider, fresh lemonade and hot or iced herb teas offer additional alternatives to soft drinks.

10. Fruit juices are nutritionally superior to and a better economic value than fruit drinks. Fruit drinks are simply a small amount of fruit juice (usually about 10 percent) with sugar, water and artificial flavor and color added.

Special Considerations for Serving Children's Lunches

1. Lunch should supply at least one-third of a child's daily nutritional needs.

2. A good source of vitamin C should be included in lunches or snacks *every day*.

3. Serve small portions so children will have enough, but won't be forced to eat more than they comfortably can. Seconds should always be available for those with bigger appetites.

4. Records of children's food allergies should be kept so that appropriate substitutions can be made in their meals, when necessary.

5. It is a good idea to keep breakfast foods on hand if possible, for children who are given no breakfast at home.

6. Food can broaden a child's experience; instead of just peas, carrots and corn, try serving more unusual vegetables like broccoli and Brussels sprouts, so children are exposed to foods they may not get at home.

7. Here's a good pattern for children's lunches:

Main dish for protein	Vegetable and/or fruit for vitamins A & C	Bread & butter for vitamins B & D, fiber, fat	Milk for minerals, vitamins, protein

Some Sample Menu Plans

These are examples of nutritionally sound meals that were popular with the students and patients to whom they were served.

Head Start

This six-week menu plan was designed for the Lehigh Valley, Pennsylvania, Head Start program by Anita Hirsch, home economist in charge of the Rodale Press dining room at Fitness House. These menus are adequate for children two to six years of age and were planned around wholesome meals that make the best use of government commodities available under the Head Start program.

Menus include lunch and a snack each day and provide hot food at each meal. Each day there is served a good to excellent source of vitamin C; a dark green leafy or yellow vegetable is served every other day. Desserts are an integral part of the meal, used to supply nutrients other than calories. Whole grain breads and cereals are used, as are full strength fruit juices. Whole grain cereal or bread, milk, fresh fruit and dried fruit and nuts are always on hand.

Teachers reported that the foods have been generally well-accepted by the children.

1975–76 TERM

WEEK ONE

Monday

Chicken Noodle Soup
Tuna Fish Salad with Lettuce
Whole Wheat Bread
Carrot Sticks
Milk
Pineapple Chunks packed in
    unsweetened pineapple
    juice

Snack: orange juice
        graham cracker

Tuesday

Spaghetti with Meat Sauce
Lettuce with Russian
    Dressing
Whole Wheat Bread/Butter
Milk
Applesauce

Snack: orange juice
        celery with peanut
        butter

Wednesday

Baked Chicken
Baked Potato
Cooked Green Beans
Whole Wheat Bread/Butter
Milk
Fresh Orange Sections

Snack: grape juice
        fresh pear half

Thursday

Beef Stew
Corn Bread
Cole Slaw
Milk
Fruit Cup

Snack: apple cider
        cheese cubes

WEEK TWO

Monday

Cream of Tomato Soup
Baked Cheese Sandwich on
    Whole Wheat Bread
Sliced Fresh Carrots and
    Cucumbers
Milk
Fresh Raw Apple

Snack: orange juice
        graham cracker

Tuesday

Sliced Hot Turkey
Cranberry Relish
Baked Sweet Potato
Tossed Salad
Whole Wheat Bread
Milk
Sliced Bananas in Orange
    Juice

Snack: fruit juice
        peanut butter raisin
        cookies

Wednesday

Chili Con Carne
Rice
Hot Corn Bread
Green Pepper Slices
Carrot Sticks
Milk
Fruit Gelatin

Snack: orange juice
        celery with
        peanut butter

Thursday

Lentil Soup
Turkey Salad Sandwich on
    Whole Wheat Bread
    with Lettuce
Milk
Apple Crisp

Snack: orange juice
        raisins and walnuts

WEEK THREE

Monday

Chicken Rice Soup
Cottage Cheese
Applesauce
Carrots, Celery, Pepper
    Sticks
Whole Wheat Bread
Bananas stuffed with peanut
    butter and rolled in
    wheat germ

Snack: orange juice
        cheese cubes

Tuesday

Fried Beef Liver
Baked Potato
Spiced Carrots
Whole Wheat Bread
Pears

Snack: orange juice
        graham cracker

Wednesday

Split Pea Soup Hungarian
Hard Cooked Egg
Carrot and Celery Sticks
Whole Wheat Bread
Oatmeal Cookie

Snack: orange juice
        bananas and
        peanut butter

Thursday

Baked Hamburger Patty
Buttered Noodles
Steamed Yellow Beans
Milk
Pudding

Snack: orange juice
        raisins and walnuts

WEEK FOUR

Monday

Winter Vegetable Soup
Corn Bread
Milk
Apples and Peanut Butter

Snack: orange juice
             cinnamon toast

Tuesday

Hamburger and Noodle
       Casserole
Brussels Sprouts
Whole Wheat Bread
Milk
Orange Slices

Snack: apple cider
            ½ egg, hard cooked

Wednesday

Baked Fish
Steamed Carrots and
    Potatoes
Lettuce and Tomato Slice
Fresh Fruit Cup with Raisins

Snack: orange juice
            peanut butter balls

Thursday

Meat Loaf
Spanish Rice
Buttered Spinach
Milk
Ice Cream

Snack: orange juice
            graham cracker

WEEK FIVE

Monday

Oven Browned Fish Fillet
Oven Browned Potatoes
Buttered Peas
Whole Wheat Bread
Milk
Sliced Oranges and Coconut

Snack: apple juice
            cinnamon toast

Tuesday

Beef Bar BQ
Bun
Waldorf Salad
Lima Beans and Corn
Milk
Peanut Butter Raisin Cookie

Snack: orange juice
            cheese chunks

Wednesday

Sautéed Meatballs and Beans
Baked Squash
Carrot Sticks
Whole Wheat Bread
Fresh Fruit in Season

Snack: orange juice
            graham cracker

Thursday

Chicken Chow Mein
Chinese Noodles
Steamed Rice
Whole Wheat Bread
Sliced Peaches

Snack: orange juice
            celery and
            peanut butter

WEEK SIX

Monday

Spinach and Rice Casserole
Scalloped Tomatoes
Celery and Peanut Butter
Whole Wheat Bread
Sliced Apples and Oranges

Snack: fruit juice
           cheese chunks

Tuesday

Frankfurters
Baked Beans
Mashed Potatoes
Lettuce and Tomato Slice
Milk
Oatmeal Cookies

Snack: orange juice
           celery stuffed
           with cottage
           cheese

Wednesday

Macaroni & Cheese
Steamed Broccoli
Whole Wheat Bread
Sunshine Dessert

Snack: grape juice
           graham cracker

Thursday

Beef & Barley Soup
Egg Salad Sandwich on
      Whole Wheat Bread
Cold Beets
Cinnamon Crispies

Snack: orange juice
           apple quarters

Volunteers of America Day-Care Center (Allentown, Pennsylvania)

These dishes are all made from scratch and are based on nutritional concepts very much like those for the Head Start menus. No government commodities are used. The lunches fill at least one-third of the daily nutritional needs of four-, five- and six-year-olds. Snack foods are chosen for nutritional value as well as for their appeal to children's tastes.

Whole grain breads are baked on the premises and contain no artificial preservatives or other chemical additives.

SPRING, 1976

WEEK ONE

Monday

Rice-Spinach Casserole
Carrot-Raisin-Pineapple
    Salad
Mock German Chocolate
    Cake
Milk

Tuesday

Poached Haddock
Baked Potatoes
Mixed Vegetables
Green Salad
Peach Kuchen
Milk

Wednesday

Split Pea Soup
Homemade Bread & Swiss
    Cheese
Chewies
Fresh Fruit
Chocolate Milk

Thursday

Corned Beef
Creamed Cabbage & Peas
Waldorf Salad
Chocolate Chip Cookies
Milk

Friday

Pastitsi (Greek hamburg &
    macaroni dish)
Steamed Carrots
Greek Salad
Fresh Fruit
Milk

Rye, whole wheat or cracked wheat bread is served at each meal.

Snacks: A.M. various juices; cereals, oatmeal & raisin cookies, cheese and crackers, graham crackers & pretzels
P.M. cookies, raisin bread, apple wedges, honey & jelly bread, raisins, corn curls, cheesettes, etc.

WEEK TWO

Monday

Scrambled Eggs
Sausage
Steamed Broccoli
Cole Slaw
Fresh Fruit
Milk

Tuesday

Beef Stew
Homemade Bread
Chewies
Date Bars
Milk

Wednesday

Barbequed Soybeans
Baked Corn
Egg & Lettuce Salad
Ice Cream
Chocolate Milk

Thursday

Simmered Chicken
Gnocchi
Peas
Garden Salad Supreme
Fresh Fruit
Milk

Friday

Lentil Shepherd's Pie
Brussels Sprouts
Golden Gelatin Salad
Homemade Tapioca Pudding
Milk

WEEK THREE

Monday

Tuna Noodle Casserole
Peas
Cole Slaw
Fruit
Milk

Tuesday

Eggplant Parmesan
Green Beans
Tossed Salad
Tapioca Pudding
Milk

Wednesday

Porcupine Beef Balls
Cauliflower w/Cheese Sauce
Carrot-Raisin Salad
Sherbet
Chocolate Milk

Thursday

Hearty Vegetable Soup
Whole Grain Bread & Cheese
Chewies
Fresh Fruit
Milk

Friday

Chicken Fried Rice
Brussels Sprouts
Nutty Fruit Salad
Applesauce Spice Cake
Milk

WEEK FOUR

Monday

Chili w/Crackers
Chewies
Oatmeal Cookies
Milk

Tuesday

Pork Loin
Scalloped Potatoes
Beets
Golden Gelatin Salad
Fresh Fruit
Milk

Wednesday

Soybean Vegetable Casserole
Egg & Lettuce Salad
Gingerbread
Chocolate Milk

Thursday

Beef Stew
Homemade Bread
Chewies
Fresh Fruit
Milk

Friday

Crusty Corn Casserole
Steamed Broccoli
Green Salad
Apple Crisp
Milk

WEEK FIVE

Monday

Potato Soup
Bread & Butter
Chewies
Milk

Tuesday

Spaghetti Pie
Tossed Salad
Sherbet
Milk

Wednesday

Broccoli Souffle
Sprouted Lentil, Bean & Rice
    Salad
Banana-Peanut Butter Cake
Chocolate Milk

Thursday

Cashew-Millet Casserole
Steamed Carrots
Cole Slaw
Fresh Fruit
Milk

Friday

Curried Beef on Brown Rice
Green Beans
Golden Gelatin Salad
Poor Man's Cookies
Milk

WEEK SIX

Monday

Chili w/Crackers
Chewies
Fresh Fruit
Milk

Tuesday

Soybean Rice Surprise
Spinach Salad
Carrot Cake
Milk

Wednesday

Yankee Red Flannel Hash
Brussels Sprouts
Pear w/Shredded Cheese
Oatmeal Raisin Cookies
Chocolate Milk

Thursday

Baked Chicken
Mashed Potatoes
Mixed Vegetables
Green Salad
Fresh Fruit
Milk

Friday

Macaroni & Cheese
Jellied Fruit-Cottage Cheese
Salad
Date Bars
Milk

Milwaukee School District

These menus, from the school district voted as having the best school lunch in the nation, emphasize conventional rather than specifically natural foods. Government commodities are used, and meals are planned to meet federal Type A lunch requirements.

Although these menus are not representative of a strictly "natural" food service, they indicate the high quality foods that can be turned out by a conventional food service. Remember that all foods served are of the best quality and are properly prepared; all meals are nutritionally sound, and all baked goods are made on the premises without preservatives or other artificial additives.

The foods contained in all menus, including meats, vegetables, fruits and desserts, were all chosen by the Inter-High School Lunch Committee, the student testing panel. Menus identified as prepared by this committee were published exactly as written by the students.

MENU—October, 1975

ALL MILWAUKEE
PUBLIC SCHOOLS

Meal Prices: Elementary   30¢
Secondary   35¢
Adults   50¢
plus 10¢ for beverage

(One-half pint milk served with all meals)

WEEK ONE

Monday

Italian Spaghetti w/Meat
  Sauce
Autumn Harvest Vegetable
  w/ Celery Seed Dressing
Buttercrust Pan Roll
Chilled Sweetened
  Applesauce

Tuesday

Baked Chicken Maryland
Whipped Potatoes
  w/Country Gravy
Mixed Fruit Salad
Cranberry Coffee Cake

Wednesday

Bratwurst on Submarine Bun
  w/Mustard
Buttered Peas and Carrots
Crunchy Cucumber Sticks
Chewy Ginger Cookie

Thursday

Juicy Chuckburger on Onion
  Bun w/Relishes
Lyonnaise Potatoes
Chilled Orange Juice
Marble Cake w/Pastel Green
  Frosting

Friday

Western Meat Loaf w/Ranch
  Gravy
Parslied Buttered Rice
Lettuce and Tomato Salad
  w/French Dressing
Whole Wheat Pan Roll
Chilled Peach Slices

WEEK TWO

Monday

Barbecue Beef on Oatmeal
  Bun
Buttered Green Beans
Fresh Orange Wedges
Chocolate Brownie

Tuesday

Breaded Fish w/Tartar Sauce
Hash Brown Potatoes
Red & White Cole Slaw
  w/Creamy Dressing
Poppy Seed Pan Roll
Peanut Butter Cookie

Wednesday

Pizza w/Meat and Cheese
  Topping
Shades 'O' Green Vegetable
  Salad w/Sweet Sour
  Dressing
Crusty Garlic Bread
Chilled Pear Slices

Thursday

Sliced Turkey in Gravy on
  Rolled Wheat Bun
Tender Green Peas in Sauce
Shredded Carrot & Celery
  Salad
Cran-Apple Cake w/Lemon
  Glaze

Friday

Oven Baked Salisbury Steak
  w/Onion Gravy
Mashed Potatoes
California Orange Juice
Buttercrust Bread
Cornmeal Crisp Cookie

WEEK THREE

Monday

Hot Dog on Cheese Bun
  w/Catsup
Buttered Whole Kernel Corn
Chilled Fruit Punch
Ginger Cake w/Lemon Glaze

Tuesday

Old World Lasagna
Parslied Head Lettuce
  w/Vinegar & Oil
  Dressing
Cinnamon Surprise
  Coffee Cake
Chilled Peaches in Syrup

Wednesday

Baked Mock Chicken Leg
  w/Mushroom Gravy
Paprika Buttered Potatoes
Crisp Celery Sticks
Anadama Bread
Orange Oatmeal Cookie

Thursday

Ham and Cheese Submarine
  Sandwich
French Fries
Buttered Green Beans
Circus Fruit Salad
Chocolate Chip Cookie

Friday

Juicy Meatballs in Brown
  Gravy
Buttered Noodles
Salted Cucumber Sticks
Golden Pilgrim Roll
Baked Apple Crisp
  w/Whipped Topping

WEEK FOUR

Monday

Melted Cheese on Whole
    Wheat Bun
Baby Peas w/Onion Bits
Tossed Lettuce & Radish
    Rings w/Russian Dr.
Brown Sugar Refrigerator
    Cookie

Tuesday

Chuckburger on Buttercrust
    Bun w/Catsup
Hash Brown Potatoes
Crisp Apple Quarters
Chocolate Cake w/Lemon
    Cream Frosting

Wednesday

Baked Sliced Turkey in
    Gravy on Salted Bun
Buttered Green Beans
Frosty Fruit Salad
Cinnamon Crisp Cookie

Thursday

Beef Taco w/Shredded
    Lettuce, Cheese & Diced
    Tomato
Black-eyed Peas w/Bacon
Jellied Orange Salad
Peanut Butter Coffee Cake
    w/Streusel Topping

Friday

Breaded Fish Steak w/Tartar
    Sauce on Buttercrust
    Bun
Whole Kernel Corn Niblets
Green Pepper Cole Slaw
    w/Slaw Dressing
Vanilla Pudding w/Fudge
    Sauce

Lewis and Clark College

These menus emphasize fresh, wholesome foods, prepared as simply as possible. An effort was made to cut down on sugar, saturated fat and chemical additives, and to bring more fiber into student diets by serving more fresh vegetables and whole grain breads.

WEEK ONE

Breakfast

Orange Juice
Tomato, Prune or Pineapple Juice
Grapefruit Half
Stewed Rhubarb
Applesauce
Millet cooked in Milk
Scrambled Eggs
Cornmeal-Soy Pancakes—Syrup/Honey
Hash Brown Potatoes
Brown Rice
Granola
Grapenuts, Shredded Wheat, Bran Flakes, Raisin Bran, All Bran
Whole Grain Breads
Beverages

Lunch

Beef Noodle Soup—Whole Grain Crackers
Salads:
    Tossed Green Salad
    Cottage Cheese Salad w/Radish Slice
    Frozen Fruit Salad
    Orange-Banana-Apple Salad
    Cucumber in Sour Cream

Entrées:
    Hot Beef Sandwich—Wheat Bread
    Chili Con Carne w/Beans
    Spinach-Cheese Casserole

Green Beans
Mixed Fresh Vegetable Medley
    Zucchini, Crookneck Squash, Onions and Tomato
Peanut Butter-Nut Cookies
Assorted Fruits

Yogurt
Whole Grain Breads
Beverages

Dinner

Cream of Mushroom Soup—Whole Grain Crackers
Salad Bar
Entrées:
Grilled Cube Steak
Baked Meat & Vegetable Loaf
Healthy Chop Suey w/Soybeans over Brown Rice
Brown Rice
Steamed Whole Potato
Cut Broccoli
Braised Celery & Peas
Whole Grain Bread Pudding w/Raisins
Apple Cobbler
Whole Grain Breads
Beverages

Breakfast

Orange Juice
Tomato, Prune or Grapefruit Juice
Banana
Peach Slices
Stewed Prunes

Wheatena with Oats

Fried Eggs

Skillet Fried Cornmeal-Wheat Germ Mush
Hash Brown Potatoes
Bulgur
Granola
Grapenuts, Shredded Wheat, Bran Flakes, Raisin Bran, All Bran
Whole Grain Breads
Beverages

Lunch

Lentil Soup—Whole Grain Crackers
Salads:
Combination Salad
Cottage Cheese w/Tomato Cube
Relish Plate
Cole Slaw
Cream Cheese Stuffed Celery
Entrées:
Hoagie Sandwich on Whole Wheat Bun

Ground Beef Shepherds Pie
Nut-Oatmeal Casserole

Spinach, Cabbage and Carrot Scramble

Molasses Cookies
Assorted Fruits
Yogurt
Whole Grain Breads
Beverages

Dinner

Boston Clam Chowder—Whole Grain Crackers

Salad Bar

Entrées:

Baked Fish w/Lemon
Braised Beef Cubes w/Vegetables
Whole Wheat Spaghetti w/Mushroom Sauce

Baked Potato
Whole Wheat Berries
Green Peas
Honey Baked Banana Squash

Whole Fresh Fruit
Whole Grain Breads
Beverages

Breakfast

Orange Juice
Tomato, Prune or Apple Juice
Fresh Orange
Pear Slices
Purple Plums

Cornmeal & Sesame Cereal

Poached Egg
Peanut Butter French Toast—Syrup/Honey
Hash Brown Potatoes
Buckwheat Groats
Granola
Grapenuts, Shredded Wheat, Bran Flakes, Raisin Bran, All Bran
Whole Grain Breads
Beverages

Lunch

Tomato Bisque Soup—Whole Grain Crackers

Salads:

Chefs Salad
Cottage Cheese w/chopped Parsley

Molded Fruit & Cheese
Mixed Fruit Salad
Peas & Cheese Medley

Entrées:
Italian Sausage Sandwich on Whole Wheat Roll
Spanish Macaroni
Sliced Avocado, Egg, Tomato & Alfalfa Sprouts
on Whole Grain Bread

Carrots
Braised Lettuce Greens

Date Nut Bars
Assorted Fruits
Yogurt
Whole Grain Breads
Beverages

Dinner
Beef Barley Soup—Whole Grain Crackers
Salad Bar
Entrées:
Broiled Top Butt Steak
Deluxe Fruit Plate with Cheese
Au Gratin Potatoes
Savory Soybeans
Green Beans
Baked Honey Glazed Acorn Squash
Rice Pudding w/Raisins (Brown Rice)
Pineapple Muffins
Whole Grain Breads
Beverages

Brunch
Orange Juice
Tomato, Prune and Pineapple Juice
Melon Wedge
Dried Fruit Compote
Applesauce
Malto-Meal w/Oats

Farmer's Omelet

Buckwheat Pancakes—Syrup/Honey
Hash Brown Potatoes
Cornmeal Mush
Granola
Grapenuts, Shredded Wheat, Bran Flakes, Raisin Bran, All Bran
Whole Grain Breads
Beverages

Dinner

Hearty Vegetable Soup—Whole Grain Crackers
Salad Bar
Entrées:
Roast Pork w/Spicy Applesauce
Grilled Chopped Steak
Egg Foo Yong over Brown Rice
Twice Baked Potato
Brown Rice
Green Peas & Onions
Cauliflower w/Wheat Germ Topping
Ice Cream Sundae—Choice of Toppings
Whole Grain Breads
Beverages

Breakfast

Orange Juice
Tomato, Prune or Grape Juice
Grapefruit Half
Stewed Rhubarb
Pear Slices

Roman Meal

Poached or Soft-Boiled Egg

Cottage Cheese Whole Grain Pancakes—Syrup/Honey
Hash Brown Potatoes
Brown Rice w/Sesame Seeds
Granola
Grapenuts, Shredded Wheat, Bran Flakes, Raisin Bran, All Bran
Whole Grain Breads
Beverages

Lunch

Split Pea Soup—Whole Grain Crackers
Salads:
Tossed Green Salad
Cottage Cheese w/Pineapple Chunks
Peach Half w/Fruit Cocktail
Deviled Egg Salad
Carrot & Celery Salad
Entrées:
Cold Cut & Cheese on Whole Grain Bread
Baked Tuna & Noodles w/Wheat Germ Topping
Tossed Garden Medley w/Cheese & Nuts
Stewed Tomatoes
Black-eyed Peas

Better Food for Public Places

    Peanut Butter-Nut Cookies
    Assorted Fruits
    Yogurt
    Whole Grain Breads
    Beverages

Dinner
    Cashew-Carrot Soup—Whole Grain Crackers
    Salad Bar
    Entrées:
        Veal Parmesan
        Oven Broiled Fish w/Lemon
        Curried Vegetables w/Soybeans and Sunflower Seeds
    Oven Browned Potatoes
    Bulgur Pilaf
    Green Peas
    Mashed Squash
    Tapioca Cream
    Assorted Fruits
    Whole Grain Breads
    Beverages

Breakfast
    Orange Juice
    Tomato, Prune and Grapefruit Juice
    Banana
    Pineapple Chunks
    Stewed Prunes
    Wheatena
    Scrambled Eggs
    Hot Baked Wheat Bread Pudding—Syrup/Honey
    Hash Brown Potatoes
    Seven Grain Mixture
    Granola
    Grapenuts, Shredded Wheat, Bran Flakes, Raisin Bran, All Bran
    Whole Grain Breads
    Beverages

Lunch
    Minestrone Soup—Whole Grain Crackers
    Salads:
        Combination Salad
        Cottage Cheese & Green Pepper Cube
        Waldorf w/Raisins
        Macaroni Salad

Pickled Beet Salad

Entrées:
Pizza w/Wheat Germ
Beef Noodle Casserole
Potato Pancakes w/Sour Cream or Yogurt

Green Beans
Succotash

Date Nut Bread
Assorted Fruits
Yogurt
Whole Grain Breads
Beverages

Dinner
Cream of Potato Soup—Whole Grain Crackers
Salad Bar

Entrées:
Roast Turkey w/Corn Bread Dressing
Beef Stew w/Vegetables
Green Peppers Stuffed with Brown Rice, Cheese & Tomato Sauce

Mashed Potatoes
Corn Bread Dressing
Zucchini and Tomato Bake
Brussels Sprouts

Whole Fresh Fruit
Whole Grain Breads
Beverages

Breakfast
Orange Juice
Tomato, Prune or Apple Juice
Fresh Orange
Peach Slices
Fruit Cocktail

Millet

Fried Eggs
Baked Cheese Sandwich—Syrup/Honey
Hash Brown Potatoes
Wheat Berries
Granola
Grapenuts, Shredded Wheat, Bran Flakes, Raisin Bran, All Bran
Whole Grain Breads
Beverages

Lunch

Chicken Gumbo Soup—Whole Grain Crackers

Salads:

Chefs Salad
Cottage Cheese w/Shredded Carrot
Kidney Bean Salad
Fresh Fruit Salad
Country Cole Slaw

Entrées:

Hamburger on Whole Wheat Bun w/Trimmings
Eggs & Mushrooms in Cheddar Sauce
Peanut Butter, Alfalfa, Cheese Sandwich on Whole Wheat Muffin

Leaf Spinach
Carrot Coins

Wheat Germ Squares
Assorted Fruits
Yogurt
Whole Grain Breads
Beverages

Dinner

Corn Chowder—Whole Grain Crackers
Salad Bar

Entrées:

Honeyed Chicken
Beef Chow Mein over Brown Rice
Baked Noodle and Cottage Cheese Casserole w/Poppy Seeds

Steamed Whole Potatoes
Brown Rice
Cauliflower
Kale

Pumpkin Muffins w/Raisins
Banana Cream Pudding
Whole Grain Breads
Beverages

WEEK TWO

Breakfast

Orange Juice
Tomato, Prune or Grape Juice
Banana
Stewed Prunes
Pear Slices

Roman Meal
Poached or Soft Cooked Eggs
Raisin Wheat Pancakes—Syrup/Honey
Hash Brown Potatoes
Buckwheat Groats
Granola
Grapenuts, Shredded Wheat, Bran Flakes, Raisin Bran, All Bran
Whole Grain Breads
Beverages

Lunch
Lima Bean Soup—Whole Grain Crackers

Salads:
Combination Salad
Cottage Cheese Salad w/Green Pepper Garnish
Relish Plate
Banana-Nut Salad
Carrot-Raisin Salad

Entrées:
French Dip
Baked Macaroni & Cheese w/Wheat Germ Topping
Ratatouille

Corn O'Brien
Braised Celery w/Poppy Seeds
Sesame Seed Cookies
Assorted Fruits
Yogurt
Whole Grain Breads
Beverages

Dinner
Beef Barley Soup—Whole Grain Crackers
Salad Bar

Entrées:
London Broil
Turkey a la King w/Peas
Fritata

Oven Browned Potatoes
Bulgur Pilaf
Cauliflower w/Wheat Germ Topping
Green Beans w/Bean Sprouts
Baked Custard
Raisin-Nut Muffin
Whole Grain Breads
Beverages

Better Food for Public Places

Breakfast
Orange Juice
Tomato, Prune & Pineapple Juice
Fresh Orange
Purple Plums
Applesauce
Oatmeal w/Raisins
Scrambled Eggs
Blueberry Wheat Pancakes—Syrup/Honey
Hash Brown Potatoes
Brown Rice
Granola
Grapenuts, Shredded Wheat, Bran Flakes, Raisin Bran, All Bran
Whole Grain Breads
Beverages

Lunch
Cream of Carrot Soup—Whole Grain Crackers
Salads:
    Tossed Green Salad
    Cottage Cheese Salad w/Tomato Cube
    Frozen Fruit Salad
    Pineapple w/Cream Cheese
    Marinated Bean Salad
Entrées:
    Fish & Chips
    Sloppy Joe on Whole Wheat Bun
    Apple Cheese Entrée
Carrot Coins
Stir-Fried Bean Sprouts, Onions, and Green Peppers
Peanut Bars
Assorted Fruits
Yogurt
Whole Grain Breads
Beverages

Dinner
Manhattan Clam Chowder—Whole Grain Crackers
Salad Bar
Entrées:
    Baked Salmon Steak w/Lemon Butter
    Chinese Pepper Steak
    Baked Nut Loaf
Au Gratin Potatoes
Wheat Berries
Spinach w/Savory Sauce
Honey Glazed Beets

Whole Fresh Fruit
Whole Grain Breads
Beverages

Breakfast

Orange Juice
Tomato, Prune & Grapefruit Juice
Melon Wedge
Peach Slices
Pineapple Chunks

Wheatena

Fried Eggs
Whole Grain French Toast—Syrup/Honey
Hash Brown Potatoes
Bulgur
Granola
Grapenuts, Shredded Wheat, Bran Flakes, Raisin Bran, All Bran
Whole Grain Breads
Beverages

Lunch

Hearty Vegetable Soup—Whole Grain Crackers

Salads:
> Chef Salad
> Cottage Cheese Salad w/Shredded Carrot
> Peanut Butter Stuffed Celery
> Waldorf Salad
> Spring Salad

Entrées:
> Meatball Sandwich on Whole Wheat Rolls
> Turkey & Vegetable Scramble
> Pinto Bean Casserole w/Sour Cream

Stewed Tomatoes w/Chopped Green Peppers
Yellow Squash, Turnips, Zucchini Sauté
Oatmeal-Nut Cookies
Assorted Fruits
Yogurt
Whole Grain Breads
Beverages

Dinner

Chicken Gumbo Soup—Whole Wheat Crackers
Salad Bar
Entrées:
> Broiled Top Butt Steak
> Deluxe Fruit Plate w/Cheese

Better Food for Public Places

Baked Potato
Buckwheat Groats
Cut Broccoli
Green Peas and Onions

Hunters Pudding
Tapioca Cream Pudding
Whole Grain Breads
Beverages

Brunch

Orange Juice
Tomato, Prune & Apple Juice
Grapefruit Half
Fruit Cocktail
Pear Slices

Oatmeal w/Wheat Germ

Scrambled Eggs w/Cream Cheese

Buckwheat Pancakes—Syrup/Honey
Hash Brown Potatoes
Skillet Fried Cornmeal w/Wheat Germ
Granola
Grapenuts, Shredded Wheat, Bran Flakes, Raisin Bran, All Bran
Whole Grain Breads
Beverages

Dinner

Beef Noodle Soup—Whole Grain Crackers
Salad Bar
Entrées:

Roast Beef Au Jus
Shrimp w/Vegetables over Brown Rice
Carrot Cheese Nut Loaf w/Parsley Sauce

Oven Browned Potatoes
Brown Rice
Brussels Sprouts
Succotash

Ice Cream Sundae—Choice of Toppings
Whole Grain Breads
Beverages

Breakfast

Orange Juice
Tomato, Prune & Grape Juice

Fresh Orange
Stewed Prunes
Apricot Halves

Malto-Meal

Scrambled Eggs

Soy-Wheat Pancakes—Syrup/Honey
Hash Brown Potatoes
Wheat Berries
Granola
Grapenuts, Shredded Wheat, Bran Flakes, Raisin Bran, All Bran
Whole Grain Breads
Beverages

Lunch
Minestrone Soup—Whole Grain Crackers

Salads:
> Combination Salad
> Cottage Cheese w/Radish Ring
> Molded Nut and Cheese Salad
> Mixed Fruit Salad
> Cole Slaw

Entrées:
> Pizza w/Wheat Germ
> Egg Salad Sandwich on Whole Grain Bread
> Cheese Fondue

Zucchini w/Parmesan Cheese
Stir-Fried Cabbage

Molasses Cookies
Assorted Fruits
Yogurt
Whole Grain Breads
Beverages

Dinner
Tomato Bisque—Whole Grain Crackers

Salad Bar

Entrées:
> Oven Fried Chicken
> Short Ribs of Beef w/Vegetables
> Pasta-Bean Casserole

Steamed Whole Potatoes
Black-eyed Peas
Honey Baked Banana Squash
Herbed Green Beans

Banana-Nut Bread
Assorted Fruits
Yogurt

Better Food for Public Places

Whole Grain Breads
Beverages

Breakfast
Orange Juice
Tomato, Prune & Pineapple Juice
Grapefruit Half
Stewed Rhubarb
Applesauce
Millet
Fried Eggs
Peanut Butter French Toast—Syrup/Honey
Hash Brown Potatoes
Brown Rice
Granola
Grapenuts, Shredded Wheat, Bran Flakes, Raisin Bran, All Bran
Whole Grain Breads
Beverages

Lunch
Cream of Mushroom Soup—Whole Grain Crackers
Salads:
    Tossed Green Salad
    Cottage Cheese Salad w/Red Onion Ring
    Pear Half w/Fruit Cocktail
    Potato Salad
    Marinated Garden Salad
Entrées:
    Hamburger on Whole Wheat Bun w/Trimmings
    Tuna Loaf w/Vegetable Sauce
    Fruit Plate w/Assorted Cheese and Whole Grain Crackers
Creamed Celery and Spinach
Herb Steamed Squash (or Pumpkin)
Wheat Germ Squares
Assorted Fruit
Yogurt
Whole Grain Breads
Beverages

Dinner
Split Pea Soup—Whole Grain Crackers
Salad Bar
Entrées:
    Country Fried Steak
    Oven Broiled Halibut Steak w/Lemon Butter

Vegetarian Lasagna
Mashed Potatoes
Savory Soybeans
Honey Glazed Carrots
Braised Lettuce Greens
Whole Fresh Fruit
Whole Grain Breads
Beverages

Breakfast

Orange Juice
Tomato, Prune & Grapefruit Juice
Banana
Pear Slices
Pineapple Chunks

Roman Meal w/Sesame Cereal

Shirred or Soft Cooked Eggs

Cornmeal-Applesauce Pancake—Syrup/Honey
Hash Brown Potatoes
Corn Chowder
Granola
Grapenuts, Shredded Wheat, Bran Flakes, Raisin Bran, All Bran
Whole Grain Breads
Beverages

Lunch

Cream Soup w/Vegetables—Whole Grain Crackers
Salads:
    Chefs Salad
    Cottage Cheese Salad w/Chopped Parsley
    Cucumber in Sour Cream
    Orange-Coconut Salad
    Relish Plate
Entrées:
    Hot Turkey Sandwich on Whole Wheat Bread
    Tamale Pie
    Noodle Surprise
Bean Sprouts, Mushroom & Green Bean Scramble
Steamed Turnips
Peanut Butter-Nut Cookies
Assorted Fruit
Yogurt
Whole Grain Breads
Beverages

Dinner

    Lima Bean Soup—Whole Grain Crackers

    Salad Bar

    Entrées:

        Grilled Liver w/Onions
        Whole Wheat Spaghetti w/Meat Sauce
        Spinach-Nut Entrée

    Steamed Whole Potatoes
    Brown Rice
    Green Peas
    Sweet & Sour Cabbage

    Orange Millet Pudding
    Assorted Fruits
    Whole Grain Breads
    Beverages

WEEK THREE

Breakfast

    Orange Juice
    Tomato, Prune & Apple Juice
    Fresh Orange
    Purple Plum
    Peach Slices

    Malto-Meal

    Fried Eggs

    Oatmeal Griddle Cakes—Syrup/Honey
    Hash Brown Potatoes
    Wheat Germ Loaf
    Granola
    Grapenuts, Shredded Wheat, Bran Flakes, Raisin Bran, All Bran
    Whole Grain Breads
    Beverages

Lunch

    Cheese Chowder—Whole Grain Crackers

    Salads:

        Combination Salad
        Cottage Cheese Salad w/Pimiento Garnish
        Mixed Fruit Salad
        Macaroni Salad
        Claremont Salad

    Entrées:

        Cold Meat & Cheese Sandwich on Whole Grain Bread

Beef Noodle Casserole
Green Peppers Stuffed w/Bulgur

Creamed Spinach
Buttered Sliced Beets

Date Nut Bars
Assorted Fruits
Yogurt
Whole Grain Breads
Beverages

Dinner

Fruit Soup—Whole Grain Crackers

Salad Bar

Entrées:

Baked Ham w/Raisin Sauce
Meat Loaf w/Mushroom Gravy
Cheese Enchilada Bake

Baked Sweet Potatoes
Bulgur Pilaf
Cut Broccoli
Wax Beans Confetti

Raisin Rice Pudding
Assorted Fruits
Whole Grain Breads
Beverages

Breakfast

Orange Juice
Tomato, Prune & Grapefruit Juice
Banana
Stewed Rhubarb
Pear Slices

Millet Cooked in Milk

Scrambled Eggs

Soy-Wheat Pancakes—Syrup/Honey
Hash Brown Potatoes
Buckwheat Groats
Granola
Grapenuts, Shredded Wheat, Bran Flakes, Raisin Bran, All Bran
Whole Wheat Breads
Beverages

Lunch

Boston Clam Chowder—Whole Grain Crackers

Salads:

Chefs Salad

Cottage Cheese Salad w/Parsley Garnish
Marasweet Salad
Grapefruit & Apple Salad
Pickled Beet Salad

Entrées:
Tuna Melt on Whole Wheat English Muffin
Chili Con Carne w/Beans
Peanut Butter-Carrot & Raisin Salad on Whole Wheat Bread

Green Peas & Mushrooms
Whole Kernel Corn

Sesame Seed Cookies
Assorted Fruits
Yogurt
Whole Grain Breads
Beverages

Dinner
Chicken Noodle Soup—Whole Grain Crackers
Salad Bar

Entrées:
Oven Broiled Fillet of Perch
Roast Leg of Lamb—Mint Sauce
Cheese Pizza w/Wheat Germ

Mashed Potatoes
Wheat Berries
Green Beans w/Slivered Almonds
Honey Baked Turnips

Whole Fresh Fruit
Whole Grain Breads
Beverages

Breakfast
Orange Juice
Tomato, Prune & Pineapple Juice
Fresh Orange
Fruit Cocktail
Apricot Halves

Oatmeal w/Raisins

Poached or Soft Cooked Eggs

French Toast—Syrup/Honey
Hash Brown Potatoes
Wheat Berries and Brown Rice
Granola
Grapenuts, Shredded Wheat, Bran Flakes, Raisin Bran, All Bran
Whole Grain Breads
Beverages

Lunch
Cashew-Carrot Soup—Whole Grain Crackers

Salads:
> Tossed Green Salad
> Cottage Cheese Salad w/Green Onion Slice
> Frozen Fruit Salad
> Banana-Nut Salad
> Sliced Tomato Salad

Entrées:
> Hamburger on Whole Wheat Bun w/Trimmings
> Hot Turkey Salad w/Sesame Seeds
> Baked Macaroni & Cheese w/Wheat Germ Topping

Vegetable Medley
Creamed Onions
Peanut Butter-Nut Cookies
Assorted Fruits
Yogurt
Whole Grain Breads
Beverages

Dinner
Beef Barley Soup—Whole Grain Crackers

Salad Bar

Entrées:
> Broiled Top Butt Steak
> Deluxe Fruit Plate with Cheese

Twice Baked Potatoes
Brown Rice
Cauliflower
Carrot Coins

Carrot Cake
Assorted Fruits
Whole Grain Breads
Beverages

Brunch
Orange Juice
Tomato, Prune & Grapefruit Juice
Melon Wedge
Stewed Prunes
Applesauce
Wheatena with Sesame Seeds
Scrambled Eggs w/Onions & Green Peppers
Banana-Nut Pancakes—Syrup/Honey
Hash Brown Potatoes

      Brown Rice Pudding
      Granola
      Grapenuts, Shredded Wheat, Bran Flakes, Raisin Bran, All Bran
      Whole Grain Breads
      Beverages

Dinner

      Potato Leek Soup—Whole Grain Crackers

      Salad Bar

      Entrées:

           Roast Turkey w/Whole Wheat Bread Dressing
           Braised Beef Cubes w/Vegetables
           Fresh Vegetable Omelet

      Steamed Whole Potato
      Buckwheat Groats
      Baked Acorn Squash
      Brussels Sprouts

      Ice Cream Sundae—Choice of Toppings
      Whole Grain Breads
      Beverages

Breakfast

      Orange Juice
      Tomato, Prune & Grape Juice
      Grapefruit Half
      Diced Fruit Compote
      Pineapple Chunks

      Seven Grain Cereal

      Fried Eggs

      Hot Baked Bread Pudding—Syrup/Honey
      Hash Brown Potatoes
      Honeyed Barley
      Granola
      Grapenuts, Shredded Wheat, Bran Flakes, Raisin Bran, All Bran
      Whole Grain Breads
      Beverages

Lunch

      Lentil Soup—Whole Grain Crackers

      Salads:

           Chefs Salad
           Cottage Cheese Salad w/Pickle Slice
           Cole Slaw w/Green Pepper
           Cheese & Pineapple Salad
           Carrot & Celery Salad

Entrées:
> Spanish Mac
> Tossed Tuna Salad
> Nut-Oatmeal Casserole

Turnip Greens
Succotash

Oatmeal Nut Cookies
Assorted Fruits
Yogurt
Whole Grain Breads
Beverages

Dinner
Chicken Gumbo Soup—Whole Grain Crackers
Salad Bar
Entrées:
> Veal Cutlet w/Celery Sauce
> Meatballs w/Brown Rice
> Chiles Rellino Casserole

Buttered Whole Wheat Spaghetti
Brown Rice
Zucchini Slices
Braised Lettuce Greens

Hunters Pudding
Assorted Fruits
Whole Grain Breads
Beverages

Breakfast
Orange Juice
Tomato, Prune & Apple Juice
Banana
Fruit Cocktail
Pear Slices

Roman Meal

Scrambled Eggs

Buckwheat Pancakes—Syrup/Honey
Hash Brown Potatoes
Bulgur
Granola
Grapenuts, Shredded Wheat, Bran Flakes, Raisin Bran, All Bran
Whole Grain Breads
Beverages

Lunch
Hearty Vegetable Soup—Whole Grain Crackers

Salads:
- Combination Salad
- Cottage Cheese Salad w/Poppy Seeds Garnish
- Molded Fruit & Cheese Salad
- Orange-Banana Salad
- Cucumber in Sour Cream

Entrées:
- Hamburger Hero on Wheat Roll
- Egg & Mushroom in Cheddar Cheese Sauce over Brown Rice
- Cream Cheese-Date-Nut on Whole Grain Bread
  w/Shredded Coconut

Green Peas
Honey Glazed Beets

Molasses Cookies
Assorted Fruits
Yogurt
Whole Grain Breads
Beverages

Dinner
French Onion Soup—Whole Grain Crackers

Salad Bar

Entrées:
- Beef Stroganoff over Egg Noodles
- Baked Fillet of Flounder Almondine
- Cabbage Stuffed w/Bulgur & Cheese

Mashed Potatoes
Wheat Egg Noodles w/Poppy Seeds
Leaf Spinach
Stewed Tomatoes w/Green Pepper & Onion Cubes

Whole Fresh Fruit
Whole Grain Breads
Beverages

Breakfast
Orange Juice
Tomato, Prune & Pineapple Juice
Fresh Orange
Stewed Rhubarb
Applesauce

Millet Cooked in Milk

Poached or Soft Cooked Eggs

Peanut Butter French Toast—Syrup/Honey
Hash Brown Potatoes
Wheat Berries

Granola
Grapenuts, Shredded Wheat, Bran Flakes, Raisin Bran, All Bran
Whole Grain Breads
Beverages

Lunch

Minestrone Soup—Whole Grain Crackers

Salads:

Tossed Green Salad
Cottage Cheese Salad w/Tomato Cube
Peas and Cheese Medley
Mixed Fruit Salad
Marinated Bean Sprouts

Entrées:

Turkey Salad Sandwich
Gourmet Casserole
Sliced Avocado, Egg, Tomato & Alfalfa Sprouts
on Whole Grain Bread

Mashed Squash
Cut Broccoli

Peanut Bars
Assorted Fruits
Yogurt
Whole Grain Breads
Beverages

Dinner

Lima Bean Soup—Whole Grain Crackers

Salad Bar

Entrées:

Swiss Steak
Beef Chow Mein over Brown Rice
Carrot Loaf w/Tomato Sauce

Steamed Whole Potatoes
Brown Rice
French Cut Green Beans Sauté
Braised Celery & Onions & Chopped Parsley
Date-Nut Muffins
Banana Cream Pudding
Whole Grain Breads
Beverages

Meadowbrook Hospital

Meadowbrook is a 50-bed hospital located near New Orleans. It is devoted to caring for patients with degenerative disease conditions, and applies preventive techniques as well. In 1974 the food service began using all natural foods. Their efforts to provide high quality meals as part of an individualized patient care program have been most successful.

First Day

Breakfast
3-minute Eggs
Apple Pancakes
Blueberry Syrup
Butter
Herb Tea or Coffee
Fruit Juice

Lunch
Baked Fish (Lemon Sauce)
Carrot Coins-Honey
French Green Beans
Stuffed Prune with Cottage Cheese
Whole Wheat Bread
Butter
Lemonade

Dinner
Beef Meat Loaf
Creamed Potatoes (with skin)
Steamed Greens
Sliced Tomato Salad
Whole Wheat Bread
Butter
Fruit Punch

Second Day

Breakfast
¼ Slice Melon
Cooked Cracked Wheat
3-minute Eggs
Sausage—All Beef
Whole Wheat Biscuits
Butter
Hot Herb Tea
Coffee

Lunch
Baked Chicken in Orange Juice
Asparagus Spears
Yellow Squash
Stuffed Celery
Whole Wheat Bread
Butter
Fruit Punch

Dinner
Liver & Onions
Steamed Brown Rice
Steamed Spinach
Tossed Green Salad
Toasted Wheat Bread
Butter
Hot Herb Tea

Third Day

Breakfast
Grapefruit Sections
Cheese Omelet
Soya Muffins
Butter
Honey
Hot Herb Tea or Coffee
Fruit Juice

Lunch
Large Bowl Vegetable Soup
Grilled Cheese Sandwich
Lettuce Wedge
Iced Tea (Peppermint)

Dinner
Baked Leg of Lamb (Mint Jelly)
Baked Sweet Potato
Broccoli Spears
Tossed Green Salad (Emerald Dressing)
Hot Tea (Peppermint)

Chapter 9

Quantity Recipes

These recipes have come from many different kitchens where natural foods are being prepared for large groups of people. The recipes are from such diverse places as the Fitness House kitchen here at Rodale Press; Friends' Boarding School in Barnesville, Ohio; Pacific Union College in Angwin, California; Glaydin School in Leesburg, Virginia; Head Start of the Lehigh Valley and nutritionist Rose McDowell. All the recipes have proven successful in institutional use, and all were popular among people to whom they were served.

The recipes are grouped into soups, salads, meatless main dishes, meats, vegetables, desserts, baked goods and miscellaneous dishes.

How to Change
the Size of a Recipe

Since there are no quantity natural foods cookbooks designed for food service, setting up your institutional kitchen will probably mean adapting a lot of smaller recipes and changing ingredients in conventional quantity recipes to

215

meet your needs. Knowing how to change the size of a recipe will be essential, and here's how it's done:

Above all, remember that a recipe should not be simply doubled or tripled or halved, etc. The first step is to decide how many servings you will need. Then divide that number by the number of servings the recipe makes as written to get a "factor." Next, multiply the amount of each ingredient by the factor to get the amount you need. Convert any fractions to the nearest measure—fractions of pounds are then expressed in ounces, cups become tablespoons, gallons become cups, and so on. It is lots easier to follow a recipe that calls for one cup than a recipe that specifies ¼ quart.

Another good idea, particularly when increasing the size of a recipe, is to use a bit less seasoning than the converted recipe calls for. Seasonings don't always have to be increased as much as other ingredients, and until the new recipe becomes familiar, it is better to underseason a bit and season the cooked food to taste before serving than to have the food turn out too salty or too spicy.

When multiplying a recipe, you will probably find that the multiplied version makes proportionately more servings than the original recipe. A recipe for eight to ten servings when doubled almost invariably serves 20 rather than 16. When you change the size of a recipe, it's also wise to consider who will be eating the meal (the same recipe will serve more children than adults), the season of the year (people tend to eat more in winter than they do in summer), and what other dishes are included in the menu (if other hearty foods are being served, smaller portions will satisfy most appetites).

To clarify the procedure for adjusting recipes, we'll take the following recipe for Baked Custard, which serves 42, and compute the ingredients needed for 100 servings.

The recipe as written calls for:

milk	3 quarts
honey	¾ cup
eggs, beaten	15

salt	1½ teaspoons
vanilla	2 tablespoons

Our first step must be to find the factor.

$$100 \div 42 = 2.4 \text{ (when rounded off)}$$

Each of the ingredients is now multiplied by the factor 2.4:

	42	**100**
milk	3 quarts × 2.4 = 7.2 quarts	or 7 quarts + ⁴/₅ cup
honey	¾ cup × 2.4 = 1.8 cups	or 1⁴/₅ cups
eggs, beaten	15 × 2.4 = 36.0	or 36
salt	1½ teaspoons × 2.4 = 3.6	or 3³/₅ teaspoons
vanilla	2 tablespoons × 2.4 = 4.8	or 4⁴/₅ tablespoons

When making the expanded version for the first time, it might be a good idea to reduce slightly the amounts of honey, salt and vanilla and taste the mixture before adding the rest of the flavorings.

HAM AND BEAN SOUP

	25	**50**	**80**	**100**
ham stock	5¾ pounds	11½ pounds	19 pounds	23 pounds
chopped celery	2½ cups	5 cups	8 cups	10 cups
chopped onion	2½ cups	5 cups	8 cups	10 cups
chopped potatoes	6¼ cups	12½ cups	20 cups	25 cups
green beans	4½ pounds	9 pounds	14 pounds	18 pounds
cooked dried limas	1 cup	2 cups	3 cups	4 cups
cooked dried kidney beans	1 cup	2 cups	3 cups	4 cups
salt and pepper				

1. Prepare stock and add celery and onion.
2. Simmer about 45 minutes and add remaining vegetables.
3. Simmer about 45 minutes longer.

217

HEARTY VEGETABLE SOUP

	50
turnips cut in chunks	3 cups
carrots, chunks	3 cups
potatoes, chunks	5 cups
celery, chopped	1 bunch
onions, diced	3 pounds
cabbage, diced	1 large
elbow macaroni, uncooked	2 cups
brown rice, uncooked	1 cup
water	5 quarts
soybeans, cooked	4 cups
kidney beans, cooked	4 cups
green string beans, cooked	4 cups
tomato paste	2 cups
whole kernel corn	2 cups
soy sauce	¾ cup
garlic, minced	6 cloves
Vegemite*	6 tablespoons

1. Cook together turnips, carrots and potatoes until just slightly tender; set aside.
2. Cook together celery, onions and cabbage until slightly tender; add to other vegetables.
3. Cook macaroni and rice together in 5 quarts of water; add to vegetables.
4. Mix together remaining ingredients; add to macaroni, rice and vegetables; simmer until thoroughly heated.

*a natural, yeast-based concentrate used for flavoring purposes. Available in health food stores and the gourmet section of many supermarkets.

BEEF BARLEY SOUP

	25	**50**	**80**	**100**
beef stock	9¼ quarts	18½ quarts	30 quarts	37 quarts
barley	1¼ cups	2½ cups	3½ cups	5 cups
chopped onion	2½ cups	5 cups	8 cups	10 cups
chopped celery	2 cups	4 cups	6 cups	8 cups
chopped carrot	2½ cups	5 cups	8 cups	10 cups
salt and pepper				

1. Prepare stock.
2. Add vegetables and simmer until tender.

CABBAGE SOUP

	25	50	80	100
beef stock	¾ quart	1¾ quarts	3 quarts	4 quarts
sausage cut in ½-inch pieces	3¾ pounds	8½ pounds	12 pounds	17 pounds
chopped onion	2½ cups	5 cups	8 cups	10 cups
chopped celery	2½ cups	5 cups	8 cups	10 cups
diced carrots	2 cups	4 cups	6 cups	8 cups
coarsely shredded cabbage	2 large heads	4 large heads	6 large heads	8 large heads
diced potato	2¾ cups	5½ cups	9 cups	11 cups
salt and pepper				

1. Prepare stock using meat.
2. Add vegetables.
3. Simmer until hot and vegetables are tender.

CORN CHICKEN SOUP

	25	50	80	100
chicken stock	12½ quarts	25 quarts	40 quarts	50 quarts
chicken	2¼ chickens	4½ chickens	7 chickens	9 chickens
onions, chopped	3¼ cups	6½ cups	10 cups	13 cups
celery, chopped	2½ cups	5 cups	8 cups	10 cups
potato, chopped	3¼ cups	6½ cups	10 cups	13 cups
corn	2 bags	4 bags	5 bags	8 bags
salt and pepper				

1. Prepare stock using chicken.
2. Add onions and celery.
3. Cook for 45 minutes and add the rest of the vegetables.
4. Simmer for another 45 minutes.

JULIENNE SOUP

	25	50	80	100
beef stock	9¼ quarts	18½ quarts	30 quarts	37 quarts
chopped turnips	6¼ cups	12½ cups	20 cups	25 cups
chopped onions	6¼ cups	12½ cups	20 cups	25 cups
cut tomatoes	9¼ cups	18½ cups	30 cups	37 cups
chopped celery stalks	3 cups	6 cups	10 cups	12 cups
head cabbage	1	2	3	4
peas	3 cups	6 cups	10 cups	12 cups
chopped carrots	6¼ cups	12½ cups	20 cups	25 cups
salt and pepper				

1. Prepare beef stock.
2. Add all vegetables and simmer until vegetables are tender.

MINESTRONE SOUP

	25	50	80	100
beef stock	12½ quarts	25 quarts	40 quarts	50 quarts
dried kidney beans	1¼ cups	2½ cups	4 cups	5 cups
chopped onions	2½ cups	5 cups	8 cups	10 cups
chopped celery	2½ cups	5 cups	8 cups	10 cups
cabbage	1¼ heads	2½ heads	4 heads	5 heads
green beans	2½ cups	5 cups	8 cups	10 cups
tomatoes	3¼ cups	6½ cups	10 cups	13 cups
frozen corn	5/8 pound	1¼ pounds	2 pounds	2½ pounds
frozen limas	5/8 pound	1¼ pounds	2 pounds	2½ pounds
cooked noodles	5/8 pound	1¼ pounds	2 pounds	2½ pounds
thyme	1 teaspoon	1¾ teaspoons	1 tablespoon	1¼ tablespoons
marjoram	1 teaspoon	1¾ teaspoons	1 tablespoon	1¼ tablespoons
garlic salt	1½ teaspoons	1 tablespoon	2 tablespoons	2¼ tablespoons
salt and pepper				

1. Prepare stock using beef bones.
2. Add dried kidney beans, onions, and celery. Simmer until beans are tender.
3. Add the remaining vegetables and simmer until hot.
4. Right before serving add cooked noodles and seasoning.

LENTIL SOUP

	25	50
lentils	8 cups	2 pounds (16 cups)
cold water	2 quarts	4 quarts
beef bone	1	2
onions, diced	2 medium	4 medium
carrots, diced	2	4
celery, diced	½ cup	1 cup
potato, peeled and grated	1	2
bay leaves	2	4
salt	to taste	to taste
thyme	¼ teaspoon	¼ teaspoon
pepper (optional)	½ teaspoon	½ teaspoon
lemon juice	2 teaspoons	2 teaspoons

1. Put lentils into large pot with water. Add the beef bone, vegetables, bay leaves, salt, thyme and pepper.
2. Place over medium heat and bring gently to a boil; lower heat and simmer until vegetables are soft.
3. Remove beef bone and bay leaves. Skim off excess fat. Remove meat from bone, dice and return to soup.
4. Slowly stir in lemon juice and serve immediately.

Note: Makes a very thick soup.

SPLIT PEA SOUP

	25	50	80	100
ham stock	6¼ quarts	12½ quarts	20 quarts	25 quarts
peas	3¾ cups	8½ cups	12 cups	17 cups
bacon, small pieces	⅝ pound	1¼ pounds	2 pounds	2½ pounds
chopped celery	2 cups	4 cups	6 cups	8 cups
chopped onion	2½ cups	5 cups	8 cups	10 cups
diced carrots	3¾ cups	8½ cups	12 cups	17 cups
salt and pepper				

1. Prepare ham stock. Soak peas overnight.
2. Add all ingredients but carrots. Simmer slowly for 1½ hours and keep covered.
3. Add carrots and simmer for another ½ hour.

SPLIT PEA SOUP HUNGARIAN

	12	25	50
split peas, green or yellow	1 pound	2 pounds	4 pounds
ox tails	½ pound	1 pound	2 pounds
green pepper, finely chopped	⅛ pound	¼ pound	1 pound
onions, finely chopped	½ pound	1 pound	2 pounds
garlic, minced	1 clove	½ tablespoon	1 tablespoon
oil	1 ounce	2 ounces	4 ounces
tomatoes, canned	1 cup	2 cups	1 quart
paprika	1 tablespoon	2 tablespoons	4 tablespoons
caraway seeds	½ tablespoon	1 tablespoon	2 tablespoons
salt	to taste	to taste	to taste
stock	3 quarts	1½ gallons	3 gallons
potatoes, cubed	2 cups	1 quart	2 quarts

1. Sauté lightly ox tails, onions, green pepper and garlic in oil. Add crushed tomatoes, seasonings and stock and split peas. Bring to a boil.
2. Reduce heat and allow to simmer 2 hours or until split peas are tender.
3. Remove ox tails, cut meat from bones and return to the soup.
4. Add potato cubes a short time before serving so that they retain their shape and texture.

POTATO SOUP

	25	50	80	100
ham stock	12½ quarts	25 quarts	40 quarts	50 quarts
chopped celery	2 cups	4 cups	6 cups	8 cups
chopped onion	2½ cups	5 cups	8 cups	10 cups
diced potatoes	7½ cups	15 cups	24 cups	30 cups
mashed potatoes	4½ cups	9 cups	14 cups	18 cups
skim milk powder	2½ cups	5 cups	8 cups	10 cups
water	2½ cups	5 cups	8 cups	10 cups
salt and pepper				

1. Prepare ham stock.
2. Add vegetables.
3. Mix skim milk powder and water and add to mixture.
4. Just before serving add chopped fresh parsley.

CHEESE-POTATO SOUP

	100
milk	4 gallons
potatoes, diced	2 gallons
onions, diced	16
salt	½ cup
paprika	3 tablespoons
longhorn or mild cheddar cheese, grated	1 pound or more
parsley, chopped*	2 cups

1. Heat milk in double boiler. Add potatoes and onions and cook until tender.
2. Whip soup to partially mash potatoes.
3. Add remaining ingredients and mix thoroughly. Serve immediately, garnished with additional paprika and chopped parsley.

Note: This soup is a delicious way to use leftover potatoes. Increase the quantities of potatoes and cheese for a thicker, richer consistency.

*If using dried parsley flakes, use only ⅔ cup.

BASIC TOSSED SALAD

	100
lettuce, head-type	4 pounds
spinach, chopped or shredded	1 pound
onions, chopped or sliced	1½ cups
cucumbers, sliced	4 pounds, 12 ounces
carrots, sliced or grated	2 pounds
tomatoes, cubed or sliced	5 pounds, 12 ounces
radishes, sliced	2 pounds

Toss all ingredients together and serve with a choice of dressings. For 100 servings, about a quart of dressing will be needed; slightly more if the dressing is thick.
Salads can be varied with:

endive, romaine, escarole, watercress and
other greens when available

      green pepper pieces or rings
      celery chunks
      mushrooms, sliced or whole
      leftover cooked beans or red beets
      zucchini chunks
      cabbage, shredded
      olives
      pimiento strips
      crumbled cheese
      sesame, sunflower and pumpkin seeds
      assorted nuts (unsalted)

HAM, CHICKEN OR TURKEY SALAD

	30	60	90
meat cooked and diced	5 pounds	10 pounds	15 pounds
diced celery	½ quart	1 quart	1½ quarts
chopped hard-boiled eggs	15	30	45
cooked salad dressing	½ quart	1 quart	1½ quarts
mayonnaise	½ quart	1 quart	1½ quarts
salt and pepper			

Toss ingredients together lightly, blending the salad dressing and mayonnaise. Chill.

EGG SALAD

	25	50	75	100
hard-boiled eggs	33	65	98	130
mayonnaise	1 cup	2 cups	3 cups	4 cups
grated onion	1 small	2 small	3 small	4 small
chopped celery	1½ cups	3 cups	4½ cups	6 cups

Chop the eggs and blend together. Chill.

TUNA SALAD

Portion: one ice cream scoop per sandwich

	30 sandwiches	50 sandwiches
celery, chopped	3 stalks	5 stalks
light tuna	3 (12-ounce) cans	5 (12-ounce) cans
eggs, hard cooked, chopped	18	30
onion, chopped	1 medium	1½ onions
carrots, chopped	½ cup	¾ cup
mayonnaise	¾ cup	1¼ cups

Mix all ingredients together.
If eggs are omitted, add more tuna fish.

CURRIED CHICKEN SALAD

	25
brown rice, cooked	4 cups
lemon juice	¼ cup
salad oil	½ cup
curry powder	1 tablespoon
chicken or turkey, cooked and cubed	8 cups
celery, chopped	4 cups
mayonnaise	2 cups
seasoning salt	to taste

1. Combine first four ingredients and chill several hours.
2. Then add remaining ingredients and toss lightly.
3. Serve on lettuce leaves, garnished with green pepper rings and pimientos. Can also be served as salad plate meal, along with tomatoes, hard-boiled eggs, raw and/or cooked vegetables.

PINEAPPLE CHICKEN SALAD

	25
mayonnaise	4 cups
lime juice	1 cup
curry powder	1 tablespoon
seasoning salt	to taste
chicken or turkey, cooked and diced	2 quarts
pineapple chunks, fresh or canned in juice	1 quart
celery, diagonally sliced	1 quart
almonds, lightly toasted	2 cups

225

1. Combine first four ingredients in large bowl and mix well.
2. Stir in remaining ingredients, and allow salad to marinate at least 1 hour in refrigerator before serving.
3. Serve on crisp salad greens, as a main course or as salad with a vegetable plate.

COMPLETE PROTEIN MEATLESS CASSEROLES

50 servings

16 cups (4 quarts) cooked	8 cups (2 quarts) cooked	sauce:16 cups (4 quarts) leftover soup or sauce	vegetables to make 12 cups	approx. 2 cups topping
brown rice	soybeans	cream of tomato soup or tomato sauce	sautéed celery and green onions	wheat germ
whole wheat macaroni	lima beans	cream of potato soup	mushrooms and bamboo shoots	slivered almonds
corn	peas	cream of mushroom soup or mushroom sauce	green pepper and garlic	whole wheat bread crumbs
whole wheat spaghetti	kidney beans	cream of celery soup	cooked green beans	sesame seeds
bulgur	black beans	cheese sauce	cooked carrots	brewer's yeast
whole wheat noodles	chick-peas	cream of pea soup or pea puree	sautéed onion and pimiento	sunflower seeds

1. Choose one ingredient from each of the five columns (ingredients in the first two columns are complementary proteins).
2. Mix together ingredients from first four columns.
3. Pour into large greased casserole dish or two tray pans. Bake for 30 minutes at 375° F.
4. Top with one choice from column five and bake 15 minutes longer at 325°F.
5. Each person may add salt to taste when served. Serve with bread and a salad.

Note: Casserole suggestions come from Anna Gordon, Nutrition Educator, Community Food and Nutrition Program, Chester County, Pa.

CASHEW CASSEROLE

2 - #20 scoops per serving

	25	50
onions, chopped	1 pound 5 ounces	2 pounds 10 ounces
celery, chopped	1 pound 1 ounce	2 pounds 2 ounces
mushrooms, chopped	4 cups	8 cups
butter	½ cup	1 cup
flour	½ cup	1 cup
milk	5 cups	2½ quarts
water	4 cups	2 quarts
cornstarch	2 tablespoons	4 tablespoons
raw cashews, broken	1 pound 1 ounce	2 pounds 2 ounces
Chinese noodles (crisp)	1 pound 9 ounces	2 pounds
chicken seasoning	2 tablespoons	4 tablespoons

1. Simmer chopped onions, celery and mushrooms in butter.
2. Add flour, then milk, and cook until thickened.
3. Add water and cornstarch, roasted cashews, all but ¼ pound of noodles and chicken seasoning.
4. Place in warming pan and top with remaining noodles.
5. Bake at 325°F. for 45 minutes.

CHEDDAR CHEESE PIE

Crust:	**1 pie (serves 6)**
whole wheat pastry flour	2 cups
cheddar cheese, grated	½ cup
salt	½ teaspoon
water	⅔ to 1 cup

Filling:	
cheddar cheese, grated	1 cup
cottage cheese	⅓ cup
corn, canned or frozen	1 cup
peas, cooked	1 cup
salt	½ teaspoon
paprika	½ teaspoon
whole wheat flour	1 tablespoon

Topping:	
wheat germ	½ to 1 cup

1. Set oven for 350°F.
2. Mix crust ingredients. Knead well and roll out. Put into greased pie plate.
3. Combine filling ingredients and fill pie shell.
4. Top with wheat germ.
5. Bake 30 minutes.

CHEESE MUSHROOM PIE

	25	**50**
butter, melted	3 tablespoons	6 tablespoons
mushrooms, diced	1 pound, 2½ ounces	2 pounds 5 ounces
onions, chopped	½ pound	1 pound
flour	2½ ounces	5 ounces
cheddar cheese	2 pounds	4 pounds
evaporated milk (check label)	2 pounds	4 pounds
eggs	17	34
salt	1 tablespoon	2 tablespoons

1. Braise mushrooms and onions in butter.
2. Add flour.
3. Add cheese, milk, eggs, salt.
4. Pour into unbaked pie shells (1 quart per 9-inch pie shell).
5. Bake 15 minutes at 400°F., reduce to 300° and bake for 30 minutes or until done.

EGGPLANT PARMESAN

	25	50
eggplant, medium, sliced thick (½ inch)	5	10
eggs, well beaten	10	20
wheat germ	7 cups	3½ quarts
whole wheat flour	¾ cup	1½ cups
oil for sautéing		
mozzarella, Swiss or provolone cheese, sliced thin	1¾ pounds	3½ pounds
Italian type tomato sauce (with oregano, thyme, basil, garlic, salt and pepper)	1 gallon	2 gallons
Parmesan cheese, grated (Sardo Italian cheese, grated)	2½ cups	5 cups

1. Dip eggplant in flour, then egg, then in wheat germ and flour mixture.
2. Sauté in oil till brown on both sides.
3. Arrange in baking pans. Add layer of mozzarella, then of tomato sauce, sprinkle Parmesan on top.
4. If pan permits, repeat layers.
5. Bake 20 minutes at 400°F.

MACARONI AND CHEESE

	10	45	90
onions, halved and thinly sliced	½ cup	2 cups	4 cups
green peppers, diced	¼ cup	1 cup	2 cups
celery, diced	¼ cup	1 cup	2 cups
tomatoes, drained	1½ cups	6 cups	#10 can
tomato sauce	½ cup	13 ounces	2 (13-ounce) cans
macaroni, whole wheat	1 pound	2½ pounds	5 pounds
boiling water			
salt	1 teaspoon	1½ tablespoons	3 tablespoons
butter	1 tablespoon	6 tablespoons	¾ pound
whole wheat flour	¼ cup	1¼ cups	2½ cups
salt	½ teaspoon	1 tablespoon	2 tablespoons
hot milk	2 cups	3½ quarts	7 quarts
garlic salt	½ teaspoon	1 tablespoon	2 tablespoons
dry mustard	1 teaspoon	1⅓ tablespoons	2⅔ tablespoons
cheese, shredded (colby & cheddar)	1 pound	3 pounds 6 oz.	7 pounds

1. Combine first five ingredients and cook until vegetables are tender.
2. Cook macaroni in boiling salted water. Drain.
3. Melt butter; blend flour and salt. Stir in milk. Cook and stir constantly until thickened.
4. Add seasonings and half of cheese to sauce, stir until blended.
5. Mix macaroni, cheese mixture and tomato mixture.
6. In greased baking pans layer noodle mixture, then some grated cheese. Keep layering, ending with cheese.
7. Bake at 300°F. for 50 minutes or until brown.

PECAN NUT PATTIES

2 patties per serving

	25	50
pecans, coarsely chopped	⅞ pound	1¾ pounds
almonds, finely ground	7 ounces	14 ounces
bread crumbs, fine	6 ounces	12 ounces
onions, finely chopped	1 pound	2 pounds
cheddar cheese, shredded	½ pound	1 pound
butter, melted	2¾ ounces	5½ ounces
Vegex	2¼ ounces	4½ ounces
eggs	15	30
milk	½ cup	1 cup

1. Combine all ingredients and mix thoroughly.
2. Form patties and drop on greased pan on medium heat. *Turn once.*
3. Serve with brown gravy or parsleyed sauce, or a sauce of your choice.

SPINACH AND RICE CASSEROLE

	15	30	45
cooked brown rice	4 cups	8 cups	12 cups
grated cheddar cheese	2 cups	4 cups	6 cups
parsley, chopped	8 tablespoons	1 cup	1½ cups

eggs, beaten	8	16	24
salt	2 teaspoons	4 teaspoons	2 tablespoons
fresh spinach, chopped	2 pounds	4 pounds	6 pounds
oil	2 tablespoons	4 tablespoons	6 tablespoons
wheat germ	8 tablespoons	1 cup	1½ cups

1. Preheat oven to 350°F.
2. Combine the cooked rice and cheese.
3. Add parsley, eggs, and salt.
4. Stir in the raw spinach and pour into an oiled casserole or warming pan.
5. Top with wheat germ which has been mixed with the oil.
6. Bake in preheated oven for 35 minutes.

Variation: Use beet greens instead of spinach.

TOFU CROQUETTES

	12	**25**	**50**
tofu	2¼ pounds	4⅜ pounds	8¾ pounds
eggs, beaten	4	9	19
cornstarch	¼ cup	¼ pound (½ cup)	½ pound (1 cup)
carrots, grated	½ pound	1 pound	2 pounds
salt	2 teaspoons	⅝ ounces	1¼ ounces
onions, grated fine	1 medium	¼ pound	½ pound
soy sauce	1 tablespoon	1¼ tablespoons	2½ tablespoons
cracker crumbs			

1. Drain the tofu for one hour or until most of water is drained out. Mash with a paddle in large mixing bowl.
2. Add eggs, cornstarch, carrots, salt, onions and soy sauce. If mixture is too thin for frying, add cracker crumbs.
3. Drop into deep fat using No. 40 dipper. Deep fat fry, drain and serve hot. This is a thin mixture—not thick like meatballs. Some cracker crumbs may be used. Do not use bread crumbs. Try frying before adding too much of anything. Test and taste.

TWO-BEAN CASSEROLE

	12	25	50
lima beans, dry	1 cup	1½ cups	3 cups
kidney beans, dry	1 cup	1½ cups	3 cups
boiling water	1½ quarts	2¼ quarts	4½ quarts
butter	3 tablespoons	¼ cup	½ cup
celery, minced	¼ cup	½ cup	1 cup
onion, minced	3 tablespoons	¼ cup	½ cup
flour	2 tablespoons	3 tablespoons	6 tablespoons
sugar (or honey)	2 teaspoons	3 teaspoons	2 tablespoons
basil	½ teaspoon	¾ teaspoon	1 tablespoon
salt	½ teaspoon	¾ teaspoon	1½ teaspoons
pepper	dash	dash	¼ teaspoon
milk	1 cup	1½ cups	3 cups
tomato, peeled and sliced	1 cup	1½ cups	4 cups
bread or cracker crumbs	¼ cup	⅓ cup	⅔ cup

1. The day before serving, sort and wash the beans.
2. Add beans to boiling water.
3. Boil 2 minutes. Remove from heat. Cover and let soak 1 hour or if more convenient, use cold water and let beans soak overnight in refrigerator.
4. Throw away soaking water. Add more water to cover beans and cook about 1½ hours until tender. Add more water if necessary to keep beans moist during cooking.
5. Grease a casserole. In medium heat in hot butter, cook celery and onion until tender, about 5 minutes. Stir in flour, sugar or honey, basil, salt and pepper until blended. Gradually stir in milk and cook, stirring constantly until mixture is thickened.
6. In casserole, gently mix drained lima and kidney beans with mixture. Top with tomato slices, then sprinkle with bread or cracker crumbs.
7. Bake for 30 minutes at 350°F. until bubbly. Serve with meatballs (recipe follows).

Note: Servings are meant for children, and will serve roughly half as many adults.

MEATBALLS

	12	25	50
ground chuck	1 pound	2 pounds	4 pounds
bread crumbs	2 tablespoons	4 tablespoons	½ cup
egg, unbeaten	1	2	4
onion, chopped	¼ cup	½ cup	1 cup
salt	½ teaspoon	1 teaspoon	2 teaspoons
pepper	dash	dash	⅛ teaspoon
oil	¼ cup	½ cup	1 cup

1. Combine all ingredients. Form into tiny meatballs.
2. Put oil in skillet and brown meatballs. Meatballs may also be baked in oven.
3. Add to Two-Bean Casserole.

BEEF BAR BQ

	20	40	80
ground beef	4 pounds	8 pounds	16 pounds
onion	2 cups	4 cups	8 cups
green pepper, chopped	½ cup	1 cup	2 cups
tomatoes (blend in blender)	4 cups	8 cups	16 cups
ketchup	1 cup	2 cups	4 cups
vinegar	¼ cup	½ cup	1 cup
honey	¼ cup	¼ cup	½ cup
tamari or Worcestershire sauce	2 tablespoons	¼ cup	½ cup
salt	4 teaspoons	8 teaspoons	16 teaspoons
pepper	1 teaspoon	2 teaspoons	4 teaspoons

1. Brown ground beef, onion, and pepper in oil.
2. Add remaining ingredients and simmer.
3. Rolled oats can be added if necessary to soak up moisture and thicken mixture.

233

CHILI CON CARNE

	20	30	50
ground beef	2 pounds	3 pounds	5 pounds
onion, chopped	2	3	5
celery, chopped	2 cups	3 cups	5 cups
green pepper, chopped	1 cup	1½ cups	2½ cups
garlic, minced	2 cloves	3 cloves	5 cloves
oil	3 tablespoons	3 tablespoons	6 tablespoons
tomatoes, fresh or canned	6 cups	9 cups	15 cups
cumin, ground	4 teaspoons	6 teaspoons	10 teaspoons (3T + 1t)
chili powder	4 teaspoons	6 teaspoons	10 teaspoons (3T + 1t)
salt	2 teaspoons	3 teaspoons	5 teaspoons
kidney beans, cooked	10 cups	15 cups	25 cups (8C dry = 20C cooked

1. Day before, cook kidney beans. Soak beans in water and remove beans that float. After soaking for 2 hours the beans can be drained and frozen. In the morning of the next day, remove beans from freezer and add water to cover in large pot. Cook until tender, at least 1 hour. Drain beans, then save water.

2. In heavy skillet, brown ground beef, onion, celery, green pepper and garlic in oil.

3. Stir in tomatoes. Add seasonings. Divide the ingredients into pans. Each pan will hold 4 cups of meat (or a pound of meat), 5 cups of beans, 3 cups tomatoes, 1 cup vegetables, 2 teaspoons chili powder, 2 teaspoons cumin and salt.

4. Cover warming pans with aluminum foil and bake in oven at 350°F. until ready to serve.

MEAT LOAF WITH OATMEAL

	18	40	46-48
lean ground beef (chuck or round)	6 pounds	10 pounds	12 pounds
wheat germ	1 cup	2 cups	2⅓ cups
oatmeal	1½ cups	3 cups	3½ cups
parsley, chopped	6 tablespoons	½ cup	⅝ cup
pepper	1½ teaspoons	3 teaspoons	3½ teaspoons
salt	2 teaspoons	2 teaspoons	1 tablespoon
onion, chopped	1½ cups	3 cups	3½ cups
oil	¼ cup	¼ cup	⅜ cup

eggs, lightly beaten	6	12	14
skim milk powder	¾ cup	1½ cups	1¾ cups
water	1½ cups	3 cups	3½ cups
tomato juice	1½ cups	3 cups	3½ cups

1. Preheat oven to 350°F. In a large mixing bowl, combine ground beef, wheat germ, oatmeal, chopped parsley, pepper and salt; set aside.
2. Sauté onion in oil until tender but not brown; add to meat mixture.
3. Beat eggs lightly. Combine skim milk powder and water, using a wire whisk, and add to eggs. Blend together and add to meat mixture; then add tomato juice. Mix thoroughly.
4. Oil a 9 x 5 x 3 pan. Turn meat mixture into pan, packing down well. Allow to rest 10-15 minutes in refrigerator.
5. Run spatula around edge of meat loaf to loosen. Carefully turn out into a lightly oiled shallow baking pan, keeping original shape as much as possible. Brush surface with oil.
6. Place meat loaf on middle rack of preheated oven and bake for 1 hour and 15 minutes. Remove from oven when nicely browned and allow to rest 10 minutes before serving.
7. Serve with ketchup.

BRAISED LIVER

	15	30	45
liver	2⅔ pounds	5½ pounds	8 pounds
flour	3 tablespoons	⅓ cup	½ cup
onion, sliced	2	4	6
oil	3 tablespoons	⅓ cup	½ cup

1. Remove connective tissue from liver and cut in small pieces. Dredge with flour to which salt has been added.
2. Brown with onions in oil.
3. Place in oiled baking dishes or pan. Cover and hold in moderately low oven (325°F.) until serving time.

OVEN FRIED CHICKEN

1. Allow ¼ chicken per serving. Wash, dry and remove any visible fat. Remove skin if so directed by physician or patient.
2. Brush chicken lightly with oil; then dip in flour mixture.
   Flour mixture: For each 1 cup whole wheat flour used, mix in 1½ teaspoons seasoning salt.
3. Arrange chicken on baking dish and bake at 325°F. until tender.

Note: Any type of flour may be used, such as soya, rye, rice, oat or wheat. Or use a mixture.

PARMESAN FRIED CHICKEN

Follow directions for Oven Fried Chicken except substitute ½ cup Parmesan cheese (grated) for ½ cup flour.

Note: For patients on a low carbohydrate diet, all the flour may be replaced with Parmesan cheese. To simplify the procedure, brush the chicken lightly with oil and sprinkle the Parmesan cheese over the chicken. Or omit the oil and sprinkle the Parmesan cheese over the chicken.

Dry Italian herbs or poultry seasoning sprinkled lightly on the chicken before cooking makes an interesting yet simple dish.

BAKED FISH

	25	50
frozen fish fillets	4½ pounds	9 pounds
skim milk (liquid)	1 cup	2 cups
butter	¼ pound	½ pound
paprika	dash	dash

1. Place frozen fish fillets in oiled baking pans. Cover the fish with milk. More milk can be used as necessary. Dot with butter. Sprinkle with paprika.

2. Bake in 350°F. oven until fish is flaky and white, approximately 20 to 30 minutes.

Note: Portions are meant for children, and will serve roughly half as many adults.

BASIC VEGETABLE GLAZE

	25
butter	¾ cup
honey	¾ cup
orange rind, grated	2 tablespoons
seasoning salt, optional	2 tablespoons

1. Heat ingredients together in saucepan until hot.
2. Pour over vegetables and toss gently until coated. Serve hot. Serve with beets, carrots, parsnips or sweet potatoes.

TANGY CONFETTI DIP FOR VEGETABLES

	about 1½-2 pints
yogurt	2 cups
mayonnaise	1½ cups
chopped chives	¼ cup
finely minced onion	¼ cup
chopped green pepper	¼ cup
chopped fresh parsley	¼ cup
chopped pimiento	¼ cup
powdered kelp or salt	1½ teaspoons
paprika	½ teaspoon
cayenne	⅛ teaspoon

1. Mix yogurt and mayonnaise in medium-sized bowl.
2. Add remaining ingredients and blend together thoroughly. Adjust seasoning if necessary.
3. Cover and refrigerate several hours or overnight to blend flavors.
4. Serve with assorted raw, fresh vegetables and whole grain crackers.

STEAMED CARROTS AND POTATOES

	12	26	40
potatoes, pared and cubed	2½ pounds	5 pounds	8 pounds
carrots, sliced in circles	1 pound	4 pounds	4½ pounds

1. Mix carrots and potatoes together in pot.
2. Add two inches of water and bring to a boil.
3. Cover pot and steam until tender, approximately 20 minutes.

BUTTERED CARROTS AND CELERY

	25
carrots, fresh or frozen	4 pounds
celery	4 pounds
butter	¾ cup
marjoram leaves	2 teaspoons
seasoning salt	2 teaspoons
parsley, minced	

1. Clean vegetables well; cut diagonally.
2. Steam carrots and celery until just tender.
3. Add seasoning and mix well. Serve sprinkled with parsley.

PEAS AND CELERY

	25
celery, diced	2 bunches
green peas, shelled or frozen	2½ pounds
water	1 cup
seasoning salt	2 teaspoons

1. Steam celery until slightly tender but still crisp.

2. Add peas and steam until tender; season to taste.

Variations: Add chopped, sautéed mushrooms and/or chopped pimiento for flavor and color.

MUSHROOMS AND RICE

	25
brown rice, raw	4 cups
water	2 quarts
vegetable bouillon cubes	8
(or use broth instead of water)	
oil	½ cup
fresh mushrooms, sliced or chopped	1½ pounds
seasoning salt	
soy sauce, optional	

1. Cook rice in liquid.
2. When rice is done, sauté mushrooms in oil.
3. Add rice to the mushrooms and stir gently until mixed.
4. Season with seasoning salt and soy sauce.

ORANGE-BUTTERED PARSNIPS

	25
parsnips, medium size	30
butter	½ cup
honey (optional)	½ cup
orange peel, grated	1 tablespoon
orange juice	1 cup

1. Wash and scrub parsnips; steam until tender; cut in sticks (as carrots). Discard center core if woody.
2. Melt butter in saucepan; blend in remaining ingredients. Heat until hot.
3. Add parsnips and simmer until parsnips are hot, stirring occasionally to coat each piece with mixture. Serve hot.

239

SPANISH RICE

	12	25	50
oil	6 tablespoons	½ cup	¾ cup
onion, chopped	2 cups	4 cups	8 cups
green pepper	1 cup	2 cups	4 cups
tomatoes	2 pounds	4 pounds 3 ounces	8 pounds 6 ounces
tomato sauce	1 pound	2 pounds	4 pounds
water	1 cup	2 cups	4 cups
salt	2 teaspoons	4 teaspoons	8 teaspoons
rice, uncooked	2⅔ cups	5⅓ cups	10⅔ cups

1. Sauté onion and pepper in oil until tender, about 5 minutes.
2. Cut up tomatoes. Add tomatoes and liquid, tomato sauce, water and salt. Heat to boiling.
3. Remove from heat and stir in rice, pour into cassrole.
4. Cover casserole and bake in a moderate oven 35 minutes or until rice is tender.

BROILED TOMATOES

sliced tomatoes — allow 2 to 3 slices per serving
(about a dozen medium
tomatoes for 25 people)

Muenster, brick or other cheese, grated

1. Place tomato slices on baking sheet. Sprinkle with Italian seasoning and spread small amount of mayonnaise on each slice.
2. Sprinkle with grated cheese.
3. Broil in hot oven for about 3 minutes, or until cheese melts. Serve hot.

SCALLOPED TOMATOES

	15	30
tomatoes, cored	2 pounds	4 pounds
green peppers, chopped	¼ cup	½ cup
celery and tops, chopped	¼ cup	½ cup

onions, chopped	¼ cup	½ cup
salt	½ teaspoon	1 teaspoon
pepper	dash	¼ teaspoon
basil	dash	¼ teaspoon
parsley	dash	¼ teaspoon
cornstarch	1 tablespoon	2 tablespoons

1. Chop tomatoes and put in blender for a few seconds. Place in baking pan.
2. Sauté green peppers, celery and onions in oil. Add to tomatoes.
3. Add spices and cornstarch.
4. Toasted croutons can be placed on top.
5. Bake in oven at 300°F. for 30 minutes.

FRESH FRUIT CUP

	15	30	45
oranges, large, juicy	3	6	9
bananas	1⅓ pounds	2⅔ pounds	4 pounds
apples, whole, cored	1⅓ pounds	2⅔ pounds	4 pounds
raisins	¼ cup	½ cup	¾ cup

1. Peel oranges and cut into chunks. Cut over bowl to save juice.
2. Peel and slice bananas; add to oranges.
3. Cut unpeeled apples into chunks and add, along with raisins, to other fruit.
4. Mix well and chill in refrigerator 30 minutes to blend flavors.

SUNSHINE DESSERT

	25
pineapple, sliced, fresh	1
oranges, sliced	6
coconut, shredded	

Arrange sliced pineapple and sliced oranges on a platter. Sprinkle with coconut.

BAKED CUSTARD

42

milk	3 quarts
honey	¾ cup
eggs, beaten	15
salt	1½ teaspoons
vanilla	2 tablespoons

1. Preheat oven to 325°F.
2. Heat milk until hot and add honey. Cool to lukewarm.
3. Mix eggs and seasonings. Add to cooled milk mixture and mix well.
4. Pour into oiled custard cups; set cups in pan of hot water.
5. Bake at 325°F. for 40 minutes or until firm. Makes 42 custard cups.

NO-KNEAD WHOLE WHEAT BREAD

4 loaves

whole wheat flour	15 cups
dry yeast	4 tablespoons
lukewarm water	2 cups
honey	2 tablespoons
molasses	½ cup
warm water	2 cups
salt	4 tablespoons
warm water	4 cups

1. Place whole wheat flour in large bowl and set it in a very low oven for about 20 minutes, to warm flour and bowl. Set oven at lowest temperature.
2. Dissolve yeast in lukewarm water and add honey.
3. Mix molasses with warm water.
4. Combine yeast mixture with molasses mixture and add with salt to warmed flour. Add enough water to make a sticky dough.
5. Oil two large loaf pans, put mixture directly into pans. No kneading involved. Let rise 1 hour. Meanwhile preheat oven to 400°F.
6. Bake for about 50 minutes or until crust is brown. Turn off

the oven. Remove loaves from pans and leave them on oven rack for about 15 minutes to get crustier. Cool before slicing.

Variation: Substitute 7½ cups triticale flour for 7½ cups of the wheat flour if desired.

BANANA BREAD

	8 loaves
bananas, ripe	16-18 (about 8 cups)
eggs	8
honey	3½ cups
oil	2 cups
whole wheat flour	14 cups
salt	2⅓ tablespoons
baking soda	3⅓ tablespoons

1. Preheat oven to 325°F.
2. Sift together flour, salt and baking soda; set aside.
3. Mash bananas well with fork. Beat in wet ingredients. Then add dry ingredients and beat well.
4. Pour into oiled and floured loaf pans (8½ x 4½ x 2½ inches).
5. Bake 1 hour in preheated oven.

FITNESS HOUSE CAROB BROWNIES

	16 squares	**32 squares**	**48 squares**
carob powder	1 cup	2 cups	3 cups
oil	⅔ cup	1⅓ cups	2 cups
honey	½ cup	1 cup	1½ cups
eggs	4	8	13
peanut flour	1 cup	2 cups	3 cups
rye or whole wheat flour	5 table-spoons	½ cup + 2 tablespoons	¾ cup + 3 tablespoons
walnuts, chopped	1 cup	2 cups	2 cups
vanilla	2 teaspoons (9 x 9 pan)	4 teaspoons (9 x 13 pan)	2 tablespoons (1-9 x 9 and 1-9 x 13 pan)

1. Preheat oven to 325°F.
2. Oil a pan.

3. In a small bowl, combine carob powder, oil and honey.

4. In a large bowl, beat eggs until light. Beat in carob mixture.

5. Stir in peanut flour, rye flour and mix well. Add nuts and vanilla.

6. Spread batter evenly in the prepared pan. Bake 30 minutes or just until surface is firm to the touch.

7. Remove from oven and cool about 10 minutes. Cut into squares.

BLUEBERRY BUCKLE

	24-25
honey	1½ cups
eggs	3
oil	¾ cup
milk	1½ cups
whole wheat flour	6 cups
baking powder	2 tablespoons
salt	1 tablespoon
blueberries	6 cups

1. Preheat oven to 375°F.

2. Mix honey, eggs and oil. Add milk and beat well.

3. Sift together flour, baking powder and salt and add to liquid mixture, stirring until thoroughly mixed. Carefully blend in the blueberries.

4. Spread batter in greased and floured tray pan. Sprinkle with streusel topping.

   Streusel topping: 1½ cups brown sugar, ½ cup flour, 2 tablespoons cinnamon, ½ cup softened butter. Mix all ingredients together.

5. Bake at 375°F. for 45 to 60 minutes.

FRUIT COFFEE CAKE

	24
whole wheat flour	4½ cups
salt	1½ teaspoons
baking powder	2 tablespoons

eggs	3
honey	1⅓ cups
oil	½ cup
milk	1½ cups

1. Preheat oven to 350°F.
2. Sift together flour, salt and baking powder.
3. Beat eggs and add honey, oil and milk. Blend thoroughly, and add to flour mixture, stirring just enough to moisten flour.
4. Pour into oiled pan. Spread with fruit topping, then cover all with honey spread.

   Fruit Topping: Use fresh or canned and drained fruit such as cherries, berries, crushed pineapple or chopped apples. Press fruit into batter.

   Honey Spread: Mix together 1 cup whole wheat flour, 1 cup softened butter and 1 cup honey. Spread over fruit.
5. Bake at 350°F. approximately 35 minutes.

HONEY ORANGE CAKE

	24
oil or butter	1½ cups
honey	2 cups
eggs	6
whole wheat flour	6 cups
baking powder	2 tablespoons
salt	1 teaspoon
orange peel, finely grated	2 tablespoons
orange juice	¾ cup

1. Preheat oven to 350°F.
2. Blend oil and honey, and beat in eggs.
3. Sift dry ingredients and add orange peel.
4. Add alternately dry ingredients and orange juice to egg mixture, beginning and ending with additions of dry ingredients.
5. Spread in well-buttered pan. Bake at 350°F. until cake tests done. Serve plain, iced or with fruit sauce.

WALNUT HONEY CAKE

	25
whole wheat flour	7 cups
baking soda	1½ tablespoons
salt	1 tablespoon
cinnamon	1½ teaspoons
cloves, ground	1 teaspoon
oil or softened butter	2 cups
honey	2 cups
eggs	3
walnuts, chopped	1½ cups
hot water	3 cups

1. Preheat oven to 325°F.
2. Mix flour, baking soda, salt and spices together. Set aside.
3. Cream oil or butter with honey. Add eggs and blend well.
4. Stir in dry ingredients until well mixed, then add nuts.
5. Quickly and thoroughly stir in the hot water. Bake at 325°F. until cake tests done.
6. While cake is baking, prepare topping: Blend ⅓ cup butter, ⅔ cup honey and 1 cup chopped walnuts (optional). Set aside until cake is baked. Then spread evenly over hot cake, and broil the cake 8 inches from the heat, until topping is bubbly and lightly browned. Serve warm or cold with whipped cream or applesauce.

BETTER PEANUT BUTTER

Peanut butter is one nutritious and popular food available under the government commodities program. Unfortunately, it tends to be dry and certainly isn't as tasty as the homemade kind. Here's a way to make peanut butter taste better, boost its nutritional value and make it go twice as far:

	6 #10 cans
peanut butter	3 #10 cans
sesame seeds	1 quart
wheat germ	2 cups
dry milk	2 cups

honey	1 cup
brewer's yeast	⅔ cup

Mix ingredients well, using heavy-duty mixer or hand-powered kneading machine. Store in a cool, dry place.

YOGURT

	50
water	2½ quarts
powdered milk	2½ quarts
whole milk	2½ quarts
yogurt (for starter)	2 pints

1. Mix all ingredients in large bowl or other container.
2. Cover and place near pilot light or other warm place overnight.
3. Refrigerate until ready to serve.

SHIRRED EGGS

	24
eggs	24
milk or cream	1½ cups
salt and pepper	
cheese, grated (optional)	

1. Preheat oven to 350°F.
2. Place each egg in individual buttered custard cup.
3. Pour 1 tablespoon milk or cream over each egg. Season with salt and pepper. Sprinkle with grated cheese if desired.
4. Bake in moderate oven 6 to 10 minutes, or until just firm.

POACHED EGGS

Fill a shallow, heavy pan ⅔ full of boiling water. Break each egg into a saucer and gently slip it into the water. Do not allow water to boil while eggs are cooking. Let stand for about 5 minutes, then carefully remove eggs with slotted spoon.

SOFT-BOILED EGGS

Place eggs in a pan with enough water to cover. Bring slowly to a boil, then reduce heat and simmer for 3 minutes. Eggs that are taken directly from the refrigerator require longer cooking.

Appendix

Resources For Additional Information

Natural Snack Foods
FLAVOR TREE FOODS, INC.
2645 N. Rose St.
Franklin Park, IL 60131

This company markets a line of delicious all-natural snack foods that are suitable for both over-the-counter and vending machine sales. Available products include Cheddar Chips, French Onion Crisps, Nut and Snack Mix, Sesame Sticks, Sunflower Nuts and Sesames, Sesame Buds, Caro-Sel Raisins and Caro-Sel Raisins and Nuts.

No artificial ingredients are used in these products. Most are made with unbleached flour. Vegetable oil is used instead of hard shortenings (which contain saturated fats); brown sugar is used instead of white sugar.

The company is most willing to supply nutritional and ingredient information on their products. (Requests to several leading purveyors of conventional vending machine products turned up lots of promotional material but not a bit of nutritional information.)

The following firms also market individually packaged, all-natural snack foods, which are suited to over-the-counter sales and possibly vending machines as well. These products are often found in health food stores.

BARBARA'S BAKERY, INC.
So. San Francisco, CA 94080

This firm specializes in baked goods; they market several kinds of all-natural cookies and cupcakes, a type of fudge, a sesame crunch bar and other snack products.

HOFFMAN PRODUCTS
York, PA 17405

Well-known for their high-protein, high-energy candy bars, made from such foods as peanut butter, carob, honey and tiger's milk.

CARACOA, a line of carob products distributed by
El Molino Mills
Division of ACG Co.
City of Industry, CA 91746

Snack items include various kinds of carob candy bars and carob-coated raisins.

COUNTRY NATURAL FOODS, INC.
Milford, NJ 08848

PLUS PRODUCTS
Irvine, CA 92705

One possible way to find out about available snack products is to contact a local health food store for information.

Additive-Free Frozen Soups

BILALIAN PRODUCTS, INC.
8135 N. Monticello
Skokie, IL 60076

This company markets a line of frozen soups intended for institutional use. The soups contain no artificial flavors, colors or preservatives; available varieties include navy bean, green split pea and vegetarian vegetable.

Manufacturers of Juice Machines

ROTO-RICO CO.
490 N. Raleigh Ave.
El Cajon, CA 92020
(714) 442-2202

WESTERN ROTO JUICER
15164 Golden West Circle
Westminster, CA 92683

Recommended Books and Publications

Creative Food Experiences for Children, by Mary T. Goodwin, Public Health Nutritionist. 191 pages. $4.00 per copy. $2.00 per copy on orders of 10 or more. Available from Center for Science in the Public Interest, 1757 S St., NW, Washington, DC 20009.

A guide to practical, inventive ways to acquaint children with different foods and introduce them to basic nutritional principles. Full of activities and recipes that make it fun to learn about food. Of value to parents, teachers and cooks who feed children.

Nutrition Kit for the Community, by Mary T. Goodwin, Public Health Nutritionist. $3.00 per kit. Available from Montgomery County Health Department, 611 Rockville Pike, Rockville, MD 20852. Make check or money order payable to Montgomery County Government.

A valuable group of materials assembled to raise public consciousness as to the overall state of our food supply. Contains information on school food, vending, snacks, complementary proteins, junk foods and basic nutritional principles. Also includes suggested nutrition projects, a listing of available films and publications and a book of shopping tips, nutrition information and recipes to help you eat better for less money. Of value to parents, teachers, administrators and anyone involved in feeding others. Includes "How To Improve Your School Lunch Program," reprinted in part in chapter 2.

If We Had Ham, We Could Have Ham and Eggs...If We Had Eggs, A Study of the National School Breakfast Program, prepared by the Food Research and Action Center. 145 pages. Available from the Food Research and Action Center, 25 West 43rd St., New York, NY 10036.

A thorough report on the successes and failures of the Breakfast Program, with suggestions for improvements. Essential for administrators and managers involved in the program.

FRAC's Guide to the National School Breakfast Program, prepared by the Food Research and Action Center. 20 pages.

A regularly updated step-by-step guide to bringing the Breakfast Program into your school.

Food for People Not for Profit, edited by Catherine Lerza and Michael Jacobson. 466 pages. 1975. Ballantine Books, New York.

For anyone who doesn't understand what's wrong with our food. Discusses food production, the food industry, food costs, nutrition, the world food situation and many ideas for alternative actions that can be taken.

Diet for a Small Planet, by Frances Moore Lappé. 411 pages. Revised edition 1975. Ballantine Books, New York.

The best book available on complementary proteins and

vegetarian cooking. Contains a sound analysis of the ethical, social and economic reasons for vegetarianism, and an explanation of how to plan meatless meals in accordance with good nutritional principles. Includes charts, tables, appendixes and recipes. Useful to the home cook, as well as food service personnel unfamiliar with vegetarian cookery.

Recipes for a Small Planet, by Ellen Buchman Ewald. 366 pages. 1973. Ballantine Books, New York.

Companion volume to Ms. Lappé's book, this one contains a condensed discussion of protein complementarity and many additional recipes.

Why Your Child Is Hyperactive, by Ben F. Feingold, M.D. 1975. Random House, New York.

Dr. Feingold describes his work with hyperactive children, in which he has found that food additives are the probable cause of many cases of hyperactivity. His elimination diet, in which patients eat strictly additive-free foods, brings relief from symptoms of hyperkinesis in many children. Anyone involved in feeding children should be aware of Dr. Feingold's work.

Notes

Chapter 1

1. Ross Hume Hall, from a lecture to The New Nutrition Conference, Institute on Man and Science, Rensselaerville, N.Y., July 18–20, 1975. See also Ross Hume Hall, *Food for Nought: The Decline in Nutrition* (Hagerstown, Md.: Harper and Row, 1974).

2. Mary K. Head, "Nutrient Losses in Institutional Food Handling," *Journal of the American Dietetic Association* (October 1974): 423–27.

3. Ibid.

4. Dr. Louis A. Saporito, quoted by Richard Trubo, "Youth Sink Teeth Into Junk Food at Alarming Rate," *Evening Chronicle* (Allentown, Pa.), 21 April 1976, p. 20.

5. "Citizen's School Lunch Committee," *Newsletter*, Board of Education, Greenburgh Central School District No. 7, Hartsdale, N.Y., December 1975.

Chapter 2

1. U.S., Office of Child Development, *Notice of Program Performance Standards* (Washington, D.C.: Government Printing Office), pp. 33–35.

2. USDA Agriculture Economic Report No. 10, *Lunch Programs in the Nation's Schools*, June 1971.

3. "Lunch Program Expands," *Nutrition Action* (December 1975): 3.

4. USDA Agriculture Information Bulletin No. 341, p. 54.

5. Ibid., p. 51.

6. Mary K. Head and Roma J. Weeks, "Major Nu-

trients in the Type A Lunch," *Journal of the American Dietetic Association* 67 (October 1975): 356–60.

7. See note 4.

8. *Journal of the American Dietetic Association* 67 (November 1975).

9. Pat Brown Kelly, "Solving the School Lunch Problem," *Washington Post,* 7 March 1974.

10. *If We Had Ham, We Could Have Ham and Eggs...If We Had Eggs,* a study of the National School Breakfast Program, Food Research and Action Center (New York, 1972), p. 19.

11. Ibid., p. 20.

12. Ibid., p. 35.

13. Ibid., p. 85.

14. Marian Burros, "Let Them Eat Cupcakes, the USDA Decrees," *The Morning Call* (Allentown, Pa.), 12 July 1974.

15. *If We Had Ham,* pp. 94–96.

16. Ibid., p. 105.

17. Patricia Camp, "A Visit From Mr. Breakfast Highlights the School Day," *Washington Post,* 13 November 1975.

18. Ben F. Feingold, *Why Your Child Is Hyperactive* (New York: Random House, 1975), p. 79.

19. Greenburgh Central School District No. 7, *Report to Consumer Assembly '76,* Hartsdale, N.Y., January 22, 1976, pp. 4–5.

20. Ibid.

21. Mabel A. Walker and Louise Page, "Nutritive Content of College Meals," *Journal of the American Dietetic Association* 68 (January 1976): 31–38.

22. Kenneth R. Nielsen, correspondence to Jane Kinderlehrer, November 12, 1975.

23. *Congressional Record,* 94 Cong., 1 sess., 16 June 1975, vol. 121, no. 94, pp. 1–2.

24. Christine McGovern, "The Five-State Nutrition Education Project: A Team Teaching Success," *Food and Nutrition* (June 1975): 6–8.

Chapter 3

1. P. Ross, "Personal View," *British Medical Journal* 3, no. 5977 (26 July 1975): 225.

2. Charles E. Butterworth, Jr., "The Skeleton in the Hospital Closet," *Nutrition Today* (March/April 1974): 4.

3. Bruce R. Bistrain et al., "Prevalence of Malnutrition in General Medical Patients," *Journal of the American Medical Association* 235, no. 15 (12 April 1976): 1567–70.

4. "Doctor Blames Hospitals for Creating Malnutrition," *Washington Post*, 30 January 1975, p. D–5.

5. "Basic Nutritional Principles Are Said to Be Ignored in Hospital Patients' Care," *Family Practice News* 4, no. 13 (1 July 1974): 36.

6. Charles E. Butterworth and George L. Blackburn, "Hospital Malnutrition," *Nutrition Today* (March/April 1975): 8.

7. Butterworth, "Skeleton in the Hospital Closet," p. 8.

8. Richard L. Meiling, "The Institutional System," *Nutrition Today* 9, no. 4 (July/August 1974): 34–35.

9. Ibid., p. 35.

10. Butterworth and Blackburn, "Hospital Malnutrition," pp. 9–18.

11. Velma L. Kerschner, *Nutrition and Diet Therapy for Practical Nurses*, 2d ed. (Philadelphia: F.A. Davis Co., 1976).

12. *The News* (State University of New York) 4, no. 5 (March 1975): 9.

13. Commonwealth of Massachusetts Department of Elder Affairs, Title VII Nutrition Program, *Project and Site Directory*, April 1975.

Chapter 7

1. "Clout Counts: Co-op Buying Can Cut Costs 20%," *Institutions* 76, no. 12 (15 June 1975): 29–30.
2. Ibid., pp. 35, 37.

Chapter 8

1. Information from "Quantity Recipes for Type A School Lunches," *USDA Bulletin PA631*.
2. Ibid.

Index